MW00683091

MYSTERIOUS ENCOUNTERS

PERSONAL ACCOUNTS OF THE SUPERNATURAL IN CANADA

JOHN ROBERT COLOMBO

MYSTERIOUS ENCOUNTERS

PERSONAL ACCOUNTS OF THE SUPERNATURAL IN CANADA

HOUNSLOW

Mysterious Encounters
Personal Accounts
of the Supernatural in Canada

Copyright © 1990 by J.R. Colombo

All Rights Reserved.

ISBN 0-88882-121-2

DEDICATION
In Memory of R. S. Lambert

Publisher: Anthony Hawke
Designer: Gerard Williams
Compositor: Accurate Typesetting Limited
Printer: Gagné Printing Ltd.
Front Cover Photograph: Gerard Williams

Pages 313-316 constitute
an extension of the copyright page.

Publication was assisted by
The Canada Council and
The Ontario Arts Council.

Hounslow Press
A Division of Anthony R. Hawke Limited
124 Parkview Avenue
Willowdale, Ontario, Canada
M2N 3Y5

Printed and bound in Canada.

He who cannot pause to wonder is as good as dead.
Albert Einstein

The absence of evidence is not evidence of absence.
Terence Dickinson

Make way for objective mystery!
Paul-Emile Borduas

We live in an empty place filled with wonders.
Peter C. Newman

Contents

Preface

"He who cannot pause to wonder is as good as dead."

Those words have been attributed to Albert Einstein. With them the famous mathematician and physicist affirmed that a sense of wonder and mystery is central to the human condition. Whoever does not ponder the wonders of the world, the mysteries of life, and the drama of human existence does not live a full life.

Indeed, a sense of wonder is something of a "sixth sense." Through this sense we enlarge our appreciation and understanding of ourselves and our place in the universe. Through this sense we are able to explore the borderlands and hinterlands of human experience. That is good because that in essence is the theme of this anthology.

Natural and unnatural mysteries and wonders exist in abundance. As the proverb has it: "Wonders never cease." The expression is as true today as it was the day it was first uttered. And when was that? One would think that the proverb is ages old, or that it is at least as old as the English language. The truth is that it made its first appearance in print in an English publication in 1823, where it appeared in the future tense: "Wonders will never cease." Thirteen years later the expression was given wide popularity in this form by Thomas Chandler Haliburton, the British-Canadian man-of-letters, in his work of humour *The Clockmaker*.

There are seventy-two wonders of Canadian origin and interest

1

in this anthology. They take the form of first-person narratives contributed by Canadians or by non-Canadians who have a direct connection with this country. The narratives are astonishing to read, yet each is astonishing in its own way, shedding light on different aspects of human life and thought — if not of other dimensions of reality. Taken together the narratives offer the reader a rich and varied reading experience: a remarkable range of events and experiences along with a variety of approaches and responses to them.

For the purposes of this anthology, a "mystery" is a happening — it may be a psychological experience, a physiological occurrence, or a physical event — which seems unreasonable or unnatural. A "mystery" apparently goes contrary to human expectation and goes against the laws of nature. (Whether it does or not, whether it is an illusion or a delusion, a deceit or a misunderstanding, is a matter that will be pondered later.) A "mystery" is certainly unexpected and usually unexplained. Thus there is no essential difference between a "mystery," a "marvel," and a "wonder." Is the world a "wonderful" place in this sense of the word? Is Canada a "marvelous" country? Do we live in a place of "mysterious" happenings? These questions may be asked, and should be asked, but the principal purpose of this anthology is to supply some evidence that wonders are worth knowing, not to affirm or deny them.

The anthology is arranged in nine sections. To some degree these sections reflect the passage of time from the early period to the late. Within each section appear eight passages — accounts, narratives, documents, texts, etc. — generally arranged in chronological order.

o "Native Mysteries" records some of the surprising beliefs and practices of the Inuit and the Indian. These accounts are presented sometimes in the words of the native people themselves, sometimes in the words of explorers or ethnologists. These beliefs and practices are based on an all-pervasive animism and pantheism which seems ageless — and shamanistic. Not all the native wonders in the book appear in this section. The categories are not meant to be confining.

o "Animal Mysteries" records in brief form some descriptions of sightings of strange creatures, not always animalistic in form. Such beasts and beings as Windigos and Sasquatches haunt the lakes and woods of the country — as well as the imaginations of Canadians. And they have done so from the earliest of times to the present.

o "Spiritualistic Mysteries" brings together some texts that shed light on the origins of the Spiritualist movement, one of the most popular and pervasive movements of all time. This movement found its source in the mid-19th century at the hands of two Canadian-born teenagers, the noted or notorious Fox Sisters. The movement they sparked is far from being merely an historical movement. The effects of the Spiritualist movement may be felt today in activities as varied as the Philip Phenomenon and the channelling of the New Age.

o "Psychic Mysteries" looks at those men and women who are out of the ordinary in the sense that they claim some form of contact with powers and possibilities that are imminent or transcendent. Opinion remains divided on the reality of such contacts or powers.

o "Natural Mysteries," the shortest section, could well have been the longest. There is seemingly no end of natural marvels to represent. These take the form of unexpected occurrences in the world of nature as seen through the eyes of trained observers who are concerned with such matters as cause and effect and perception and illusion. There are oddities in the world of nature, as in the world of mankind.

o "Human Mysteries" puts a human face on the extraordinary experiences of ordinary men and women — that is, people who maintain they have no psychic abilities whatsoever and yet have much to report in this field. The range is wide, extending from relics of the Buddha to mental control over hydroelectric power.

o "Ghostly Mysteries" is the zone reserved for hosts of ghosts, spectres, demons, apparitions, poltergeists, etc. These are forces or presences that are seldom seen, hardly heard, semi-sensed, or otherwise partially experienced — though seldom entirely rationally entertained.

o "Visionary Mysteries" takes a peek into the psyches of others to consider the dynamics of inner life. Fantasy, imagination, alternative states of consciousness, and levels of spiritual existence are briefly dramatized. This section begs the following question: Are dreams precognitive or clairvoyant?

o "Alien Mysteries," the most contemporary of all the sections and concerns, looks at encounters with flying saucers, UFOs, abductions, alien beings, and extraterrestrial intelligences. It has been said the fairy-folk have taken to outer space. Whether this is true or not in any symbolic sense, here is evidence that they have made the leap.

If there is something common like a thread that links all nine sections, it is not "the golden cord" which is said to be the vital link between the physical body and the astral body. Instead, it is the expressive value of these narratives, as well as whatever evidential value they may possess.

Another way of looking at the contents of this collection is to call it "paranormal Canadiana." When it comes to the paranormal, the public is often divided into the believers and the skeptics — the sheep and the goats. This simple-minded division leaves little or no room for those who neither affirm nor deny — the agnostics. Agnosticism has been defined as the modest man's religion because it makes no claims and requires no commitments whatsoever. In parapsychological terms, if the believers are the sheep and the skeptics are the goats, perhaps the agnostics are the porcupines. The porcupine is a prickly beast, but it knows its own mind. Although it seldom goes on the attack, it does have a characteristic defensive posture.

Perhaps this characteristic defensive posture is required today, as fundamentalisms of all sort — from the irreligious to the rigidly religious — are the bane of civilized values. Since the dawn of time matters of the spirit have perplexed mankind. Yet such matters have failed to generate a consensus among reasonable men and women, so the posture of the porcupine remains honourable and reasonable.

Mankind — and Canada — are wealthy in accounts of anomalous experiences and inexplicable phenomena. But we are destitute of proof that such things do in reality happen or exist. While there is much evidence for the operation of the paranormal in everyday life, its quality is suspect. As James Randi (a contributor to this collection) once expressed it, there is plenty of evidence for the existence of Santa Claus; the problem is that the evidence is not very good.

The evidence for the existence of the paranormal — "that such things be" — has more appeal to the humanist than to the scientist. The evidence is not impressive to the scientist, at least not for long. The "hard" scientist — the engineer or the physicist — requires evidence that will stand up in the laboratory, evidence that yields replicable results. The evidence that does exist is not of this sort, for it is in the main spontaneous and evanescent. But it has an appeal to those concerned with the "soft" sciences — the statistician, the social scientist, the psychologist, the scholar, and the literary critic. Some work has been done by scientists in laboratories and by statisticians in research centres which might lead one to accept the thesis that minds may have a direct influence over matter, but those studies have yet to receive widespread acceptance in critical circles. Practically all the evidence for the operation of the paranormal in everyday life emerges from anecdotal accounts which are rich in subjectivity.

That is the sort of evidence that has been collected in this anthology. It has a fascination all its own. Over and above its verifiability, its verisimilitude, it makes great reading. The anecdotal evidence is sufficiently compelling that it would be a shame not to take a serious look at the effects that are reported here, if not the assigned causes. Accounts like these are what must "give one pause" and "make one wonder" — short of finding proof acceptable to the "hard" scientist, should this occur.

Tales of the incredible come from the earliest of recorded times to the present, from all the races of mankind, from across all known cultures and civilizations, from all continents. Most of the tales are offered as expressions of fancy or as works of the imagination, with symbolic and other overtones, but some of the tales are offered as straight-forward records of amazing experiences and events. Deeply buried in the psyches of men and women through the ages is the felt need to relate such wonders to one another. Story-telling seems a universal trait. We are a tale-telling species, and the tales we tell involve signs and wonders.

To the psychologist, as distinct from the parapsychologist, the mind of man is constantly making perceptual and conceptual mistakes. Experiences are erroneously interpreted, recalled, and reported. While this is undeniably true, the parapsychologist, unlike the psychologist, entertains the possibility that the human mind may be capable of transcending its material limitations or of employing its physical nature in totally unexplained ways. Psychologists are prepared to consider a limited number of states of consciousness such as waking, dream, trance, etc. Parapsychologists focus on intuitive, alternative, or transpersonal states. Psychology is comfortable with the actual, parapsychology with the possible. Both disciplines (to the extent that the latter is a discipline at all) are prepared to admit that extraordinary experiences tell us something about man; whether they tell is something about nature and the cosmos is a matter that concerns the parapsychologist.

Whatever interpretation we care to bring to events and experiences that seem to violate the natural order of things, we are left with the tales themselves, and with the fact that relating them and responding to them through the medium of either speech or print is a deeply satisfying human experience. As activities go, this is a distinctly human one, shared with no other creatures on this planet.

The fantastic narratives included here are matters of fact, or at the very least they are offered as such. It is possible that those who originally narrated them were themselves deceived or sought to deceive others. Perhaps the narrators are mistaken, insufficiently critical, or prone to jump to conclusions acceptable to some segments of society and not to other segments. Maybe they are mistaken in judging others as incredulous as themselves. The possibility of deliberate deception remains ever-present. Yet some of the accounts refer to events that have been widely and independently observed; other accounts refer to experiences limited to a single person. Whether they are experiences or events, some of the happenings are more mysterious than others. The gamut runs from the probable to the improbable, from the unlikely to the impossible.

There is an interesting distinction between "psychic" and "psychical." The word "psychic" refers to a possible dynamic activity which is not amenable to direct study. The word "psychical" refers to the evidence that exists for that possible dynamic activity — its history, theory, practice, interpretation, evidence, effects, etc. The *psychical* may be studied directly, the *psychic* indirectly, if at all. Clairvoyance is reported, but is not a proven fact; the study of clairvoyance does exist and has a remarkable history. It should even be possible to discuss the nature and characteristics of clairvoyance based solely on the study of its literature. After all, it is routine for "hard" scientists, like astronomers, to discuss the characteristics of Black Holes, despite the fact that these are theoretical constructs. They may correspond to known facts but no one has seen or sensed one and they may or may not exist.

This anthology collects the literature about the subject, rather than the subject itself. So an examination of these writings in light of related literature is worthwhile. The narratives in this collection may be seen in light of the literature of high imagination: fantastic literature.

Students of fantastic literature distinguish between fantasy fiction and science fiction; the distinction is fundamental and has immediate relevance to these narratives. It is important to note at the onset that the accounts in this book are not fiction at all; they are non-fiction. They are neither fantasy fiction nor science fiction. Yet the accounts have more in common with science fiction than they do with fantasy fiction.

Fantasy fiction offers the reader a universe in which pretty well everything is permitted. In practice, the writer of fantasy diminishes the number of irregularities pretty quickly. The natural order, as the reader experiences it on a daily basis, is violated by actions described on the printed page. Once upon a time, a magic lantern is lost or found, a genii appears or disappears, a carpet flies through the air, a hero is transported hither and yon, remarkable coincidences occur, and everyone lives happily ever after. All and everything seems possible in the universe of fantasy fiction. This is definitely not "consensus reality."

In the world of science fiction, only the real and the rational are possible. The clock strikes thirteen; society has adopted the twenty-four-hour clock. An android opens the door; every home has such servo-mechanisms these days. Star ships flash from galaxy to galaxy; faster-than-light flights have been routine for at least half a century now. This is definitely "consensus reality" plus the *novum*. Something new has been added, but something that seems reasurringly reasonable. Fantasies are impossible fictions; science fictions seem possible — and plausible.

At first it might seem that the accounts published here are fantasy fiction. Initially, at least, everything seems possible. Yet that is not so. Natural law has not been waived; cause and effect are not been overruled. There is no wholesale violation of expectation. The narratives, unlike fantasy fiction but like science fiction, imply a "consensus reality." Yet there is one instance in each narrative of a violation of the natural order of things. News of an illness in a family is normally carried from city to city by telephone, not clairvoyance. Yet what is described is an instance of clairvoyance, a crisis apparition of unknown causation. The operative word is "unknown." The *ovum* is unexplained. Perhaps the higher cause is the hyperactivity of the power of intuition which normally dormant in the human psyche. (The rationale is that it lies closer to the surface of consciousness in the primitive, the fool, the artist, the child, the aged, or the saint.) In this way the narrative resembles science fiction. Yet wanting is the scientific or technological rhetoric or rationale. Why is this latent power activated in the first place? It is presumed that there is an explanation which involves some "higher reason" or "superpower." The question may be unanswerable, but there are parapsychologists and spiritualists who will supply explanations. Thus these narratives are closer to the world of science fiction than they are to the universe of fantasy.

The narratives project the image of a "consensus reality" plus one "wild talent." Everything is reasonable as long as recourse to "higher reason" — a rhetorical flourish like "it was meant to be" or "I lived here in an earlier incarnation" — is considered part of that condition. The poet Samuel Taylor Coleridge, who spoke about "the willing suspension of disbelief," distinguished between facts of "fancy" and acts of "imagination." The former simply combined known elements into impossible amalgams: unicorns, sphinxes, etc. The latter, deeply rooted in reality, generated new, living forms: Ancient Mariners, etc. Perhaps the fact that these narratives are closer to genuine imagination than to spurious fancy accounts for their hold over the popular imagination.

Another way to examine extraordinary events and experiences is to distinguish between puzzles and mysteries. A puzzle is a logical problem which is missing some element or component.

There is a solution to every puzzle, though the solution may not be immediately apparent. One must deduce the existence of the missing piece or pieces. The charm of the puzzle is that it is merely... puzzling. It is solved by a single person, not by a group of people. Some of the narratives here, especially those of the natural-wonder variety, resemble puzzles. Without question there are meteorological reasons why a "dark day" occurs, yet it is unlikely that those Montrealers who experienced a "dark day" in the 19th century knew many or any of these reasons.

If a puzzle is puzzling, a mystery is mysterious. Mysteries by definition have no solutions. An individual solves a puzzle; a group responds to a mystery. A mystery is something of a convention. There are fashions in mysteries as there are in *haute couture*. For instance, the vogue for what was called physical mediumship (the production of ectoplasm and other physical effects) passed with the Great Depression. Society establishes conventions and psychics work within them, though there are occasions (the Fox Sisters are one instance) when psychics set the conventions and society accepts them. Yet even for the Fox Sisters the time was "ripe." A mystery like the Shaking Tent may be a ritual act, a rite, and a ceremony which involves showmanship and some degree of shaman-ship. A mystery may also be pure show, pure spectacle, like a magic act, having no other purpose than the naked effect. One simply suspends disbelief and appreciates the conjuring.

The reader is on safe ground should he or she wish to regard these narrative accounts as folklore and not as naturalistic narratives. Folklorists collect stories and tales, which quite often include supernatural motifs, as a matter of course. Some of these stories and tales are offered as true accounts of actual incidents. The folklorist does not worry about the truth or falsity of the accounts; the folklorist is concerned with the nature of oral transmission: delivery, description, and documentation. There is also the undeniable element of drama. Some motifs and tale types are found in one form or other throughout the world; others are restricted to specific localities or societies. There are tales that are palpably the product of diffusion, and tales that are probably the result of independent creation. Whatever the origin and nature of the tale that they preserve and study, there is a term that folklorists have on occasion used to refer to the first-person narrative. That term is *memorate*.

Memorates are "personal experience narratives." A memorate is the account of a noteworthy event or experience that has been reported in the first-person by the person to whom it occurred. Memorates are easily distinguished from tall tales and legends. A tall tale is a highly exaggerated story that is alleged to be true, but no one holds the narrator strictly accountable for the veracity of the tale. Everyone has heard the tall tale of "the fish that got away." The tall tale may or may not be reported in the first-person. Memorates differ from tall tales in a number of ways. The memorate is told as true and it is narrated in the first person by the person to whom the incident allegedly occurred. As well, the incident defies belief — or requires it. Memorates serve to preserve experiences; they are not told to impress listeners.

Memorates are unlike legends. A legend is set in the past and explains how the past has influenced the present. Legends are addressed to groups of people, entire societies, and not to individuals. A memorate is set within the lifetime of a living person, it records one living person's experience, and it is usually addressed to a single person or to some like-minded people, not generally to the public at large. Legends familiar to most readers refer to events that took place in the Ancient World or during the Middle Ages. A legend may account for a single fact or truth about humanity or history. A memorate accounts for a single person's experience. A memorate is personal whereas a legend is impersonal.

One of the purposes served by the memorate is the validation of the individual's experience. The truth is in the telling. Memorates are oral compositions; they are only written down upon request. They are reserved for a select audience, one that shares the "sense of wonder" of the narrator.

Folklorists have studied a form of legend which does shed some light on the memorate. This type of narrative, which has yet to be considered, is called the "urban legend." In some ways the memorate resembles the urban legend. Unlike the legend *per se*, the urban legend refers to contemporary conditions, well within the experience of the narrator. Everyone has heard the urban legend about "alligators in the New York sewer system" or "the phantom hitchhiker." The memorate and the urban legend share the present, so to speak, and they refer to events that are improbable (science fiction) though not to events that are impossible (fantasy fiction). Yet urban legends differ from memorates in one important particular. The urban legend recalls the experience of someone other than the narrator. The unlikely incident that is being described happened to someone else. It was observed by someone who is unnamed but who has some relationship with somebody whose name is known. The person to whom it all happened is "a friend of a friend," a familiar formulation that has come to be known through its acronym: FOAF. It all happened to the FOAF who picked up the Vanishing Hitchhiker or who encountered the alligator in the New York sewer system. The charm of the urban legend is that it masquerades as a truthful account. The weakness of the urban legend lies in the fact that the narrator remains unknown. The strength of the memorate emanates from the identity of the narrator and the knowledge that the narrator may be trusted to tell the truth as it appeared at the time.

Although the memorate differs from the tall tale, the legend, and the urban legend, many of the features of such folklore shed light on characteristics of the memorate. As Jan Harold Brunvand wrote in *The Vanishing Hitchhiker: American Urban Legends and Their Meanings* (New York: W. W. Norton & Company, 1981): "Legends can survive in our culture as living narrative folklore if they contain three essential elements: a strong basic story-appeal, a foundation in actual belief, and a meaningful message or 'moral.'"

Brunvand's "three essential elements" apply to memorates as well as to narrative folklore. Brunvand went on to list other characteristics of urban legends which relate to the fantastic accounts in this book. He wrote:

> For legends in general, a major function has always been the attempt to explain unusual and supernatural happenings in the natural world. To some degree this remains a purpose for urban legends, but their more common role nowadays seems to be to show that the prosaic contemporary scene is capable of producing shocking or amazing occurrences which may actually have happened to friends or to near-acquaintances but which are nevertheless explainable in some reasonably logical terms. On

the one hand we want our factual lore to inspire awe, and at the same time we wish to have the most fantastic tales include at least some hint of a rational explanation and perhaps even a conclusion.

Yet there are important differences between Brunvand's folklore and the accounts in the present collection. The accounts presented here are written narratives rather than oral lore. They are *believed in* rather than reported to be remarkable. They are presented as testimonies rather than as tall tales. Their narrators are witnesses of wonders rather than uninvolved story-tellers.

A memorate is a factual, first-hand account of an incident which relates a mystery, a marvel, or a wonder that is accepted by the narrator at face value. Folklorists do not limit memorates to mysterious events and experiences. For the purposes of this anthology, however, a memorate involves the supernatural, the paranormal, or the mysterious. There may be no proof of the existence of the supernatural, the paranormal, or the mysterious, but there is some evidence for it. That evidence generally takes the form of the memorate.

Memorates deal with the irrational, and skeptics are quick to point out that the irrational is dangerous. They see the irrational as the opposite of reasoned thought and behaviour. They hold to the views of man's mental evolution advanced almost a century ago by the cultural anthropologist James Frazer. Throughout the thirteen volumes of *The Golden Bough*, Frazer elaborated an evolutionary theory which depicted mankind as evolving in his conception of causation from primitive magic, through religious notions, to scientific thought. Today to explain anything in other than scientific terms is considered intellectual backsliding or slumming. To account for an action or a reaction in religious or magical terms is an atavistic reversion to earlier forms of thought and feeling. Yet the irrational — whether it is the opposite of reason or its absence — is ever-present in everyday life. One has only to read newspaper headlines or watch television programs to be aware of how rational thought leads to irrational behaviour. Bureaucratic thinking, which is highly rationalized and organized, is only one instance of how rational thought leads to decisions and actions that are illogical. At the same time, one has only to experience contemporary advertising techniques to appreciate how through calculation irrational factors, especially emotive elements, are employed to direct action, notably purchasing power.

How better to experience the irrational than through reading about it? Skeptics are mistaken when they maintain that thinking about the irrational leads to irrational thinking. It is a confusion of categories. Indeed, the reverse is true. Failure to consider the nature of the irrational leads to a failure to consider the strengths of reason.

The reader should feel free to savour these experiences, and to shiver while doing so. Never fear that levitation will become the norm, that "distant viewing" will turn into an everyday occurrence, or that teleportation will be a common practice. What an surreal world it would be if there were a miracle a minute! How awful it would be if such feats as these could be commonplace! How frightening if your friend or enemy could read your mind at will; if your neighbour could levitate across the hall or the backyard; or if your billfold could apport and disport across the country whenever it wanted!

There are five billion people living on Earth today, and about one billion of them call themselves Christians. Some are nominal and some are practising Christians. It is assumed that both groups subscribe to the basic beliefs of the Christian church. They apparently accept the following reports as facts: a man was born of a virgin; as a child he confounded sages; he changed water into wine; he walked on water; he cured the sick; he raised the dead; he confounded the devil; he predicted his own death; he died and three days later he rose from the dead; he appeared in splendour before family members and followers; he died for the sins of all mankind; then he ascended into heaven, where he sits at the right hand of God the Father Almighty and watches over the living and the dead....

Is such a creed rational or irrational? Does adherence to or acceptance of religious or spiritual irrationality enhance human life? Are men and women better persons for a *soupçon* of the supernatural? Are they more human for it? The events and experiences which are recalled so dramatically in the pages of this book may be incredible, they may be improbable, and they may be impossible, but are they as mind-boggling as these Christian beliefs, which are presumably held by one billion Christians today?

Wonders never cease.

Acknowledgements

I am pleased to acknowledge the contributions made to this collection by contributors both living and dead, both willing and unwitting. Were all the contributors alive and well today, no doubt many of them would be surprised and perhaps delighted with the company they now keep.

I personally benefitted from discussions concerning the intriguing issues raised in these pages with diverse and talented people who have little if anything in common other than the fact that they discussed these matters with me. No doubt a few of them will take issue (even violent issue) with my interpretations and explanations. (My counsel to them runs along these lines: Never mind, we may both be wrong.) Among the talented people are Robin Armstrong, Ritchie Benedict, Edith Fowke, Terry Green, Cyril Greenland, Terry Kelly, Mark Leiren-Young, Ted Mann, Judith Merril, Alice M. Neal, Robert J. Sawyer, Robin Skelton, Allen Spraggett, Charles Taylor, Andrew Weiner, and Dwight Whalen.

Fellow researchers who lent a hand include Philip Singer, Farbod Riahi, Michael Richardson, the gentleman who cares to be known as Mr. X, as well as the aforementioned Dwight Whalen. Much of the research was conducted in the North York Public Library system and at the Metropolitan Toronto Reference Library. Good use was made of the facilities of Ben Abraham Books in Toronto.

Once again I am grateful to Anthony R. Hawke of Hounslow Press for his interest in the subject of this book. I am indebted to my

wife Ruth who makes all these projects and publications possible
— even the impossible ones. The text was composed on a Philips
3100 Personal Computer using the software system Nota Bene 3.0.

I continue to collect "mysterious encounters." Readers who wish
to share their accounts, or who wish to draw my attention to
previously published Canadian accounts, are invited to do so by
letter. Address letters to me care of the publisher whose mailing
address appears on the copyright page.

Now it is time to pause to wonder about the mysterious encounters that lie ahead. It is time to ponder what lurks — in Stephen
Leacock's felicitous phrase — "behind the beyond."

1. Native Mysteries

Mysterious and Overwhelming Delight

Aua

K*nud Rasmussen, the Danish explorer and anthropologist, spent much time with Aua, an Iglulik Eskimo and* angakoq, *in the Barren Lands of the Northwest Territories during the early 1920s. The explorer was part Danish and part Eskimo, and he recalled his first sight of Aua alighting from a sledge pulled by fifteen white dogs: "A little man with a large beard, completely covered with ice, leapt out and came towards me, holding out his hand white man's fashion." The Dane found the Eskimo to be a kind, hospitable, and humorous man. He noted he possessed many skills and a great knowledge of Eskimo traditions and beliefs. Aua could philosophize at great length and express himself with great cogency and immediacy.*

The text which appears here is Aua's account of the activities of his two spiritual helpers and their effect on his emotional life. The text is taken from Knud Rasmussen's Intellectual Culture of the Iglulik Eskimos *(1930) translated by William Worster. The source is Volume 7, Part I, of the Report of the Fifth Thule Expedition 1921-24, issued in Copenhagen.*

EVERYTHING WAS THUS MADE READY for me beforehand, even from the time when I was yet unborn; nevertheless, I endeavoured to become a shaman by the help of others; but in this I did not succeed. I visited many famous shamans, and gave them great gifts, which they at once gave away to others; for if they had kept the things for themselves, they or their children would have died. This they believed because my own life had been so threatened from birth. Then I sought solitude, and here I soon became very melancholy. I would sometimes fall to weeping, and feel unhappy without knowing why. Then, for no reason, all would suddenly be changed, and I felt a great, inexplicable joy, a joy so powerful that I could not restrain it, but had to break into song, a mighty song, with only room for the one word: joy, joy! And I had to use the full strength of my voice. And then in the midst of such a fit of mysterious and overwhelming delight I became a shaman, not knowing myself how it came about. But I was a shaman. I could see and hear in a totally different way. I had gained my *quamaneq*, my enlightenment, the shaman-light of brain and body, and this in such a manner that it was not only I who could see through the darkness of life, but the same light also shone out from me, imperceptible to human beings, but visible to all the spirits of earth and sky and sea, and these now came to me and became my helping spirits.

My first helping spirit was my namesake, a little aua. When it came to me, it was as if the passage and roof of the house were lifted up, and I felt such a power of vision, that I could see right through the house, in through the earth and up into the sky; it was the little aua that brought me all this inward light, hovering over me as long as I was singing. Then it placed itself in a corner of the passage, invisible to others, but always ready if I should call it.

An aua is a little spirit, a woman, that lives down by the sea shore. There are many of these shore spirits, who run about with a pointed skin hood on their heads; their breeches are queerly short, and made of bearskin; they wear long boots with a black pattern, and coats of sealskin. Their feet are twisted upward, and they seem to walk only on their heels. They hold their hands in such a fashion that the thumb is always bent in over the palm; their arms are held raised upon high with the hands together, and incessantly stroking the head. They are bright and cheerful when one calls them, and resemble most of all sweet little live dolls; they are no taller than the length of a man's arm.

My second helping spirit was a shark. One day when I was out my kayak, it came swimming up to me, lay alongside quite silently and whispered my name. I was greatly astonished, for I had never seen a shark before; they are very rare in these waters. Afterwards it helped me with my hunting, and was always near me when I had need of it. These two, the short spirit and the shark, were my principal helpers, and they could aid me in everything I wished. The song I generally sang when calling them was a few words, as follows:

> *Joy, joy,*
> *Joy, joy!*
> *I see a little shore spirit,*
> *A little aua,*
> *I myself am also aua,*
> *The shore spirit's namesake,*
> *Joy, joy!*

These words I would keep on repeating, until I burst into tears, overwhelmed by a great dread; then I would tremble all over, crying only: "Ah-a-a-a-a, joy, joy! Now I will go home, joy, joy!"

My Helping Spirit

Igjugarjuk

Igjugarjuk was a Caribou Eskimo befriended by the great Danish explorer Knud Rasmussen on the trip he made in the early 1920s across the barren grounds west of the northern reaches of Hudson Bay. Igjugarjuk was an angakoq *or shaman of great skill. To Rasmussen's delight he was willing to discuss his period of training and how he acquired his well-earned and hard-won powers.*

It took Igjugarjuk well over a year to become a shaman. During his period of training and instruction, he avoided sexual relations, ate specially prepared foods, and observed all manner of special prohibitions and restrictions. He apparently lived for thirty days in a tiny igloo in below-zero weather, subsisting on two sips of water a day. Then a female spirit called Pinga appeared to him. That was the turning point in his training. Throughout the entire period of initiation he benefitted from the instruction of his father-in-law, Perqánâq.

In these two excerpts, Igjugarjuk describes two most unusual experiences in a manner that is matter-of-fact. These are his vision of Pinga and the emergence of his new-found powers and abilities. The excerpts come from Knud Rasmussen's Intellectual Culture of the Iglulik Eskimos *(1930) translated by William Worster. This is Volume 7, Part I, of the Report of the Fifth Thule Expedition 1921-24, issued in Copenhagen.*

21

The Vision

MY NOVITIATE took place in the middle of the coldest winter, and I, who never got anything to warm me, and must not move, was very cold, and it was so tiring having to sit without daring to lie down, that sometimes it was as if I died a little. Only towards the end of the thirty days did a helping spirit come to me, a lovely and beautiful helping spirit, whom I had never thought of; it was a white woman; she came to me whilst I had collapsed, exhausted, and was sleeping. But still I saw her lifelike, hovering over me, and from that day I could not close my eyes or dream without seeing her. There is this remarkable thing about my helping spirit, that I have never seen her while awake, but only in dreams. She came to me from Pinga and was a sign that Pinga had not noticed me and would give me powers that would make me a shaman.

The Powers

Later, when I had quite become myself again, I understood that I had become the shaman of my village, and it did happen that my neighbours or people from a long distance away called me to heal a sick person, or to "inspect of course" if they were going to travel. When this happened, the people of my village were called together and I told them what I had been asked to do. Then I left tent or snow house and went into solitude: *ahiarmut*, away from the dwellings of man, but those who remained behind had to sing continuously: *quiahunnialukhinarlutik*, just to keep themselves happy and lively. If anything difficult had to be found out, my solitude had to extend over three days and two nights, or three nights and two days. In all that time I had to wander about without rest, and only sit down once in a while on a stone or a snow drift. When I had been out long and had become tired, I could almost doze and dream what I had come out to find and about which I had been thinking all the time. Every morning, however, I could come home and report on what I had so far found, but as soon as I had spoken I had to return again, out into the open, out of places where I could be quite alone. In the time when one is out seeking, one may eat a little, but not much. If a shaman "out of the secrets of solitude" finds out that the sick person will die, he can return home and stay there without first having allowed the usual time to pass. It is only in cases of a possible cure that he must remain out the whole time. On the first night after returning from such a spirit wandering in solitude, the shaman must not lie with his wife, nor must he undress when going to sleep, nor lie down at full length, but must sleep in a sitting position.

These days of "seeking for knowledge" are very tiring, for one must walk all the time, no matter what the weather is like and only rest in short snatches. I am usually quite done up, tired, not only in body but also in head, when I have found what I sought.

We shamans of the interior have no special spirit language, and believe that the real *angatkut* do not need it.... A real shaman does not jump about the floor and do tricks, nor does he seek by the aid of darkness, by putting out the lamps, to make the minds of his neighbours uneasy. For myself, I do not think I know much, but I do not think that wisdom or knowledge about things that are hidden can be sought in that manner. True wisdom is only to be found far away from people, out in the great solitude, and it is not found in play but only through suffering. Solitude and suffering open the human mind, and therefore a shaman must seek his wisdom there.

The Making of a Medicine-Man

Isaac Tens

When Isaac Tens, a Gitksan, was in his thirtieth year, he found himself falling into deep trances. Visions appeared to him and terrified him. When he reported these experiences to the elders of the Gitksan community, they informed him that he was being transformed into a shaman. They told him that the transformation would be complete only when he would start to sing songs and chants that were entirely his own. Only then would he be a swanasuu *and a* halaait *and be accorded recognition as a medicine-man and a healer. It took more than a year of strain and study before the transformation was completed. By that time Tens had twenty-three songs and chants of his own.*

The narrative of Isaac Tens was collected by the folklorist and anthropologist Marius Barbeau in 1920 and appeared in Barbeau's Medicine Men of the Pacific Coast *(Ottawa: National Museums of Man, Bulletin 152, 1958, 1973).*

The Calling

THIRTY YEARS after my birth was the time when I began to be a *swanassu* (medicine-man). I went up into the hills to get firewood. While I was cutting up the wood into lengths, it grew dark towards the evening. Before I had finished my last stack of wood, a loud noise broke out over me... and a large owl appeared to me. The owl took hold of me, caught my face, and tried to lift me up. I lost consciousness. As soon as I came back to my senses I realized that I had fallen into the snow. My head was coated with ice, and some blood was running out of my mouth.

I stood up and went down the trail, walking very fast, with some wood packed on my back. On my way, the trees seemed to shake and to lean over me; tall trees were crawling after me, as if they had been snakes. I could see them. Before I arrived at my father's home, I told my folk what had happened to me, as soon as I walked in. I was very cold and warmed myself before going to bed. There I fell into a sort of trance. It seems that two *halaaits* (medicine-men) were working over me to bring me back to health. But it is now all vague in my memory. When I woke up and opened my eyes, I thought that flies covered my face completely. I looked down, and instead of being on firm ground, I felt that I was drifting in a huge whirlpool. My heart was thumping fast.

The medicine-men working over me were Kceraw'inerh...of the household of Lutkudzius, Gyedemraldo, and Meeky. While I was in a trance, one of them told me that the time had arrived for me to become a *halaait* like them. But I did not agree, so I took no notice of the advice. The affair passed away as it had come, without results.

The Initiation

There was no one in sight, only trees. A trance came over me once more, and I fell down, unconscious. When I came to, my head was buried in a snowbank. I got up and walked on the ice up the river to the village. There I met my father who had just come out to look for me, for he had missed me. We went back together to my house. Then my heart started to beat fast, and I began to tremble, just as had happened a while before, when the *halaaits* were trying to fix me up. My flesh seemed to be boiling...my body was quivering. While I remained in this state, I began to sing. A chant was coming out of me without my being able to do anything to stop it. Many things appeared to me presently: huge birds and other animals. They were calling me. I saw a *meskyawawderh* (a kind of bird) and a *mesqagweeuk* (bullhead fish). These were visible only to me, not to the others in my house. Such visions happen when a man is about to become a *halaait*; they occur of their own accord. The songs force themselves out complete without any attempt to compose them. But I learned and memorized these songs by repeating them.

During the following year I composed more songs and devoted all my time to my new experience, without doing any other work. I would lie down in my father's house, for I felt sick. Four people looked after me all the time in order to hear me sing my new songs, and they were not satisfied until they had learned them too.

The Healing

My first patient was a woman, the wife of chief Gitemraldaw. Her full name was Niskyaw-romral'awstlegye'ns...she was seriously ill, had been for a long time, and she had been treated before by various *halaaits* in turn, but without avail. I was called in to see whether I could undertake to do something for her. So I went into her house and instructed the people there to light a fire first. As I began to sing over her, many people around me were hitting sticks on boards and beating skin drums for me. My canoe came to me in a dream, and there were many people sitting in it. The canoe itself was the Otter (*watserh*). The woman whom I was doctoring sat with the others inside this Otter canoe. By that time about twenty other *halaaits* were present in the house. To them I explained what my vision was, and asked, "What shall I do? There the woman is sitting in the canoe, and the canoe is the Otter."

They answered, "Try to pull her out."

I told them, "Spread the fire out, into two parts, and make a pathway between them." I walked up and down this path four times, while the other *halaaits* kept singing until they were very tired. Then I went over to the couch on which the sick woman was lying. There was a great upheaval in the singing and the clapping of drums and the sticks on the boards. I placed my hand on her stomach and moved round her couch, all the while trying to draw the canoe out of her. I managed to pull it up very close to the surface of her chest. I grasped it, drew it out, and put it in my own bosom. This I did.

Two days later, the woman rose out of bed; she was cured. My prestige as a *halaait* gained greatly. This, because the others had failed to accomplish anything with her, and I had succeeded. More demands came to me from other parts, as far as the village of Gitsegyukla. Everything usually went well in my work. The fees for doctoring might be ten blankets, prepaid, for each patient, or it might be as little as one blanket. But if the doctored person died afterwards, the blankets were returned. The fees depended upon the wealth of the family calling for services, also upon the anxiety of the relatives of the sick person who wanted to urge the doctor to do his utmost. Should a *halaait* or *swanassu* refuse to doctor a patient, he might be suspected of being himself the cause of the sickness, or of the death should it occur. In this eventuality, the relatives would seek revenge and kill the one suspected. This was the hard law of the country. But the doctors were not known to decline any invitation to serve the people in need.

Medicine at Prince of Wales's Fort

Samuel Hearne

Samuel Hearne (1745-1792), fur trader and explorer, served as chief of Prince of Wales's Fort for six years. In 1782 he was forced to surrender the fort to the French. The fur fort, the most northerly in the world, is located on Hudson Bay, at the mouth of the Churchill River, in present-day Manitoba. In its partially reconstructed state today it is known as Fort Prince of Wales.

Hearne was interested in the practices of the Chipewyan conjurers or medicine-men and their apparent voodoo-like ability to cast fatal spells. He affixed a note to this effect to the entry for Nov. 1771 in A Journey from Prince of Wales's Fort in Hudson's Bay to the Northern Ocean *(1795). It said, in effect, that his friend and guide Matonabbee believed in the efficacy of such "art" and even beseeched Hearne, should he possess such "art," to seek "secret revenge" against Matonabbee's enemy.*

...MATONABBEE, (who always thought me possessed of this art,) on his arrival at Prince of Wales's Fort in the Winter of 1778, informed me, that a man whom I had never seen but once, had treated him in such a manner that he was afraid of his life; in consequence of which he pressed me very much to kill him, though I was then several thousands of miles distant: On which, to please this great man to whom I owed so much, and not expecting that any harm could possibly arise from it, I drew a rough sketch of two

28

human figures on a piece of paper, in the attitude of wrestling: in the hand of one of them, I drew the figure of a bayonet pointing to the breast of the other. This is me, said I to Matonabbee, pointing to the figure which was holding the bayonet; and the other, is your enemy. Opposite to those figures I drew a pine-tree, over which I placed a large human eye, and out of the tree projected a human hand. This paper I gave to Matonabbee, with instructions to make it as publicly known as possible. Sure enough, the following year, when he came in to trade, he informed me that the man was dead, though at that time he was not less than three hundred miles from Prince of Wales's Fort. He assured me that the man was in perfect health when he heard of my design against him; but almost immediately afterwards became quite gloomy, and refusing all kind of sustenance, in a very few days died. After this I was frequently applied to on the same account, both by Matonabbee and other leading Indians, but never thought proper to comply with their requests; by which means I not only reserved the credit I gained on the first attempt, but always kept them in awe, and in some degree of respect and obedience to me. In fact, strange as it may appear, it is almost absolutely necessary that the chiefs at this place should profess something a little supernatural, to be able to deal with those people. The circumstance here recorded is a fact well known to Mr. William Jefferson, who succeeded me at Churchill Factory, as well as to all the officers and many of the common men who were at Prince of Wales's Fort at the time.

A Strange Adventure

Sir Cecil Edward Denny

"*A Strange Adventure*" *is the intriguing title of this chapter in the memoirs of Sir Cecil Edward Denny. The memoirs are called* The Riders of the Plains: A Reminiscence of the Early and Exciting Days of the North-West *(Calgary: The Herald, 1905). The chapter is reproduced here in its entirety with a minimum of copy editing.*

The adventure described by Sir Cecil is more than "strange" — it is incredible. Is it possible that a well-educated officer and a seasoned observer hallucinated like this? Was Sir Cecil, through some freak of nature, clairvoyantly able to oversee the sights and overhear the sounds of some long-vanished Cree encampment? Or was he deluded and disoriented by the sudden effects of a summer storm? He discounts the latter possibility but declines to do more than puzzle about the consequences of the former explanation.

Sir Cecil Edward Denny (1850-1928) was born in Edmonton but educated in England, France, and Germany. He enlisted with the North West Mounted Police the year following its formation, and served with the Force (the forerunner of the RCMP) from 1874 to 1881. Attaining the rank of Inspector, he resigned and found subsequent employment as an Indian Agent and then as the Provincial Archivist of Manitoba. In 1921 he succeeded his half-brother in the baronetcy of Tralee Castle, County Kerry, Ireland.

FOR SOME YEARS AFTER the advent of the North West Mounted Police into the western portion of the then Prince Rupert's land, and today known as the Northwest Territories, the newness, and also the strangeness, of the country, were a source of unfailing interest to us, who belonged to that force. Game of all kinds abounded throughout the country and as we came to the foot hills of the Rockies, bear, elk and moose were often to be seen. This class of game was little molested by the tribe of Blackfeet Indians, whose home was out on the plains, and who lived altogether on the buffalo, which animals supplied them not only with meat, but nearly everything, either directly or indirectly, that they required. The streams were full of fish of many kinds, trout being the most plentiful, and near the mountains salmon trout which often weighed fifteen to eighteen pounds were easily to be caught.

In the summer of 1875 I determined to take a trip from the fort on Old Man river to the foot hills of the mountains, and up that river about forty miles for the purpose of fishing, also intending to give one day to deer hunting. Deer of two kinds were always to be found in the patches of brush and timber along the river bottom, called black and white tail by the hunters of the west. These were not a very large species, but the venison was excellent, and made a welcome addition to our mess, as a continuous course of buffalo meat was found monotonous after a while.

I took with me a pack horse, together with my blankets a few cooking utensils, and an Indian rubber boat which was made to be inflated, and when so filled was very buoyant, and impossible to overturn. It would only hold one man, who could sit comfortably in the bottom with a gun and a rod. A couple of short paddles, one for each hand, was enough to guide the light boat away form any rocks or to the shore when required. This, rolled into a small compass, was packed on the top of the blankets. I took an Indian with me, as I intended after a day's shooting to return to the fort by water, and the Indian would take back the horses with any game we might shoot.

The Blackfeet were very friendly with us, and I expected to come across one of their camps up the river, as I had been told some Indians had gone up towards the mountains intending to cut lodge poles, which they did every summer, never using the same poles for more than one year.

We made a quick ride up the river about thirty miles, that being far enough to come down by boat in one day, which I should have to do, not being able to carry any blankets or cooking utensils. The distance by water would be about double that by land owing to the winding of the channel, and I was not at all sure that there might not be rapids or even falls between there and the fort.

We shot only two deer, myself and the Indian one each. The one I killed was altogether by chance, as in walking down a buffalo path through a patch of wood, I thought I saw something stir in the brush to my right. I was passing on when I thought I would fire a shot in that direction, which I did, without any apparent result. Still I had an idea that I had seen something move, and on walking through the brush in that direction I had gone about fifty yards when in drawing back a bush to make my way through I almost fell over a fine buck lying dead. On examining him I found that my bullet had severed his jugular, and he had dropped without a sound. He had a splendid pair of horns, which, together with the meat, were taken down by the Indian to the fort on the following day.

We made a pleasant camp that night in a clump of wood near the river, and having caught some trout, they, together with some steaks cut from one of the deer, made a first-class supper, to which we did ample justice. On the following morning we packed the deer and our camp outfit on the two spare horses, and the Indian made an early start with them for the fort. I remained with the boat ready to go down by the river, keeping only my gun and a light overcoat, with a bite of cold meat and bread for lunch.

I made good way down the river during the morning, which was fine and warm, only once having any trouble, at a rather nasty rapid, in the middle of which I stuck on a flat rock. In getting off the boat I upset it, and I got a thorough ducking before I could catch it again. The gun, which was fastened by a cord to the side of the cushion, was not lost, although rendered useless for the time by water. I, therefore, camped early for dinner, eating the bread and meat, which, although rather sodden, was better than nothing. I got my clothes partially dried in the sun. All my matches were wet, and a fire was not to be had.

While camped about noon the weather began to look threatening, heavy banks of clouds gathering in the north, and now and then the growl of thunder in the distance could be heard. As I was not more than half way, I started again on my downward journey as soon as possible, but the farther I went the darker it grew, and I soon saw that I was in for a heavy storm, which, to say the least, was by no means pleasant. The thunderstorms along the mountains, although seldom of long duration, were often very severe while they lasted, and by the look of things, I was in for one of the worst. I however made my way steadily down the river, and after a while the storm came down with a vengeance. There was a heavy wind, with hail, rain, and perpetual lightning, followed by deafening peals of thunder, seemingly right overhead. I found it difficult with such a light boat to make any progress, as the heavy wind would drive me from one shore to the other, and the river was lashed into quite heavy waves, so that, although the boat could not sink, I was sitting in water up to my waist, and sometimes sheets of water would be blown right over me. As it was getting quite dark, although not more than four o'clock in the afternoon, I found it impossible to make my way, and I determined to land and wait until the storm was over.

In rounding a bend in the river I saw on the south bank a good clump of timber, and determined to take shelter in it. I made for that shore, and as I approached the fury of the storm for a moment lulled, and in the stillness I could plainly hear the drums beating in an Indian camp, and the sound of the Indian "Hi-ya" mingling with it.

The sounds came from beyond the clump of trees, and I congratulated myself upon meeting with an Indian camp where I could take shelter from such a storm. I concluded that this was the camp I had been told had gone up the river. I therefore landed and drew up the boat into the brush, tying it securely, and, taking my gun, made as quickly as possible through the wood towards the point from which the sounds could now be plainly heard. The storm had now come down worse than ever, and the lightning was almost blinding. I made my way through the timber as fast as possible, it not being any too safe in such close proximity to the trees, and coming out into an open glade of quite an extent, I saw before me the Indian camp not more than two hundred yards away. I could see men and women, and even children, moving about among the lodges, and what struck me as strange was the fact that the fires in the centre of many of the tents shone through the entrances, which were open. This surprised me, as you do not often find the Indians moving about in the wet if they can help it. They generally keep their lodges well closed during a thunder storm, of which they are very much afraid. They look upon thunder as being the noise made by one of their deities called the "Old Man," while throwing great boulders form the mountains. There were, I should consider, about twenty lodges in the camp, and a band of horses could be seen grazing not far off on the other side of the camp.

I stood for a few seconds watching and considering which lodge to make for, and had taken a few steps towards the one nearest me, when I seemed to be surrounded by a blaze of lightning, and at the same time a crash of thunder followed that fairly stunned me for nearly a minute, and sent me on my back. A large tree not far off was struck. I could hear the tending of the wood, and it was afterwards found nearly riven in half. Some of the electric fluid had partly stunned and thrown me down. I was fortunate to have escaped with my life, and, as it was, it was a few minutes before I was able to rise and look around. I looked towards the place where the camp stood, but to my unutterable astonishment as well as terror, it was not there.

It was quite light, although still storming heavily, and was not much after four o'clock. A few minutes before not only a large Indian camp had stood there, and the voices of the Indians could be distinctly heard, but now all had suddenly disappeared, even to the band of horses that were quietly grazing there only a few minutes before.

I stood for a moment almost dumb with astonishment, seeing and hearing nothing, when suddenly an overwhelming sense of terror seemed to seize me, and almost without knowing what I did, I ran towards the bank overlooking the river, which was about a quarter of a mile away, dropping my gun as I ran. I did not stop until I reached the top of the bank, and there I had to rest for want of breath. Here I managed to gather my wits together, and to think of what had taken place.

The open place where the camp had stood was in plain sight from where I was, with the clump of trees behind towards the river, but it was empty, and not a tent or human being in sight. There was nothing but the trees tossed by the storm and the driving rain, and now and then a flash of lightning. I could even then hardly believe my eyes, but there was no doubt about it, and I did not remain long in sight of that spot, and being afraid to go down to my boat, I determined to walk down the river back to the fort, which must have been a good fifteen miles away. It was one of the hardest journeys I ever undertook. What with the shock from being thrown down, and then the most astonishing and inexplicable disappearance of the camp, and also being soaked to the skin, I was in a most uncomfortable condition. The storm continued until night, when it cleared up, and I made my way into the fort at about midnight, completely fagged out, turning into bed at once, with no explanation to anyone.

In the morning I told my story at breakfast to my three brother officers. I was not much the worse for my experience of the previous day, but the more I thought over the matter, the more bewildered and astonished I became. As I expected, I was only laughed at by my companions, who called it imagination. But this I am firmly convinced it was not.

I was not unduly excited when I first heard the Indian drums. I did not expect to find a camp there, but when I emerged from the wood and saw a camp before me, everything seemed perfectly natural, and in no way out of the ordinary. But the sudden and complete vanishing the camp I could in no wise explain. I however determined to again proceed to the spot that morning, and bring down my boat and gun.

I therefore took an Indian and our Blackfoot interpreter with me. We found the place without trouble, but it was vacant, and look as we could no sign of any recent camp was to be seen. A few rings of stone partly overgrown with grass showed where an old camp had been many years ago, and on questioning the Indian he stated that the Blackfeet had surprised and slaughtered a camp of Cree Indians at that place many years ago, and in fact we came across two bleached skulls lying in the grass.

The Indian did not seem to have any superstitions regarding that place. We found where a tree had been struck by lightning, and the boat and gun we brought away.

I have, until now, but seldom mentioned this circumstance, but I am today as firmly convinced as ever that the Indian camp, together with the men, women, and the horses, was most certainly there, and that I suffered under no hallucination whatever, but account for it I cannot, and look upon it as one of those inexplicable riddles which cannot be solved.

On the commissioner's arrival at Macleod, he proceeded at once to Fort Kipp, and paid the Blood Indians, together with the Piegans. This second payment passed off well. There were many traders on the ground, but they did not make as good bargains as in the previous year, as the Indians had begun to find out the value of the money paid them. This year the money was all in Canadian bills, thereby saving a great deal of trouble. Many traders from Montana came over, and did a good cash trade for horses and goods.

After the payments most of the Indians went south into Montana, after buffalo, as most of the bands had gone in that direction, and but a few scattered herds were now to be found in the Northwest Territories.

The Last Sun Dance

Richard G. Hardisty

The naming of Hardisty Lake in the vicinity of Great Bear Lake recalls the life and work of Richard G. Hardisty, an employee of the Hudson's Bay Company whose active years coincided with the opening of the West. As a young man Hardisty was privileged to witness and write about one of the last of the full-fledged Sun Dances. The ritual of endurance and celebration was performed by the Cree and Blackfoot Indians in 1875 in once-open field now part of the City of Edmonton.

Hardistry witnessed a remarkable event but reported no incredible occurrences as taking place during the Sun Dance. It extended over eight days: four days of preparation and four days of ritual. The Sun Dance was outlawed by the Indian Act from 1885 to 1951 when the ritual was legally reinstated — rehabilitated, so to speak. "The Last Sun Dance" is reprinted from Alberta Folklore Quarterly, No. 2, 1946.

I SHALL NEVER FORGET my boyhood impressions of an Indian festival of which I was an eye-witness when the last Sun Dance was held on the river-flats in the heart of the area now known as the City of Edmonton. Prior to the time of which I shall speak civilization had been slowly but surely creeping into the west, yet at that time with the exception of the employees of the Hudson's Bay Company, there were not more than ten white men between Fort Garry and

the Rocky Mountains, and they were mostly missionaries. Civilization had already affected the Indians, sometimes disastrously, for
thousands had died of smallpox and scarlet fever, and contacts with
Hudson's Bay officers and missionaries had already modified some
of the tribal rites and customs. The Sun Dance, which but a few
years earlier had been a savage and gruesome pagan rite, was
becoming a more peaceful and social gathering.

Up to the early eighteen-seventies there had been a practically
constant state of war between the Crees and the Blackfeet. The
Crees were "Woods Indians" who inhabited the timbered and park
lands through which runs the North Saskatchewan River. The
Blackfeet, Bloods and Peigans were "Plains Indians" who ranged
from Montana north to the upper waters of the same river. Fort
Edmonton was the chief trading post in the Cree country. Rocky
Mountain House, on the headwaters of the Saskatchewan, was
established to trade with the Blackfeet with the idea of keeping
them away from the trading posts used by their enemies the Crees.
The Plains Indians mainly relied on the buffalo herds for food and
clothing. The Woods Indians trapped fish and fur-bearing animals. They had no knowledge of fish nets, and when food became
scarce in the woods, which was by no means infrequently, the Crees
sent buffalo hunting expeditions to the plains. Such expeditions
into hostile country were usually made by small parties, for speed
in attack and retreat were major factors in Indian tactics.

At last the tribes met in a great peace conference near where
Wetaskiwin now stands, the Crees encamped on the north side of
the hill near the present townsite, and the Blackfeet on the south
side. Chiefs and headmen conferred on the summit of the hill, and
when finally the Pipe of Peace was smoked the hill was given the
Cree name Wetaskatwinatinac — meaning Peace Hill and the
origin of the name of the present town. Peace was never afterwards
broken between the tribes.

A few years later a great gathering of Cree Indians at Fort
Edmonton staged the last Sun Dance, and though I was but a
youngster at the time, the picture is still clear in my mind's eye after
all these years. For more than a week the Indians had been coming
in, and the river flats below the Fort were dotted with tepees of
buffalo hide. The encampment was about three-quarters of a mile

east of the Fort. The Legislative Buildings now occupy the site of the Fort and baseball and football grounds have taken the place of the Indian encampments on the flats. After sunset, camp fire glowed, the banks of the river, covered with pine and spruce, making an intensely dark background below the skyline, made the camp fires bright and dotted the plain with brilliant light. The beating of drums, the howling of dogs joined the voices of those keeping time to the drum beat. This religious gathering had been for ages an annual event at which were featured the making of sacrifices and the enduring of self-inflicted torture. The conjuror rehearsed his medicine hymns — looked to his medicine bag — fixed his rattles and bells and retouched his ghastly costume. The warriors burnished their war dress. The women made ready their finery, though all they had, such as beaded leggings, a leather girdle — decorated with brass tacks — would be contained in a small bag made of calfskin.

The selection of the tree to be used as the "Idol Pole" was carried out with great ceremony. This "Idol Pole" was set up in the centre of the enclosure. For walls, small poles were set in the ground, sloping inward, and covered with leafy branches, making a good shelter from rain or sun. The walls formed a large circle with the pole standing about 30 feet high in the centre. One opening was left as an entrance, but this was closed with a buffalo robe during the ceremony. The "Idol Pole" was decorated with different coloured clays and streamers of red and blue tape or braid. Long pieces of shaganapie, reaching from the top of the centre pole to the circumference of the lodge, carried small bells, dried bones, and in former days the scalps taken in their last battle. Strong lines made from buffalo hide swung loose to the ground from the very top of the centre pole.

The enclosure would hold, seated on the ground, about a hundred braves. No women or children were permitted to enter during the ceremony. They, however, sat outside encircling the enclosure and taking part in the pow-wow, raising shrill but musical voices to the high heavens, keeping time to the rhythm of the drum beats. This all took time — it took preparation and rehearsal. The festival lasted for six days with but one performance a day and that at noon, by the sun.

In former days any of the warriors who desired to call upon the
Sun God to favour him against his enemies in war and to supply his
needs to maintain himself against his enemies in war and to supply
his needs to maintain himself and family, took part in the ceremony, by sacrifice and self-inflicted torture. At this time, however,
the Sun was invoked to witness only the cruel ordeals of youths
who desired to become warriors and be recognized as men. In this
last Sun Dance, twelve young men qualified as braves daily. The
warriors, led by the chiefs and headmen, gathered in full war paint,
naked but for a breech cloth — brass rings hanging loose on their
ankles; dozens of brass rings on their wrists and forearms —
strings of bear claws and elk teeth round their necks. They move
towards the temple, led by conjurors and medicine men, the medicine men chanting in doleful notes and in unknown tongues,
petitionary and sacrificial hymns, their faces and bodies painted in
alternate streaks of white and yellow — their ornaments around
neck, waist and ankles are human bones. The drums beat and the
medicine men dance, going forward. The chief walks quietly
behind, but the warriors, sounding the tribal war-whoop, go
through all kinds of contortions. They enter the enclosure and sit
on the ground, their bodies moving and swaying, their voices
raised to the beat of the drums.

The medicine men, now opposite each other, dance back and
forth, chanting their incantation to the Sun to bless the gathering,
working themselves and the warriors up to a frenzy of excitement.
In the meantime, the women and youngsters have taken their place
on the outside, and their voices blend with the warriors' and the
drums beat louder.

About fifteen minutes before noon six young men, clean, their
copper skins glistening in the sun — they are naked but for the
breech cloth, no ornament, no paint — enter and dance the war
dance, facing outward from the centrepole. They look fearlessly
into the eyes of the warriors as they circle several times. Proud they
are, for they have become experts in the use of bow and arrow, in
tracking game, in trapping, in wood and prairie lore and all the
many activities of the hunter and provider. Now they are to go
through the test of courage and endurance to become warriors —
taking their place in councils of the tribe — winning the privilege of

seeking the hand of some girl — their eyes having no doubt already caught the eye of one girl.

The drums continue, the women's and children's voices grow shriller and shriller, war-whoops fill the air. Three of the boys stop before one medicine man, standing erect, their chests thrown out. Three others face the medicine man on the opposite side. The medicine man produces two short pieces of red willow, prepared for the occasion, looking somewhat like the skewers butchers use to fasten the roast of beef. The stick is about four inches long with one end pointed — the point hardened by fire and then scraped. Now the medicine man gathers as much of the flesh on the youth's chest as he can between his thumb and forefinger, forcing the stick through the flesh. The second stick is placed in the same manner on the opposite side, an equal distance from the centre of the youth's body. A loop of deer hide, about the width and length of a boot lace, is then fastened to each of the sticks. The youths face about, when all are skewered, and to the loops are attached one of the rawhide ropes hanging from the centre pole — the loops when tied are about six inches from the youth's chest, directly in the centre of his body. The drums beat, the medicine man cavorts, the war-whoop rings out, there is a frenzy of movement and sound. The young men, their legs extended, their bodies thrown back, their weight carried by that portion of their flesh punctured by the stick, sway back and forth, blood streaming down their bodies from their wounds, sweat pouring from them. They leap and tumble, but utter no sound. The agony must continue until the flesh is torn through and they are free.

As each frees himself, he rushes from the enclosure, into the midst of his family — mother, cousins and aunts — each prepared to minister to his suffering torn flesh. The wound is covered with the fine brown powder taken from dried toadstools, which to my own knowledge will stop bleeding, and is soothing and healing. It has taken less than 15 minutes for the six to complete their ordeal; immediately six others take their place.

At the same time, daily, for six days, the test is carried out, not one of the 48 young men failing to qualify as warriors. It is a great disgrace to the young man should he fail to pass the test, for in that event he is compelled to help the womenfolk around the camp gathering wood, making fires, cleaning game, drawing water — not for such as he are the pleasures of the hunt or the thrill of war. The young girls avoid him.

At the conclusion of the trials for the day, the visiting, feasting and drinking begins and continues day and night. The older women have kept the pots boiling, buffalo, moose, bear fat, beaver tail, deer tongues, ducks, geese, partridges, saskatoons and cranberries fill the pots. Tea — tea on the boil day and night. Drums beat, boys and girls shout and romp, young boys with bows and arrows aim at targets of interwoven willow hoops, which are thrown and shot at while rolling, and seldom missed.

Continual movement, family to family, lodge to lodge, eating and drinking everywhere, young braves singing and dancing. To increase the potency of the boiled tea, blackstrap and other tobaccos, saskatoons and cranberries are added. These cocktails, with the added excitement of the drum beats and noise, bring out actions very similar to present-day cocktail parties — the difference only the surroundings — instead of chesterfields or bed, the bare ground, the same ideas, however, lying down wherever sleep overtakes them — waking — eating — drinking.

The dancing lodges had been erected where dancers took their turns. The program was made up of but four dances — the "Wood Partridge," the "Prairie Chicken," the "Medicine Rattlers" and the "Kid Fox." Each in turn to vocal and rum music went through their movements. The dances are imitations of birds and animals dancing, resembling somewhat the quadrille and the lancers.

This band of Crees were prosperous — the winter catch of fur had been large. They were well provided with trade goods, chief of which were Hudson's Bay four-point blankets. The blankets, much lighter in weight than a buffalo robe, were used in place of it as part of gambling paraphernalia. The game, between two contestants who endeavoured to hide three articles, in their hands or under the blanket which covered each of the contestants' knees as they sat on the ground facing each other. The wagers were for wearing apparel, pipes, dogs, horses and, in a crisis — wives. Sharpened stakes were used for chips. Each contestant had a friend responsible for moving the stakes to the winner's side.

The manipulator shows his opponent the three articles, then he makes passes behind, before and under the blanket, then exposes them. This goes on for some minutes. He suddenly stops — both closed hands extended in the direction of his opponent. The drums are silent. The opponent claps his hands together and by certain movements of his fingers and hands indicates where he thinks the three articles are hidden. These hand signals appear to have been adopted by the present day buyer on the floor of a stock exchange.

When a correct guess was made, the three hidden articles were transferred to the winner. When a wager is won, another is made, and so continued for several nights and ays till one or the other is cleaned out. Should either of the players become weary, a friend is ready to substitute for him. Their women provide them with food and drink.

These festivities are repeated night and day for the duration of The Last Sun Dance. I had spent much of the time during the week running about, taking in everything to be seen. Yet on the morning following the last day of the festival I was up early and out on the balcony of the Big House. I looked over the flat, there was of sign of life — the flat was deserted. Nothing but the skeleton of the Sun Temple was to be seen.

The camp had moved at dawn.

A Contest between
Medicine Men

E.R.

The Shaking Tent mystery has been widely witnessed and repeatedly reported by explorers, missionaries, and traders. Indeed, preserved are over one hundred descriptions of the rite's performance between Samuel de Champlain's description of 1609 and an anthropologist's account in 1989. But rare if not unique is this account of the contest, waged by competing medicine men, which involves a Shaking Tent and the watchful gaze of both a Corporal of the Royal Canadian Mounted Police and a Factor of the Hudson's Bay Company!

The account that follows describes just such a contest held to determine which of the two medicine men — the older resident or the younger interloper — could and would hold sway over the settlement and its inhabitants. The account comes from the pen of an unnamed H.B.C. factor, a native of Winnipeg, identified by his initials — E.R.

Winifred G. Barton included E.R.'s account in her book Psychic Phenomena in Canada *(Ottawa: Psi-Science Productions Ltd., c. 1967).*

IN THE YEAR 1920 I was just a greenhorn, having recently come from England to become a clerk in the Hudson's Bay Company at a post in Northern Manitoba. The post was situated on one of several large lakes which dot this part of Manitoba. The Indian

Reserve occupied a large part of the shore line of one of these lakes, as was the usual custom.

In those days each reserve had its Medicine Man, a person who rarely did any trapping or fishing but seemed to live comfortably. He was usually considered to be something of a leech, living off the rest of the tribe, by Hudson's Bay men — an opinion shared by the R.C.M.P. and the Catholic Missionaries. The two last-named establishments utilized every means possible to discredit the Medicine Men and the superstitions they evoked.

One day a young man appeared in the village. He was from another tribe and came in search of a bride. Once this mission was accomplished he tried to establish himself as a Medicine Man within the tribe, despite the fact that this enviable position was solidly held by an aging local resident.

On several occasions the young man challenged the other's powers, claiming his own "magic" to be superior. This caused some dissension within the tribe, which soon reached the ears of the local R.C.M.P. Corporal, who, gladly seizing upon a chance to quell belief in the supernatural, decided to pit the two claimants against each other in such a way as to utterly discredit each, and force the young troublemaker to return to his own tribe. The officer was aware that in his native village the younger man's prowess was considered negligible.

To this end, the R.C.M.P. Corporal picked upon what he considered to be the young brave's most boastful claim. Arrangements were made to hold a public contest, with the Corporal supervising the demonstration. As the local Oogima (Head Man, Chief, or Boss of the Hudson's Bay Post) I was the only other white man invited to attend the proceedings.

These began shortly after daybreak a few days later. The young man was permitted to build a doorless Migawap. This consisted of four poplar poles, each about twenty feet in length, which were criss-crossed in tepee fashion and bound firmly together at the top. In addition to being secured at the top, each pole had a long rope tied to it. The base of the poles was spread out, with each of the long ropes being firmly tied to a separate tree. The poles were then covered with solid canvass to form a tent without a doorway; the only opening was a small aperture at the apex. The soundness of the structure was fully tested by many of the onlookers, including myself and the Corporal, and we agreed that no amount of shaking, pushing, or pulling would cause any of the poles to so much as tremble.

Then a tin can, partially filled with pebbles, was lowered into the tent through the hole in the apex. It was suspended by a long leather thong which reached half way to the ground.

The whole construction was built under the watchful eyes of the Corporal and myself and occupied most of the daylight hours of that wintry day. When it was completed the Corporal and I took turns in walking around the tent whilst waiting for the full moon to rise above the horizon.

As darkness descended we sharpened our vigil. The villagers began to gather in the darkness beyond the searching beam of our two lanterns. We could feel the presence of a great many people rather than see them; a snapping twig, the shuffle of leaves in the September night told us that the whole tribe had assembled to watch the contest.

At the appointed hour the young Medicine Man approached boldly, accompanied by the old man whom he hoped to dispossess. They were followed by the Chief of the Tribe in full ritual costume — pinned to his chest was a very large medal, bestowed by the great white fathers who considered show more advantageous than food in those days.

The Corporal and I stationed ourselves so that between us we could see all sides of the Migawap. The young man stepped forward and invited the older Medicine Man to do his best to rattle the pebbles, without of course making any effort to touch the tent.

The old man went into a dance routine accompanied by his own very nasal singing and chanting which had as its basic theme the invoking of spirits to shake the tent and make the stones rattle. Half an hour later nothing had happened; the old man, quite exhausted by his exertions, gave a final leap into the air and shuffled off into the darkness looking tired and dejected.

Confidently the young man leapt forward moving in animated rhythm. His intonations were louder, more forceful; his steps full of the vigour and vitality of youth. Throughout the whole proceedings it should be noted that neither man stepped within three feet of the Migawap or touched any of the ropes that held it rigid.

In less than ten minutes the tent began to vibrate, and as the crescendo of the dance mounted to a fever pitch, the loud rattling of pebbles could clearly be heard above the chanting. A low murmur went up from the onlookers, to be followed by grunts of applause.

The Corporal hesitated for a moment, then quickly stepped up to the tent and slit the canvas coating from top to bottom with his sharp hunting knife. He felt sure that, somehow, someone had managed to get into the tent to shake the tin can. But it was quite empty.

The white man had gambled and lost. There was nothing that he could say or do to undo the damage that had been done. From this time forward the old Medicine Man was decidedly second-rate in the eyes of the tribe, and the younger man's prestige rose beyond all bounds of common sense. Within a short while he had more power among the villagers than either the Chief or his council.

The R.C.M.P. lost face — but in spite of all this I somehow think that the two young and inexperienced white men gained a lot that night.

The St. Victor Petroglyphs

Mark Abley

Mark Abley is an talented author and able commentator on cultural matters. He was born in Leamington Spa, England, and raised in Lethbridge and Saskatoon. He now lives and writes in Montreal. In 1985, he made a sentimental journey by automobile across the Prairie provinces. He kept detailed notes of the sights he saw and the emotions he felt. He published a highly readable account of his experiences as Beyond Forget: Rediscovering the Prairies (Vancouver: Douglas & McIntyre, 1986).

Abley has a sharp eye for shapes indicative of contrast and discontinuity. His sympathies are readily sparked by the marginal and the marginalized. In the following passage from Beyond Forget, he reacts with feeling to the sight of the indecipherable and enigmatic Indian petroglyphs at St. Victor, Southern Saskatchewan. There are hundreds of such sites across Canada. It seems that once a site has been consecrated to a noble purpose, it retains its special, spiritual qualities. It puts other places into its perspective.

EVEN SO, SOME PLACES on the continent hold a special power: places where the spirit becomes manifest in a sign, a song, a dream; places where a young man's quest for a vision might find a strong reward. One such place is a sandstone outcrop high above the western plains.

To reach the outcrop, I slipped past the Dirt Hills in the wind's teeth. I veered westward to the town of Assiniboia, then left its Empire Road for a chain of dark, rising rectangles of farmland. A side road led me to a tiny village in the shadow of a steepled, white-painted church. The village's name happens to be St. Victor. Another side road breasts the farms on its ascent to the carvings of a vanished people: the St. Victor petroglyphs.

The gravel car-park was empty. A narrow path squeezed down from it into a rumpled valley, thick with poplars and chokecherry bushes, and loud with the animated monologue of a brown thrasher. The path curved and rose towards a cluster of tan, contorted rocks against the sky. As I climbed, the wind sharpened and the chokecherries gave way to juniper. A mountain bluebird, swaying on a twig, watched me nervously from the peak of the outcrop. I climbed some more, and turned, and my eyes went numb with possibility.

Below the rocks, grey-green ranchland followed the ancestral contours of the earth. A few miles farther, ploughed oblongs dominated the plain. The road seemed a silver needle stitching a geometrical quilt. Far beyond the village of St. Victor and its pale adjacent lake, Assiniboia's grain elevators quivered above the town. The horizon from such a vantage point is so remote that the land merges with its sky in some liquid shimmer of the mind, as though the air and the soil are one.

I began to search for the carvings. The intense sunlight was a handicap, for petroglyphs are clearest in a damp half-light. Scrambling off the path, I walked under the outcrop, dodging the mosquitoes in the green hollows and hoping to detect in the hidden reaches the hoofprints, the faces, the toothed mouth that seekers carved here long ago as tokens of power and grace. What I found inescapable were the scrapings of vandals: all the possessive initials, the contemptuous JACKs and JANICEs who had felt a burdensome itch to scratch their own identities in stone. Once, where a slim rock pawed the air, I saw (I think) an ancient hand disfigured by BOB and his chums. A forlorn rage came over me.

Yet perhaps the vengeance of the invaders concealed a deep uneasiness. Perhaps their mockery hid fear. For in that wind-ridden solitude, I felt the Indians' presence on the prairies as a force that lingers: a power that smallpox, alcohol, despair and their confinement on little reserves have not been able to expunge. A sense of holiness can outlast its makers. I collected a few candy wrappers and tufts of loose plastic, and stuffed them into my pockets. Regrettably, I could do nothing about the broken glass. I was clambering back towards the summit, having almost abandoned hope of a good look at a carving, when a low table or rock at the corner of my eye presented a clear stick-figure man, a wayfarer in stone. The bluebird gave his quick alarm call and fled.

A blood-breasted hawk was hunting the pastureland, his shadow gliding rapidly over the spring grass. I sat cross-legged on the high prairie and wrote my name with a juniper stick in a smudge of sandy earth. The rocks received the sun, geologically patient. Below me was a foreign land. I found it sweet.

The day wore on. I got back into the car and drifted down the tall hill to the village. The province's guidebook gives its population as sixty-three and warns: "No Hotel Accommodation Available."

2. Animal Mysteries

Which Spectacle We All Beheld

Sir Humphrey Gilbert

The early explorers of the Atlantic seaboard reported seeing all manner of marine life, some comfortingly familiar, some uncomfortably unfamiliar. Sir Humphrey Gilbert (1539-1583), the English explorer, is among their number. On his second voyage to the New World, made in the Summer of 1583, he took possession of Newfoundland, the first of England's overseas colonies. He also reported a "spectacle."

It was while on the return voyage, on 31 August 1583, that Gilbert spotted a strange creature disporting in the waves of the Grand Banks off Cape Race. He likened the unfamiliar sight to "a lion in the ocean sea, or fish in shape of a lion." The sea creature was spotted by Gilbert, aboard the Squirrel, *but seen by four captains under his command, including his next-in-command, the captain of the* Golden Hind.

Perhaps the strange creature took a scunner to Gilbert or to the Squirrel. *Nine days later the* Squirrel, *encountering rough weather and icebergs, sank; all hands were lost. Over the tumult and the shouting, the captain of the* Golden Hind *reported hearing the voice of Gilbert repeatedly calling out, as if to comfort his crew, "We are as near to heaven by sea as by land!"*

Gilbert's narrative of the voyage was first published by the marine historian Richard Hakluyt in 1589. The text reproduced here derives from Selected Narratives from the Principal Navigations of Hakluyt *(Oxford: Clarendon Press, 1909) edited by Edward John Payne.*

SO UPON SATURDAY in the afternoon, the 31. of August, we changed our course, and returned back for *England*. At which very instant, even in winding about, there passed along between us and towards the land which we now forsook a very lion to our seeming, in shape, hair, and colour, not swimming after the manner of a beast by moving of his feet, but rather sliding upon the water with his whole body, excepting the legs, in sight, neither yet diving under, and again rising above the water, as the manner is of whales, dolphins, tunnies, porpoises, and all other fish: but confidently showing himself above water without hiding: notwithstanding, we presented ourselves in open view and gesture to amaze him, as all creatures will be commonly at a sudden gaze and sight of men. Thus he passed along turning his head to and fro, yawing and gaping wide, with ugly demonstration of long teeth, and glaring eyes; and to bid us a farewell, coming right against the Hind, he sent forth a horrible voice, roaring or bellowing as doth a lion, which spectacle we all beheld so far as we were able to discern the same, as men prone to wonder at every strange thing, as this doubtless was, to see a lion in the ocean sea, or fish in shape of a lion. What opinion others had thereof, and chiefly the General himself, I forbear to deliver: but he took it for *bonum omen*, rejoicing that he was to war against such an enemy, if it were the devil. The wind was large for *England* at our return, but very high, and the sea rough, insomuch as the frigate, wherein the General went, was almost swallowed up.

The Haunt of the Mammoth

David Thompson

The great explorer David Thompson (1770-1857) recorded in the narrative of his explorations references to the existence of gigantic beasts.

In the first instance, he noted the fact that the Peigan Indians believed in the existence of gigantic beasts. He heard about their traditional beliefs from members of the tribes on the bank of the Athabaska River in the vicinity of the Rocky Mountains in present-day Alberta. He recorded the tradition in the entry in his narrative for 5 Jan. 1811, where he referred to the gigantic animal in question as "the Mammoth." The passage appears, in the explorer's inimitable style, in David Thompson's Narrative of His Explorations in Western America, 1784-1812 (Toronto: Champlain Society, 1916) edited by J.B. Tyrrell.

In the second instance, Thompson was travelling in the vicinity of present-day Jasper on 7 Jan. 1811, when he and his guides came upon an extraordinary set of giant footprints. The explorer described the discovery in detail in his journal. The prints were very much on his mind when he returned to the site later that year. There he saw not only the tracks but the beast itself, as he noted in his journal on Oct. 5. The two excerpts here are taken from Travels in Western North America, 1784-1812 (1971) edited by Victor G. Hopwood. It is interesting to add in this context that Thompson's celebrated journal went unpublished until 1916.

Thompson was omnivorously curious about the natural world and possessed great powers of observation. He felt impelled to keep in check his penchant for the exotic. In this regard as in his work generally he succeeded admirably. Elsewhere he explained that as a child in Scotland he doted on highly imaginative writing, mentioning specifically two books, the Arabian Nights and Gulliver's Travels.

As an adult Thompson was aware that throughout Northern Europe and North America there were people, both European and Aboriginal, who claimed that they had seen mammoth beasts roaming the wilds at large and at will. Today these beasts or creatures could be called "prehistoric creatures," but the words would have meant little or nothing to Thompson. The concept of "prehistory" had yet to evolve, and the first fossils were yet to be systematically studied. Thompson would have equated descriptions of mammoth beasts with Job's account of the rhinoceros-like Behemoth.

The great mammals of the past are the Mastodons. A Mastodon is any one of a number of prehistoric mammals of the extinct genus Mammul, from which it is believed the modern elephant developed. During the Miocene era, Mastodons rose in the Old World and spread to the New World. They died out at the end of that era in the Old World, but in the New they survived well into the late Pleistocene or Ice Age.

One Mastodon which roamed the Northern Hemisphere was the Siberian Mammoth or Woolly Mammoth. This large, prehistoric, elephant-like creature stood nine feet tall, wore a coat of long shaggy hair, and thrust upward-curving tusks. Its appearance is familiar today through the cave paintings of Cro-Magnon man. Its ivory tusks are commonly found in Siberia, but from time to time the carcass of a Woolly Mammoth is recovered from the permafrost of the Arctic. There are even instances of the carcass being thawed out and eaten — once on site by starving peasants; once by scientists at a learned conference in Europe. The species is now extinct. It is generally held that the Woolly Mammoth has been extinct throughout the historical period, but sightings reported by native and non-native observers would tend to question that belief.

...STRANGE TO SAY, here is a strong belief that the haunt of the Mammoth, is about this defile, I questioned several, none could positively say, they have seen him, but their belief I found firm and not to be shaken. I remarked to them, that such an enormous heavy Animal must leave indelible marks of his feet, and his feeding. This they all acknowledged, and that they had never seen any marks of him and therefore could show me none. All I could say did not shake their belief in his existence.

Continuing our journey in the afternoon we came on the track of a large animal, the snow about six inches deep on the ice; I measured it; four large toes each of four inches in length to each a short claw; the ball of the foot sunk three inches lower than the toes, the hinder part of the foot did not mark well, the length fourteen inches, by eight inches in breadth, walking from north to south, and having passed about six hours. We were in no humour to follow him: the Men and Indians would have it to be a young mammoth and I held it to be the track of a large old grizzled Bear; yet the shortness of the nails, the ball of the foot, and it's great size was not that of a Bear, otherwise that of a very large old Bear, his claws worn away; this the Indians would not allow. Saw several tracks of Moose Deer.

*

I now recur to what I have already noticed in the early part of last winter, when proceeding up the Athabasca River to cross the Mountains, in company with...Men and four hunters, on one of the channels of the River we came to the track of a large animal, which measured fourteen inches in length by eight inches in breadth by a tape line. As the snow was about six inches in depth the track was well defined, and we could see it for a full one hundred yards from us, this animal was proceeding from north to south. We did not attempt to follow it, we had no time for it, and the Hunters, eager as they are to follow and shoot every animal made no attempt to follow this beast, for what could the balls of our fowling guns do against such an animal. Report from old times had made the head branches of this River, and the Mountains in the vicinity the abode of one, or more, very large animals, to which I never appeared to give credence; for these reports appeared to arise from that fondness for the marvelous so common to mankind; but the sight of the track of that large beast staggered me, and I often thought of it, yet never could bring myself to believe such an animal existed, but thought it might be the track of some monster Bear.

Creatures Half Satanic and Half Human

E. R. Young

The dread Windigo represents the spirit of cannibalism and demonic possession to the Algonkian-speaking Indians of Northeastern Canada. A single cannibalistic act will transform a man or woman into a Windigo who will then take to the woods, prey on his or her own kind, and wreak havoc upon the countryside.

The Windigo *has been derived from two Algonkian words, and according to the native writer and scholar Basil Johnston, the words mean "he for himself" — that is, extreme selfishness. The word may be pronounced and spelled any number of ways. To the Ojibway it is* Weendigo, *to the Saulteaux* Weendigo, *etc.*

Egerton Ryerson Young was a Methodist missionary who served among the Saulteaux and Cree Indians from 1868 to 1888. He established his mission centre at Norway House, north of Lake Winnipeg, Man., and among the Indians there he encountered the belief — to him the superstition — of the dread Windigo. Needless to say he dismissed the notion of the existence of such supernatural beings, yet he and his family suffered the consequences of those beliefs. In a lively fashion he recollected his experience with the Windigo-believers in Stories from Indian Wigwams and Northern Camp-Fires *(London: Charles H. Kelly, 1893).*

THAT THESE INDIANS should have in many of the tribes a most remarkable tradition of a great deluge, in which the world was overwhelmed, and the whole human race perished except one family who escaped either in a big canoe or on a great raft, is very suggestive and instructive. Among the many errors and superstitions into which they have fallen is the belief in the existence of windagoos, or gigantic creatures half satanic and half human, whom they represent as being of great size and dwelling in the dark, dreary forests. They describe them as being so powerful that when they march along they can brush aside the great pine-trees as an ordinary man does the grass of the prairies as he strides along through it. We found the Saulteaux Indians especially living in dread of these imaginary monsters. At many a camp-fire they used to tell us with bated breath that these windagoos were terrible cannibals, and that whenever they caught a lonely hunter far away from his home they soon devoured him. When I tried to disabuse their minds of these fears they proceeded to tell me of this one and that one who had been seized and devoured. The instances they brought before me were of hunters who had gone away on long journeys down dangerous rivers and treacherous rapids. On my expressing my opinion that the poor fellows had been drowned or had met with some other accident the Indians refused to be convinced. They will never admit that an accident could happen to any of their great hunters, and so the one theory always before them is that those who mysteriously disappear have been caught and devoured by the windagoos.

Of the power and grip this superstition had on these Saulteaux I had a startling and somewhat amusing illustration shortly after I had gone as their first missionary to live among them. Very cordially were we received, and much encouraged were we by the attention given to our words and the really sincere desire manifested to improve their circumstances socially as well as religiously. As there were many of their countrymen still without missionaries they used to frequently ask why it was that more missionaries with the great book were not sent among them. So one Sunday afternoon I held a kind of a missionary meeting with them. I took into the church my large maps of the world, with a number of pictures of heathens of many lands. I explained the map to them and showed them their own country, and told them that while we had a great land as regards size, yet there were many single cities with more people in them than all the Indians in our land put together. Then I showed them pictures of the cannibals of the isles of the Pacific, and described others of the wild, wicked nations of the earth, and told them that good white people were sending missionaries to a great many of these lands, and they must not expect to have them all come to them. "For," said I, "as bad as you and your forefathers were, some of these other people were much worse"; and then I particularized by describing some of the vilest and most degraded of the sinful races. I dwelt on cannibalism especially, and told of the man-eaters of the Pacific islands, who did not even object to a roasted missionary and some of his people cooked up with him. They were intensely interested, and also became very much excited before I finished, especially at what I had said about the cannibals.

The service closed and the people quickly returned to their little houses and wigwams at the Indian village, which was a little distance from the mission-house and church. The next morning, bright and early, I was up, and after breakfast and prayers started off to continue the work in which I had been engaged, namely, acting the part of a surveyor and helping the men run the dividing-lines between their little fields. To my great surprise, when I reached the first home I found that every body was away, and a stick tried across the door was the sign that they did not soon expect to return. On to the next and the next houses I went, and thus on through the whole village, and found, to my amazement, that I was literally a shepherd without a flock, a missionary without his people. Not a man, woman, child, dog, or canoe was to be found. After about an hour of aimless wandering around and wondering what had happened. I returned to my home and told my good wife of the loss of our flock. Like myself she was perplexed, and neither of us could make out what it meant.

The Indians had often, in large numbers, gone away on their great hunting excursions, but they never all went at the same time, and never without telling us of their going. So we were indeed perplexed. Toward evening I saw a solitary Indian coming from a distant island in his canoe. I quickly hurried down to the shore, and as he stopped paddling a few hundred feet from the beach I shouted to him to come to land. He immediately came in, and when at the shore I said to him:

"Where are the Indians?"

"Out there far away on that island in Lake Winnipeg," he replied.

"Why are they there?" I asked.

"Very much afraid," he said.

"Very much afraid! Of what are they afraid?" I asked.

"Windagoos! Cannibals!" he answered.

"Did any of you see any windagoos?" I asked.

"No, I don't think we did, but what you said about them in your address in the church made our hearts melt like water, and then the winds began to blow, and there from the dark forests, with the sighing winds we seemed to hear strange sounds, and some said, 'Windagoos! windagoos!' and that was enough, so we all got so alarmed that we launched our canoes, and, taking our families and dogs, away we paddled out to that distant island, and there the people all are now."

I confess I was amused as well as annoyed at the startling effect of my *moving* speech, and picking up a paddle I sprang into the canoe, and telling the Indian to show me what he could do as a canoe-man I struck in with him, and in less than an hour we had traversed the distance of several miles that lay between the mainland and that island. The Indians crowded down to the shore to meet us, and seemed delighted to see me. They wanted to shake hands and make a great fuss over me, but I repelled all their advances and would not shake hands with one of them. At this they were much crestfallen and surprised.

"Why did you leave us in this way?" I asked of the principal ones.

"Windagoos, windagoos!" they fairly shouted. "When you told us about those windagoos who used to eat the missionaries and their people you made us very much afraid, and our hearts got like water, and the more we talked the worse we got, and so we all hurried over here."

"Did I not tell you that those windagoos were more than a hundred days' journey away, even with your best canoes?" I asked.

"O, yes, you did, missionary," they said; "but we did not know but some of the might have started many days ago to come and catch us, and so we hurried out here."

"And you left your missionary and his wife and their little ones, whom you profess so to love, behind to be eaten by the windagoos, did you? And yet you say you so love us and are so thankful we have come to live among you and teach you the good way. Why, I am ashamed of you. Suppose the windagoos had come and no stalwart men had been there to help the missionary fight them off. What would he have thought of your love when he heard you had all, like a lot of old grandmothers, run away?"

Heartily shamed of themselves, they speedily launched their canoes and returned with me to their village, and very little did we hear after that about the windagoos.

The Home-Made Windigo

P.H. Godsell

P.H. *Godsell spent many years in the employ of the Hudson's Bay Company as a trader, a factor, and an inspector. When he penned the article which follows, he was serving as District Inspector of the Mackenzie River region in the Northwest Territories. The article appeared in the September 1921 issue of* The Beaver, *the journal published by The Bay.*

Godsell called his article "Overcoming Competition," and gave it the subtitle "The Story of the Home-made Weetigo." In it he recalled how in 1907 he was able to play on the fears and traditional beliefs of the Northern Indians to frustrate the life of a "free trader" and thus further the cause of the H.B.C. The native belief system included a bundle of superstitions regarding the dread Windigo, or Weentigo, *which as the spectre of starvation and cannibalism is said to stalk the northern woods and prey on unsuspecting Indians.*

Here is one of the few times that a white man boasts of hood-winking an entire native settlement. Important in this context is the author's boast: "My veracity was apparently unquestioned."

THE SPRING OF 1907 found me in charge of one of the remote out posts of the Company at a place called *Pepekwatooce*, situated in a trackless wilderness three hundred miles inland from the western shore of Hudson Bay and nine hundred miles from the nearest railroad. During the whole winter my sole companions

63

had been half-breed dog drivers employed by the Company and a few scattered families of Cree Indians.

Spring having arrived, all the Indians, with their squaws and families, had come in to the post, and were camped in their wigwams on a high ridge about a quarter of a mile in the rear of the fort.

The following day all the hunters were leaving for their final spring hunt, which consisted of overhauling their traps and shooting any beaver, musquash or otter they could find.

As the spring hunt was usually the best of the season, each man expected to return in the course of two weeks with a good catch of furs.

One night, about a week after the hunters had left, one of my half-breed employees, McKay by name, came rushing into my room to inform me that one of the squaws, while out cutting wood towards dusk, had seen a "devil," which had pursued her until she reached the encampment. McKay declared that the whole camp was in an uproar as a result of the woman's story.

For the benefit of the few who reading this article may not be conversant with Indian character, I should explain that Indians as a rule are very superstitious, with strong leanings towards the supernatural. They have a very firm belief in "devils," and in a kind of cannibal spirit, which they call a "*weetigo*." One has only to mention in the hearing of an Indian that he has seen a "*weetigo*" to turn the whole camp into a frenzy of fear.

I took a stroll over to the Indian camp, accompanied by McKay, to investigate the matter. With the exception of one wigwam, all the rest had been deserted, and the whole campful of women and children were assembled under the birch-bark covering of the dwelling of an old medicine man named *Piskonas*, who, although pale (relatively speaking) as the rest, was, by singing, beating on a drum, and sundry other incantations, endeavouring to keep the "devil" away.

The same thing occurred night after night, the whole camp remaining awake at night and snatching a little sleep in the day time.

In fact so frightened were the squaws that even in daylight they would not venture into the bush for firewood, except in bands of eight or ten.

About the sixth day after the supposed appearance of the "devil," I saw the half-breed who was in charge of a fur trade post for a tree trader in opposition to the Company. Between him and myself, as between all Hudson's Bay men and "free traders," a very keen rivalry existed, each of us endeavouring to obtain all the furs he could.

The free trader appeared to be as badly scared as the other Indians, and in a conversation that I had with him signified a very strong desire to leave the vicinity and take his wife, family and belongings to the centre of a small island about eight miles out in the nearby lake, where he thought he would be safe from the wiles of the "*weetigo*."

Seeing the way things were shaping, I did everything in my power to play upon his fears. Finally as he was leaving, he told me that should anything more be heard of the "*weetigo*" during the night he would carry out his intention of leaving his post and moving out into the lake without delay.

After the trader had left an idea ocurred to me while I lost no time in putting into execution. The sun was setting and in an hour it would be dusk; so, sending for my two men, McKay and Nazie, I informed them of what I intended doing.

My plan was to work upon my rival's fears to cause him to leave his post, by substituting a home-made "*weetigo*" for the super-natural article.

In a couple of days the hunters would probably return, and with the opposition trader away I should undoubtedly gather most of the furs.

Accordingly, announcing that we were going for a duck hunt, my half-breed companion and I embarked in a canoe, and after about an hour's paddling beached the canoe about a mile in the rear of the encampment which was hidden from view by a strip of woods skirting the lake shore. Quickly pressing through the woods we emerged into a flat swamp, plentifully covered with willow growth. It was now dark, but the conical wigwams could be seen dimly outlined against the sky about three-quarters of a mile distant. Everything in the camp was quiet.

We cut a couple of long willow sticks and secured a lantern which we had brought with us to the end of each. In the shelter of the willow bush we lighted the lamps, tying red handkerchiefs around them which caused them to emit a dull red glare.

Everything was deadly still as we hoisted the lighted lanterns overhead and gradually swung them to and fro.

Suddenly the stillness was rudely broken by an ear-splitting shriek from the direction of the camp, followed by a most awful uproar — a medley of shouts, cries, screams, and the wailing of children, with the occasional report of a muzzle-loader.

Now igniting a quantity of gunpowder, we held the lanterns side by side in the smoke. To the overwrought imaginations of the Indians on the ridge the two red lights no doubt appeared to be the blood-shot eyes of the "*weetigo*."

Suddenly the uproar subsided considerably, and we could distinctly hear the voice of a man who appeared to be addressing the women.

Presently the voice stopped and the uproar recommenced louder than ever. We still continued for a while to swing our lights in the air, intermittently moaning and shrieking as we did so.

Suddenly McKay shouted that there was someone moving in the darkness ahead. Hardly had he spoken when there was a flash, followed by the report of a rifle, and a cry from McKay, as he dropped his lantern and made off for the woods, quickly followed by Nazie.

I quickly grabbed the two lanterns, dropping them in a pool in the swamp and followed the others. Just then the rifle cracked again, and a bullet whizzed over my head — far too close to be comfortable. Meanwhile I could hear the frightened cries and shouts of McKay and Nazie in the woods ahead of me; they no doubt thought that the real "devil" was after them incensed by our mummery.

Breaking from the woods, I rushed to the beach, only to find my half-breed friends afloat and paddling for dear life. Calling to them to wait for me, I rushed waist deep into the icy cold water, and was hauled into the canoe. In the meantime the heavens had become overcast and occasional flashes of lightning dispelled the gloom. Rounding a point, there suddenly occurred a bright flash of lightning which illuminated everything, and lasted long enough for us to discern a birch bark canoe, far out in the lake, being vigorously propelled in the direction of Dog Island. I chuckled, for I had no doubt that it contained the free trader and his family.

Upon disembarking at the fort we immediately ran over to the encampment to find everybody in a state of the most extreme terror.

One young man, it appeared, upon seeing the "apparition," had uttered a shriek and immediately fainted. The camp was still in a furor when old *Piskonas*, the medicine man, returned, carrying a Winchester in his hand. Evidently it was he who had shot at us. Immediately upon arrival in camp he proceeded to recount his experiences to the band. He had, it appeared, fired two shots at the "*weetigo*," whereupon the devil had knocked him down (sic) and fled shrieking into the bush. Nobody suspected us as they thought that we had left for a duck hunt, but had returned owing to the storm.

Next morning I learned that, sure enough, F---- , upon the reappearance of the "devil" had immediately locked his store, transferred his wife, children and his belongings to his canoe, and with a plentiful supply of "grub" had left for Dog Island. As night approached, there were unmistakable signs of excitement and fear amongst my Indian friends, and shortly after dusk two boys came running into my room to say that the "*weetigo*" was about again as the women had heard him.

Rising from my chair, I picked up my Winchester and, having filled the magazine with cartridges, again walked over to the camp.

Immediately the story of the "*weetigo*'s*" reappearance was shouted in my ears from a dozen quarters. Thereupon I informed them that I was going to see if I could not kill the "devil" myself. Half a dozen voices immediately dinned into my ears the most approved methods of dealing with "*weetigos*." With my rifle under my arm, I strolled down the trail in the direction from which the latest sounds were supposed to have come. Penetrating for some distance into the woods, I stood awhile and waited. Then uttering one or two piercing shrieks, I commenced firing my rifle, as quickly as I could eject the exploded cartridges. Thus I discharged ten or twelve rounds of ammunition into the air, accompanying the shots with blood curdling yells.

Having emptied the magazine, I slowly retraced my steps to the camp, whence I could hear yells and cries of fright. Arriving inside the circle of light thrown out by a fire kindled in the middle of the camp I was assailed with questions.

In reply I informed them that I had had an encounter with the "*weetigo*" and had rendered him *hors de combat*; that the shrieks they had heard were emitted by the demon as I pumped lead into him.

I further informed them (lest some curious and sceptical member should take a notion to view the "remains") that I had treated my cartridges with a preparation known only to white men, which would penetrate the body of a "*weetigo*" and cause him to dissolve into thin air, whereas an ordinary bullet would take no effect. My veracity was apparently unquestioned. So highly appreciative were they that a withered old lady of some eighty or ninety odd summers insisted much to my distress, upon endeavour to perform the act of osculation upon my elusive person.

During the following day all the hunters returned with remarkably good catches of fur, and needless to say I lost no time in visiting them at their own firesides and relieved them of their weighty bundles of fur, which they were only too ready to render up, having heard of how I had "saved" their squaws and children from the "*weetigo*."

F---- did not reappear for three days, and I need scarcely say that by that time I had purchased every hair of fur in the Indians' possession, which information he received from his informants in gloomy silence.

Medicine Man vs. Sasquatch Man

J. W. Burns

This is an unusual account of an encounter between an Indian medicine man, whose name is Frank Dan, and a nameless Sasquatch. It was written by J. W. Burns, a teacher in the interior of British Columbia who is credited with popularizing the name Sasquatch for Big Foot, the North American Yeti. (The word Sasquatch is said to be "wild hairy men" in the language of the Salish.)

Burns's account refers to an incident that he said occurred in July 1936 along Morris Creek, a small tributary of the Harrison River which lies generally north of Chilliwack, B.C. This folklore-like account is not without charm. It is reproduced from Ivan T. Sanderson's Abominable Snowmen: Legend Come to Life *(New York: Jove/HBJ Book, 1977).*

IT WAS A LOVELY DAY, the clear waters of the creek shimmered in the bright sunshine and reflected the wild surroundings of cliff, trees, and vagrant cloud. A languid breeze wafted across the rocky gullies. Frank's canoe was gliding like a happy vision along the mountain stream. The Indian was busy hooking one fish after another hungry fish that had been liberated only a few days before from some hatchery. But the Indian was happy as he pulled them in and sang his medicine song. Then, without warning, a rock was hurled from the shelving slope above, falling with a fearful splash

69

within a few feet of his canoe, almost swamping the frail craft. Startled out of his skin, Frank glanced upward, and to his amazement beheld a weird looking creature, covered with hair, leaping from rock to rock down the wild declivity with the agility of a mountain goat. Frank recognized the hairy creature instantly. It was a Sasquatch. He knew it was one of the giants — he had met them on several occasions in past years, once on his own doorstep. But those were a timid sort and not unruly like the gent he was now facing.

Frank called upon his medicine powers, sula, and similar spirits to protect him. There was an immediate response to his appeal. The air throbbed and some huge boulders slid down the rocky mountain side, making a noise like the crack of doom. This was to frighten away the Sasquatch. But the giant was not to be frightened by falling rocks. Instead he hurried down the declivity carrying a great stone, probably weighing a ton or more, under his great hairy arm, which Frank guessed — just a rough guess — was at least two yards in length. Reaching a point of vantage a jutting ledge that hung far out over the water — he hurled it with all his might, this time missing the canoe by a narrow margin, filling it with water and drenching the poor frightened occupant with a cloud of spray.

Some idea of the size of the boulder may be gained from the fact that its huge bulk blocked the channel. Later it was dredged out by Jack Penny on the authority of the department of hinterland navigation. It may now be seen on the tenth floor of the Vancouver Public Museum in the department of "Curious Rocks"....

The giant now posed upon the other ledge in an attitude of wild majesty as if he were monarch of these foreboding haunts, shaking a colossal fist at the "great medicine man" who sat awe-struck and shuddering in the canoe, which he was trying to bail out with his shoe. The Indian saw the Sasquatch was in a towering rage, a passion that caused the great man to exude a repugnant odour, which was carried down to the canoe by a wisp of wind. The smell made Frank dizzy and his eyes began to smart and pop. Frank never smelt anything in his whole medicine career like it. It was more repelling than the stench of moccasin oil gone rotten. Indeed, it was so nasty that the fish quitted the pools and nooks and headed in schools for the Harrison River. The Indian, believing the giant was about to dive into the water and attack him, cast off his fishing lines and paddled away as fast as he was able.

An Encounter with a Windigo

Wilma Raynor

The Windigo is the spectre of cannibalism, but it also serves among native children as the bogeyman of the northern woods. Fear of the spectre or bogey man is part of the belief-system of the Algonkian-speaking Cree Indians of the Plains and the Northwest Territories.

This encounter with the Windigo was recalled by Wilma Raynor. At the time Mrs. Raynor was a nurse employed by the Health Service of the Department of Indian and Northern Affairs. For many years she served in the Arctic and sub-Arctic regions of the country. Her account of the Cree's reactions to the spectre first appeared under the title "Windigo Woman" in The Beaver, *Summer 1957.*

IT'S AN EVIL SPIRIT — feared by the Indians.

I learned this fact after I went north as a government field nurse on an Indian reservation. I felt quite strange when I found myself alone with the solemn faced Crees and quite inadequate when faced with difficult situations involved with ancient customs and superstitions. Then as I travelled from place to place I studied the ways of the people and found that a little common sense plus a friendly handshake and some self confidence was worth more than all the medicine and equipment I could carry.

Occasionally I would be told that an Indian had had an encounter with a Windigo. Sometimes it would be described as a weird animal and at other times as an evil faced woman. it had appeared to them in darkness and even in broad daylight and it was regarded as a bad omen. I decided that these strange stories were quite ridiculous and never took them very seriously until several years later when I had reason to change my views.

I was posted at the north end of Lake Winnipeg. After two years in this area I knew the Indians pretty well and most of them spoke English. One day when returning from an early morning call, I noticed a young Indian woman walking slowly to the water's edge to fill her pail. I sat down on a log and watched her from a distance. It was Christina, a nice quiet girl about nineteen years old. The water was unusually calm, and Christina stood there, pail in hand, gazing as though fascinated with the beauty of the still blue water and the islands in the distance. Suddenly I heard a piercing scream and saw Christina stumbling as she ran over the rough ground and disappeared into the cabin. A few seconds later she emerged, frantically pulling her mother toward the shore where the pail had been dropped. All this time Christina was shrieking hysterically as she pointed at something on the water. Then I watched the mother drag the girl back from the water's edge. I decided to investigate.

By the time I reached the little cabin, at least six neighbours had gathered to help and to sympathize, and as the family itself numbered nine or ten, I could scarcely squeeze myself into the room. Loud sobbing from a far corner led me to the poor girl, who was being held down on the bed by two big Indian women.

"What happened?" I asked her mother, after making a brief examination.

For a moment she just looked at me, shrugging her shoulders helplessly, then slowly she walked from the bed, out of hearing of the girl and in a low undertone murmured, "The Windigo...she seen it...she scairt."

"Where?" I enquired.

"The lake"...and little by little I was able to piece together the appearance of this creature seen only a stone's throw from the cabin door. This Windigo appeared to be a woman standing in the water up to her waist. She had long black hair hanging loosely around her evil face and she was beckoning to the girl with a long thin arm.

The mother could see nothing on the calm water and had a hard struggle to bring the girl away. Christina seemed to be drawn to this spectre like a moth to a flame.

I stayed beside Christina for some time and was able to soothe her with a sedative. I saw her several times during the next three months and although she did respond to treatment, she never fully recovered — possibly owing to what happened later. Eventually I decided that it was all due to a nervous disorder and the Windigo once more receded to the back of my mind.

Freeze-up had now come and another one of my numerous calls brought me to the same area. This time it was a very dark night when a young Indian brave went through the ice, while skating home alone. His frantic cries had been heard by another Indian but couldn't be found until too late. While taking the history of this case I learned that the young man had been visiting Christina in her home just prior to the accident.

An old Indian came up to me to describe in detail the position of the body when it was found. "Funny thing," said the old man, slowly shaking his head, "I never seen a man drown like that one…and me…I see some drown many times in my life." Then he went on: "We find hole in ice…then we shine light around the hole…and we see his head…just under the ice…very close to that hole — just like he stand there."

Next day I further investigated the accident. The open the hole in the ice left no doubt — it was the place where the Windigo had called Christina.

I Stood Still Wondering

Charles Flood

*A most interesting statuary declaration was made in
September of 1957 by Charles Flood of New Westminster, B.C. In
his declaration Flood, an old-timer and one-time prospector,
recalled a most unusual experience that had taken place more than
four decades earlier. At the time he was prospecting in the
Chilliwack Lake area of British Columbia with two of his friends.
Did they espy the Sasquatch, the hairy wildman of the rugged B.C.
Interior? Flood's declaration appeared in full in Ivan T. Sanderson's
book* Abominable Snowmen: Legend Come to Life *(New York:
Jove/HBJ Book, 1977).*

I, CHARLES FLOOD of New Westminster (formerly of Hope) declare
the following story to be true:

I am 75 years of age and spent most of my life prospecting in the
local mountains to the south of Hope, towards the American
boundary and in the Chilliwack Lake area.

In 1915, Donald McCrae and Green Hicks of Agassiz, B.C., and
my-self, explored an area over an unknown divide, on the way back
to Hope, near the Holy Cross Mountains.

Green Hicks, a half-breed Indians, told McCrae and me a story,
he claimed he had seen alligators at what he called Alligator Lake,
and wild humans at what he called Cougar Lake. Out of curiosity
we went with him; he had been there a week previous looking for a

75

fur trap line. Sure enough, we saw his alligators, but they were black, twice the size of lizards in a small mud lake.

Awhile further up was Cougar Lake. Several years before a fire swept over many square miles of mountains which resulted in large areas of mountain huckleberry growth. Green Hicks suddenly stopped us and drew our attention to a large, light brown creature about eight feet high, standing on its hind legs (standing upright) pulling the berry bushes with one hand or paw toward him and putting berries in his mouth with the other hand, or paw.

I stood still wondering, and McRae and Green Hicks were arguing. Hicks said, "It is a wild man," and McRae said, "It is a bear." As far as I am concerned the strange creature looked more like a human being. We had seen several black and brown bear on the trip, but that thing looked altogether different.

Huge brown bear are known to be in Alaska, but have never been seen in southern British Columbia.

Nessie and Ogopogo

Henry H. Bauer

The Loch Ness Monster invariably springs to mind whenever anyone mentions lake monsters or sea serpents. Since 1933, Nellie of Loch Ness in northern Scotland has been the world's best-known lake monster, the one against which all others are measured and found wanting.

Prophetic words were spoken about Nessie in my book Mysterious Canada *(1988). In the section devoted to British Columbia, Ogopogo is identified as the denizen of Okanagan Lake and described as Canada's best-known sea serpent. Indeed, it says there that "Ogopogo is usually identified as Canada's Loch Ness monster, but the reverse is true, for it is Nessie who should be identified as Scotland's Ogopogo." What the author had in mind was the fact that, native and Christian legends to one side, actual reported sightings of the Canadian monster predate by at least one year sightings of the Scottish monster.*

Since then some evidence has come to light which goes beyond proof of priority and establishes the common ancestry of the two monsters. It seems that reports of Ogo are responsible for reports of Nessie; that both monsters are creations of individuals; and that Nessie sprang full-blown from the imagination of a firm of publicists in London, England. There is no direct proof of these assertions, but there is some documentary evidence. Here it is.

Henry H. Bauer is Professor of Chemistry and Science Studies at Virginia Polytechnic Institute and State University, where he served for eight years as Dean of the College of Arts and Sciences. He is the author of Beyond Velikovsky: The History of a Public Controversy *(1984) and* The Engima of Loch Ness: Making Sense of a Mystery *(1986). Both books are serious studies of their subjects published in Urbana and Chicago by the University of Illinois Press. The first chapter of the latter book is titled "The Monster Is a Myth," and it offers some evidence for the common ancestry of Ogo and Nessie plus the reason for the popularity of the reports in the first place. Chalk everything up to hoax or fraud or tourism publicity!*

What appears below is an excerpt from that chapter, an excerpt in which Bauer quotes from some personal correspondence. He does not identify the correspondent; in fact, he deliberately withholds the identity of the letter-writer. But he does offer the careful reader a passel of clues as to the identity of the informant. Bauer explained his reluctance to identify the correspondent in an endnote in these words: "The author, whom I shall call Lester Smith, asked me not to print his well-known nom de plume: *'When the book of mine you read appeared I was inundated with letters from all over the world. I don't want that to happen again.'"*

A pleasant pastime for some literary detective might be the task of establishing the identity of the British author called "Lester Smith," and then determining in which book "Lester Smith" makes reference to both Ogo and Nessie.

Will such revelations of the mundane origin of Ogo and Nessie affect the tourist traffic to the two loch-like lakes? Is the Pope Catholic? Is the world round? Is justice rewarded? Wonders never cease....

HUMANITY'S KNOWLEDGE of natural history was low in fact and high in fancy for so long that it is a daunting task now to separate the one from the other in legends and the older records....

When I began work on this book I recalled heaving read long ago in a semi-autobiographical novel that the Loch Ness monster had been an invention of journalists. I wrote to ask the author of that book about the provenance of his story. Here is his reply:

Dear Mr. Bauer: Your letter of July 8th has only just reached me.

Let me first tell you that...[Lester Smith] writes fiction, although it may often appear otherwise. Truth with trimmings might describe it better. I am afraid I don't remember in which of my books the episode you quote may be found, but it was not necessarily the truth. The truth now follows.

In the early 1930s I, with two young partners, ran a publicity service in London. One of the partners was a native of Lossiemouth, Ramsay Macdonald's home, not far from Loch Ness. On returning from a holiday he brought us a small account. A group of hotels catering to tourists in that area wanted publicity and offered a fee of 50 pounds. We accepted.... Around the same time we were offered a more important account by [a realtor]...in the Okanagan Valley of British Columbia.... We were told and I am inclined to believe that he invented the Ogopogo, a legendary creature inhabiting Lake Okanagan. This was corn in Egypt. The Lossiemouth member of the firm then told us that for centuries a legendary creature was supposed to dwell in Loch Ness. We had never heard of it. At that time our "board room" was the saloon bar of a pub just off Trafalgar Square and over several pints of beer we became midwives of the reborn Loch Ness Monster. All we had to do was to arrange for the Monster to be sighted. This we did and the story snowballed. Thousands went north to see it and see it they did. It was, of course, pure hokum. The unwitting parent was the Ogopogo.

The technique is old and effective and has been used through the ages by organized religions. More recently did we not have soldiers wide-eyed on "seeing" the Angels of Mons!

I hope this helps you.

I could hardly believe that serendipity had thus brought me the explanation of the Loch Ness affair. Could Smith's recollection be trusted nearly fifty years after the event? Was it not implausible that he could not remember in which of his books he had told the story?

In point of fact I discovered that Smith had written under more than one pseudonym and a total of more than forty books, as well as stories, articles, scripts, and so forth, so it was not implausible that he could not remember just where he had used a by-the-way reference to Loch Ness. Over the course of several years I reread Smith's books as I could find them (most were out of print and had never been published in the United States); several references to Okanagan were tantalizing. Finally I found the following, in an account published in 1950: "...a great number of persons have sworn to having seen a creature called the Loch Ness Monster, and you may accept my assurance that the same Loch Ness Monster was born in my presence, during a conversation which took place in a London public house, under the shadow of the monument erected to the great Lord Nelson.... The Loch Ness Monster... was invented for a fee of 150 pounds by an ingenious publicity man employed by hotel-keepers." So Smith's recollection of the events had been the same in 1950 as in 1980, which makes his story all the more convincing — especially since my query to Smith had been based on a misrecollection of what I had read.

Apparently this publicity scheme of Smith and his colleagues — which doubtless involved the press, be it wittingly or unwittingly — proved to be very effective indeed. Loch Ness became the most popular destination in Britain for motorists: a patrolman for the Automobile Association recalled an occasion when 200 cars were drawn up by the side of the loch, and pandemonium would break out every time he pointed to something. Monster-hunting parties became fashionable, and all the hotels in the area were filled over the Christmas season of 1933. Inverness was flood-lit for the first time. On Boxing Day cars formed virtually a continuous line for the twenty miles from Inverness to Fort Augustus. In February 1934 the Inverness Town Council reduced its expenditure for advertising by one-third since the monster was deemed sufficient publicity.

Smith's revelation helps greatly in elucidating the course of events. The Nessie sighting that spurred the flap of 1933 was reported in the *Inverness Courier* on May 2: an unnamed couple had seen a large creature disporting itself in Loch Ness. Rupert Gould's inquiries revealed that these people were, in point of fact, the lessees of the Drumnadrochit Hotel, near Urquhart Bay on the north side of the loch (the side on which the new road had been built). The report had been given to the *Inverness Courier* by a local correspondent, Alex Campbell, who was also the water bailiff at Fort Augustus.

Campbell himself subsequently saw the monster on a number of occasions....

All of the salient features of the Loch Ness phenomenon, then, can comfortably be explained by the stimulus of legend and of public relations acting on the gullible and expectant visitor, by human misperceptions made more likely by occasional combinations of mirage-like effects working on such natural objects as birds and tree trunks. Or can they?

3. Spiritualistic Mysteries

The Hydesville Outbreak

Mrs. Margaret Fox and Mr. John D. Fox

The Hydesville Outbreak is as good a phrase as any to use to refer to the series of mysterious rappings that were heard at the Fox Family Cottage at Hydesville, N.Y. The rappings first came to public knowledge the evening of 31 March 1848. Were they evidence of "spirit communication"?

The poltergeist-like disturbance came as a welcome winter's distraction and a premature April Fool's Day diversion to the farming families that lived at Hydesville, near present-day Newark, immediately west of Palmyra, a locale sacred to the Mormons. To everyone's surprise, the rappings became an incident of national and then international import. They became a psychic phenomenon, as news of the rappings at Hydesville spread to Rochester, to New York City, and thence to the capital cities of the world. The news created a vogue for mediumship and seances. In fact, the Hydesville Outbreak is considered the beginning of modern Spiritualism.

The rappings are associated with the celebrated Fox Sisters — Kate, Maggie, and Leah — whose lives were changed by what occurred that winter and spring. The sisters were soon internationally renowned — and reviled — for their practice of mediumship, which they based on the principle of "spirit communication." But it is to the sisters' parents that is owed the first detailed descriptions of the Hydesville Outbreak and the attendant mediumship.

The events of those March evenings were recalled in statements drawn up and signed in April of that year by Mrs. Margaret Fox and Mr. John D. Fox. What about the parents? Mrs. Fox was of French, Dutch, and English ancestry; Mr. Fox was of German background, the original form of the name being Voss, then Foss, and finally Fox. They were a hardy and affectionate farming couple whose union was blessed with numerous children. There are some indications that Mrs. Fox was highly suggestible and that Mr. Fox was not terribly critical.

The Fox Family were newcomers to the Hydesville area, to Upper State New York, and indeed to the United States. They had moved into the cottage on 11 Dec. 1847, hardly four months prior to the outbreak. They had come from a similar rural community, Consecon, near Belleville, in Upper Canada, and were seeking superior farming conditions on the south shore of Lake Ontario than they had found on the north shore.

There is always the possibility that young Kate and Maggie, frisky youngsters, were playing pranks. Maybe they had learned to produce loud raps by covertly cracking their toe-joints. Perhaps it all began with a few children's games in anticipation of April Fool's Day. Yet it is a matter of historical record that in 1904 excavators, digging in the cellar of the cottage, came upon a human skeleton. Were these bones the remains of the thirty-one-year-old murdered man mentioned by Mrs. Fox?

The accounts of Mr. and Mrs. Fox are reprinted from Leslie Shepard's edition of the three-volume Encyclopedia of Occultism and Parapsychology *(Detroit: Gale Research Company, 1978; 2nd ed., 1984).*

Statement of Mrs. Fox

ON THE NIGHT of the first disturbance we all got up, lighted a candle and searched the entire house, the noises continuing during the time and being heard near the same place. Although not very loud, it produced a jar of the bedsteads and chairs that could be felt when we were in bed. It was a tremulous motion, more than a sudden jar. We could feel the jar when standing on the floor. It continued on this night until we slept. I did not sleep until about twelve o'clock. On March 30 we were disturbed all night. The noises were heard in all parts of the house. My husband stationed himself outside the door while I stood inside, and the knocks came on the door between us. We heard footsteps in the pantry, and walking downstairs; we could not rest, and I then concluded that the house must be haunted by some unhappy restless spirit. I had often heard of such things, but had never witnessed anything of the kind that I could not account for before.

On Friday night, March 31, 1848, we concluded to go to bed early and not permit ourselves to be disturbed by the noises, but try and get a night's rest. My husband was here on all these occasions, heard the noises and helped in the search. It was very early when we went to bed on this night — hardly dark. I had been so broken of my rest I was almost sick. My husband had not gone to bed when we first heard the noise on this evening. I had just lain down. It commenced as usual. I knew it from all the other noises I had ever heard before. The children, who slept in the other bed in the room, heard the rapping and tried to make similar sounds by snapping their fingers.

My youngest child, Cathie, said: "Mr. Splitfoot, do as I do," clapping her hands. The sound instantly followed her with the same number of raps. When she stopped the sound ceased for a short time. Then Margaretta said, in sport, "No, do just as I do. Count one, two, three four," striking one hand against the other at the same time; and the raps came as before. She was afraid to repeat them. Then Cathie said in her childish simplicity, "Oh, mother, I know what it is. Tomorrow is April-fool day and it is somebody trying to fool us."

I then thought I could put a test that no one in the place could answer. I asked the noise to rap my different children's ages, successively. Instantly each one of my children's ages was given correctly, pausing between them sufficiently long to individualize them until the seventh, at which a longer pause was made, and then three more emphatic raps were given, corresponding to the age of the little one that died, which was my youngest child.

I then asked: "Is this a human being that answers my questions so correctly?" There was no rap. I asked, "Is it a spirit? If it is make two raps." Two sounds were given as soon as the request was made. I then said: "If it was an injured spirit, make two raps," which were instantly made, causing the house to tremble. I asked: "Were you injured in this house?" The answer was given as before. "Is the person living that injured you?" Answered by raps in the same manner. I ascertained by the same simple method that it was a man, aged thirty-one years, that he had been murdered in this house and his remains were buried in the cellar; that his family consisted of a wife and five children, two sons and three daughters, all living at the time of his death, but that his wife had since died. I asked: "Will you continue to rap if I call my neighbours that they may hear it too?" The raps were loud in the affirmative.

My husband went and called in Mrs. Redfield, our nearest neighbour. She is a very candid woman. The girls were sitting up in bed clinging to each other and trembling with terror. I think I was as calm as I am now. Mrs. Redfield came immediately (this was about half past seven), thinking she would have a laugh at the children. But when she saw them pale with fright and nearly speechless, she was amazed and believed there was something more serious than she had supposed. I asked a few questions for her and she was answered as before. He told her age exactly. She then called her husband, and the same questions were asked and answered.

Then Mr. Redfield called in Mr. Duesler and wife, and several others. Mr. Duesler then called in Mr. and Mrs. Hyde, also Mr. and Mrs. Jewell. Mr. Duesler asked many questions and received answers. I then named all the neighbours I could think of and asked if any of them had injured him and received no answer. Mr. Duesler then asked questions and received answers. He asked, "Were you murdered?" Raps affirmative. "Can your murderer be brought to justice?" No sound. "Can he be punished by law?" No answer. He then said: "If your murderer cannot be punished by the law manifest it by raps," and the raps were made clearly and distinctly. In the same way Mr. Duesler ascertained that he was murdered in the east bedroom about five years ago and that the murder was committed by a Mr. ---- on a Tuesday night at twelve o'clock; that he was murdered by having his throat cut with a butcher's knife; that the body was taken through the buttery, down the stairway and that it was buried ten feet below the surface of the ground. It was also ascertained that he was murdered for his money by raps affirmative.

"How much was it — one hundred?" No rap. "Was it two hundred?" etc., and when he mentioned five hundred the raps replied in the affirmative.

Many called in who were fishing in the creek, and all heard the same questions and answers. Many remained in the house all night. I and my children left the house. My husband remained in the house with Mr. Redfield all night. On the next Saturday the house was filled to overflowing. There was no sounds heard during the day, but they commenced again in the evening. It was said that there were over three hundred persons present at the time. On Sunday morning the noises were heard throughout the day by all who came to the house.

On Saturday night, April 1, they commenced digging in the cellar; they dug until they came to water and then gave it up. The noise was not heard on Sunday evening nor during the night. Stephen B. Smith and wife (my daughter Marie) and my son David S. Fox and wife, slept in the room this night.

I have heard nothing since that time until yesterday. In the forenoon of yesterday there were several questions answered in way by rapping. I have heard the noise several times today.

I am not a believer in haunted houses or supernatural appearances. I am very sorry there has been so much excitement about it. It has been a great deal of trouble to us. It was our misfortune to live here at this time; but I am willing and anxious that the truth should be known and that a true statement should be made. I cannot account for these noises; all that I know is that they have been heard repeatedly as I have stated. I have heard this rapping again this (Tuesday) morning, April 4. My children have also heard it.

I certify that the foregoing statement has been read to me and that the same is true; and that I should be willing to take my oath that it is so if necessary.

(Signed) *Margaret Fox*
April 11, 1848.

Statement of Mr. Fox

I have also heard the above statement of my wife, Margaret Fox, read, and hereby certify that the same is true in all its particulars. I heard the same rappings which she has spoken of, in answer to the questions, as stated by her. There have been a great many questions besides those asked, and answered in the same way. Some have been asked a great many times and they have always received the same answer. There has never been any contradiction whatever.

I do not know of any way to account for these noises, as being caused by any natural means. We have searched very nook and corner in and about the house at different times to ascertain if possible whether anything or anybody was secreted there that could make the noise and have not been able to find anything which would or could explain the mystery. It has caused a great deal of trouble and anxiety.

Hundreds have visited the house, so that it is impossible for us to attend to our daily occupations; and I hope that, whether caused by natural or supernatural means, it will be ascertained soon. The digging in the cellar will be resumed as soon as the water settles, and then it can be ascertained whether there are any indications of a body ever having been buried there; and if there are I shall have no doubt but that it is of supernatural origin.

(Signed) *John D. Fox*
April 11, 1848.

This Dreadful Life of Deception

Margaret Fox

Remarkable is the best word to use to describe these two documents. They were originally published in the 21 Oct. 1888 issue of The New York World. They are reprinted here with a minimum of copy editing from A Skeptic's Handbook of Parapsychology (Buffalo: Prometheus Books, 1985) edited by Paul Kurtz.

The first document is called "The Medium's Statement." It consists of the confession of fraud of Margaret Fox (1838-1893) who, with her two sisters, was responsible for the launching the modern Spiritualist movement. In her statement she confesses to more than four decades of fraud and deception. Margaret, who is also known as Margaretta or Maggie, was the middle child of the three famous (or infamous) Fox Sisters. Three years younger than Margaret was Catharine (Kate) Fox (1838-1893); considerably older than Margaret was Leah (Ann) Fox (1814-1890). So, when it all began, Margaret was about ten years of age; Catharine was about thirteen; Leah was already married and living in nearby Rochester, N.Y.

Where it all began was at the Fox Family Cottage at Hydesville, a small farming community which today lies on the outskirts of Newark, N.Y. It commenced with childish pranks the evening of 31 March 1848. Thus has been established the traditional birthplace and birthdate of the modern Spiritualist movement. It is true that men and women have always and everywhere tried to communicate with the spirits of the dead; but it is also true that for the first

*time at Hydesville on that evening the modern practice and para-
phernalia of mediumistic communication with the "spirit world"
was established: raps, knocks, little tables, séances, darkened
chambers, etc.*

*The second document, "A Séance," is an unnamed journalist's
account of some of Margaret Fox's "effects." It accompanied the
confession and was intended to demonstrate that the medium
resorted to trickery to produce her raps. It also drew public attention to the fact that a public exposé of such matters at the New York
Academy of Music was scheduled for that evening. At that sold-out
event, Margaret Fox was the main speaker; her sister Catharine
cheered from the audience. Leah was out of town that evening, but
when she returned to New York she denounced the whole exposé as
a put-up job.*

*The confession and public exposé produced mixed results. Skep-
tics were confirmed in their opinion that the Fox Sisters' mediumship — and hence all other mediumship — was fraudulent and that
Spiritualism was a snare and a delusion. Believers kept their faith
but lamented the regrettable lapse of two sisters out of three. The
lapse did not last very long, however, for the two sisters, properly
penitent, returned to the fold. The following year Margaret and
Catharine recanted and reaffirmed their faith in "spirit communication." By this time, however, the public could see them as two
penniless older women who drank too much.*

*It should be noted that the Fox confession is a confused docu-
ment with more than its share of falsehoods. For instance, there is
no proof that Margaret Fox was ever married to the noted Boston
physician and Arctic explorer Elisha Kent Kane, despite the fact
that their courtship became a matter of public record. Another
instance is that Margaret and her sisters were born in the farming
community of Consecon, near Belleville, Ont., not in New York
State, as Margaret implies. The family moved from Consecon to
Hydesville on 11 Dec. 1847, about four months before the "manifestations" commenced.*

*So three Upper Canadian farm girls almost single-handedly
launched one of history's most remarkable movement — some
sense of which may be gleaned from Margaret Fox's remarkable
confession.*

The Medium's Statement

I THINK THAT it is about time that the truth of this miserable subject "Spiritualism" should be brought out. It is now wide-spread all over the world, and unless it is put down soon it will do great evil. I was the first in the field and I have the right to expose it.

My sister Katie and myself were very young children when this horrible deception began. I was eight, and just a year and a half older than she. We were very mischievous children and we wanted to terrify our dear mother, who was a very good woman and very easily frightened. At night, when we went to bed, we used to tie an apple to a string and move the string up and down, causing the apple to bump on the floor, or we would drop the apple on the floor, making a strange noise every time it would rebound. Mother listened to this for a time. She could not understand it and did not suspect us of being capable of a trick because we were so young.

At last she could stand it no longer and she called the neighbours in and told them about it. It was this that set us to discover the means of making the raps. I think, when I reflect about it, that it was a most wonderful discovery — a very wonderful thing that children so young should make such a discovery, and all through our mischief. Children will always find means to accomplish mischief. And to the thought of spirits, this never entered our brains. We were too young to know anything about that.

Our oldest sister, Mrs. Underhill, was twenty-three years of age when I was born. She was in Rochester when these tricks first began, but came to Hydesville, the little village in Central New York where we lived and were born, shortly after. My father and mother were very good, honest people and great friends with the Hyde family for whom the village was named and who lived near. They took a great fancy to us and we were especial favorites of the Hydes, both before and after the notoriety that our rappings made became widespread. All the people around, as I have said, were called into witness these manifestations. My sister, now Mrs. Daniel Underhill — she was Mrs. Fish then — began to form a society of spiritualists. There were so many people coming to the house that we were not able to make use of the apple trick except when we were in bed and the room was dark. Even then we could hardly do it so that the only way was to rap on the bedstead.

And this is the way we began. First as a mere trick to frighten mother, and then, when so many people came to see us children, we were frightened ourselves and kept it up. We were then taken by Mrs. Underhill to Rochester. There it was that we discovered how to make the other raps. My sister Katie was the first one to discover that by swishing her fingers she could produce a certain noise with the knuckles and joints, and that the same effect could be made with the toes. Finding we could make raps with our feet — first with one foot and then with both — we practised until we could do this easily when the room was dark. No one suspected us of any trick because we were such young children. We were led on by my sister purposely and by my mother unintentionally. We often heard her say, "Is this a disembodied spirit that has taken possession of my dear children?"

That encouraged our fun, and we went on. All the neighbours thought there was something, and they wanted to find out what it was. They were convinced some one had been murdered in the house. They asked us about it, and we would rap one for the spirit answer "Yes," not three, as we did afterwards. We did not know anything about Spiritualism then. The murder, they concluded, must have been committed in the house. They went over the whole surrounding country, trying to get the names of people who had formerly lived in the house. They found finally a man by the name of Bell, and they said that this poor innocent man had committed a murder in the house, and that those noises came from the spirit of the murdered person. Poor Bell was shunned and looked upon by the whole community as a murderer. As far as the spirits were concerned, neither my sister nor I thought about it.

I am the widow of Dr. Kane, the Arctic explorer, and I say to you now, as I hold his memory dear and would call him to me were it possible, I know that there is no such thing as the departed returning to this life. I have tried to do so in every form, and know that it cannot be done. Many people have said to me that such a thing was possible, and seemed to believe so firmly in it that I tried to see if it were possible. While in London, some years ago, I went to the sexton of a churchyard and asked him if I could go among the graves at 12 o'clock at night. He consented when I told him that I wanted to do this for a certain purpose. I left my servant at the gate outside. I went to each grave and stood over it, and called upon the dead, alone there in the dark, to come and give me some token of their presence. All was silent, and I found that the dead would not return. That is how I tested it. There is no test left that I have not thoroughly sifted. Mediums I do not visit. They are too low and too illiterate. Dr. H. Wadsworth, of 91 Queen Anne street, London — a very dear friend of mine — sent me money for my expenses to go over to London. I said to him when I arrived: "I think too much of you to have you deceived, and there is nothing in Spiritualism. It is a fraud."

He answered me: "I thank you for telling me about it, Maggie. I know all the rest to be humbug. I thought I would have you to come in last." I said: "There are no dead or departed spirits that have returned." He said: "If you say so, Maggie, it must be true, because I have always believed in you." But still he seemed incredulous.

To return to the story of my childhood: I said I had gone with my sister Katie to Mrs. Underhill, my oldest sister, to Rochester. It was here that Mrs. Underhill gave her exhibitions. She took us there and we were exhibited to a lot of Spiritualist fanatics. We had crowds coming to see us and Mrs. Underhill made as much as $100 to $180 a night. She pocketed this. Parties came in from all parts to see us. Many as soon as they heard a little rap were convinced. But as the world grew wiser and science began to investigate, my younger sister and myself began to adapt our experiments to our audiences. Our séances were held in a room. There was a centre-table in the middle, and we all stood around it. There were some who even believed that the spirits of living people could be materialized. There are many different forms of Spiritualism. To all questions we would answer by raps. When I look back upon this life I almost say in defence of myself that I did not take any pleasure in it. I never believed in the spirits and I never professed to be a Spiritualist. My cards always say: "Mrs. Kane does not claim any spirit power, but people must judge for themselves." Nobody has ever suspected anything from the start, in 1848, until the present day as to any trickery in our methods. There has never been a detection.

Like most perplexing things when once made clear, it is astonishing how easily it is done. The rappings are simply the result of a perfect control of the muscles of the leg below the knee which govern the tendons of the foot and allow action of the toe and ankle bones that are not commonly known. Such perfect control is only possible when a child is taken at an early age and carefully and continually taught to practise the muscles which grow still in later years. A child at twelve is almost too old. With control of the muscles of the foot the toes may be brought down to the floor without any movement that is perceptible to the eye. The whole foot, in fact, can be made to give rappings by the use only of muscles below the knee. This, then, is the simple explanation of the whole method of the knocks and raps.

Some very wealthy people, formerly of San Francisco, came to see me some years ago when I lived in Forty-second street, and I did some rapping for them. I made the spirit rap on the chair, and one of the ladies cried out, "I feel the spirit tapping me on the shoulder." Of course that was pure imagination. A great many people, however, when they hear the rapping imagine at once that the spirits are touching them. It is a very common delusion. One fanatic gives Sunday services at the Adelphi Hall yet. He is called the "Old Patriarch." He said to some one the other day: "If Mrs. Kane says that she can make these rappings without the aid of the spirits she lies." This person will be one of those who will see that I speak the truth.

As I have said before, my sister Katie and myself continued in this business until she was twelve years old and I was thirteen and a half. After we left Rochester we travelled all over the United States. I was thirteen years old when Dr. Kane took care of me and took me out of the miserable life we began in 1848, and it was in 1853 that he took me away from this thing. It was at Philadelphia he met me. He sent me to a seminary and my vacations were spent with Mrs. Waters, a sister of Senator Cockrell. She lives not at No. 7 East Sixty-second street. She was a little inclined to believe in Spiritualism herself, although she never let Dr. Kane know about it. I was taken away from all "spiritual" influences and for a long time did not see any of my old associates. When Dr. Kane came into the room at Philadelphia I told him that I hated this time, that I had been pushed into it. I explained to him that it was a trick, that I had been forced into it and did not want to go on with it. I think now that if my brain had not been very round I should have been a maniac. Spiritualists say that I am mad now, that if I attempt to expose these tricks I am mad. I have had a life of sorrow, I have been poor and ill, but I consider it my duty, a sacred thing, a holy mission to expose it. I want to see the day that it is entirely done away with. After my sister Katie and I expose it I hope Spiritualism will be given a death blow.

Every morning of my life I have it before me. When I would wake up I would brood over it, and Dr. Kane has said to me more than once, "Maggie, I see that the vampire is over you still." Dr. Kane was certainly not a believer in Spiritualism. He was often horrified at the blasphemy of those fanatics. One day he came into the room, at Philadelphia, and an old fanatic asked me to call up St. Paul. The doctor hurried in and took me out. He was shocked beyond measure. If those we love who have passed away before us can look down upon us from heaven — if we are ever to meet again — I know my dead husband is looking on me now and blessing me for my work.

I remember one time before my marriage the death of Mr. Brown, the second husband of my sister Mrs. Fish, now Mrs. Underhill. Although Dr. Kane had no great devotion to Mr. Brown, he had respect for death. He sent his body servant Morton to sit up with the corpse. When he was laid out he asked me to come and look at the dead and to see how dreadful it was to trifle with death. There were several champagne bottles in the room, I suppose for the refreshment of Morton — and as I entered the room a cork popped with a dreadful noise, and I made for the door horrified. My sister forced me to wear mourning for Mr. Brown and to go to the funeral in state. This is an example of how entirely under the influence of Mrs. Underhill I was during that dreadful time. Katie and I were led around like lambs. We went to New York from Rochester, then all over the United States. We stopped at the Burnett House. The rooms were jammed from morning until night and we were called upon by these old wretches to show our rappings when we should have been out at play in the fresh air. We made the tour of the States, and came back to New York where

Mrs. Underhill left us. Mother went on to Philadelphia and took me and that is where Dr. Kane met me and brought me away from this life.

All during this dreadful life of deception I had been protesting. I have always rebelled against it. I have been going to expose it time and time again. After I married, Dr. Kane would not let me refer to my old life — he wanted me to forget it. He hated the publicity. When I was poor, after his death I was driven to it again. I have told my sister, Mrs. Underhill, time and time again: "Now that you are rich, why don't you save your soul?" But at my words she would fly into a passion. She wanted to establish a new religion and she told me that she received message from spirits. She knew we were tricking people, but she tried to make us believe that spirits existed. She told us that before we were born spirits came into her room and told her that we were destined for great things. But we knew when to rap "yes" or "no" according to certain signs she made us during the séance. After my marriage, my sister Katie still kept up the séances. She had many wealthy patrons here in New York — Mr. Livermore, a wealthy banker, and a Dr. Gray, a well-known homeopathic physician. They used to have regular meetings privately and Katie was the medium.

I have seen so much miserable deception that I am willing to assist in any way and to positively state the Spiritualism is a fraud of the worst description. I do so before my God, and my idea is to expose it. I despise it. I never want to lay eyes on any Spiritualists again, and I wish to say clearly that I owe all my misfortune to that woman, my sister, Mrs. Underhill. The last act of treachery she did — she has been persecuting me all along until recently — was to take my boys from me. Her hand has been felt in all my sorrows and misfortunes.

Now I am, I hope, a Christian and a sincere one. I am a Catholic, baptized in the Roman Catholic Church by the Rev. Father Quinn in St. Peter's, in Barclay street. I want to do honour to my faith. Father Quinn said to me that as long as I was in this business and did not believe in it and had to support myself, to charge very high prices, so that it would at least limit the number of my patrons; that I should not give any free exhibition and never claim supernatural powers.

When Dr. Kane died he left only $5,000 in trust for me. There was a suit over the possession of some of the doctor's letters which I wanted to publish. These letters have been in the care of a Catholic priest, and also of my lawyer. Afterwards some of these letters were published, although Dr. Kane's family strongly objected. The book was called "The Love-Life of Dr. Kane." I received but little income from the book and have had few sources of revenue. I now am very poor. I intend, however, to make the exposé of Spiritualism because I think it is my sacred duty. If I cannot do it, who can? — I have been the beginning of it. I hope to reduce at least the ranks of the 8,000,000 Spiritualists now in this country. I go into it as into a holy war. I do not want it understood that the Catholic Church has advised me to make these public disclosures and confessions. It is my own idea, my own mission. I would have done it long ago if I could have had the necessary money and courage to do it. I could not find any one to help me. I was too timid to ask.

My oldest sister, Mrs. Underhill, has gone to the country, and this exposé will be a severe blow to her, and perhaps kill her. I am waiting anxiously and fearlessly for the moment when I can show to the world, by personal demonstration, that all Spiritualism is a fraud and a deception. It is a branch of legerdemain, but it has to be closely studied to gain perfection. None but a child taken at any early age would have ever attained the proficiency and wrought such widespread evil as I have.

I trust that this statement, coming solemnly from me, the first and most successful in this deception, will break the force of the rapid growth of Spiritualism and prove that it is all fraud, a hypocrisy and a delusion.

Margaret Fox Kane

A Séance

When a *World* reporter called on Mrs. Margaret Fox-Kane at the hotel, where she has been closely guarded from the attempts of certain mediums to kidnap her, a private séance was arranged to demonstrate the mysteries of the supposed spiritual knockings.

Mrs. Kane was not aware that it had been arranged to have the rappings, and she came from her room to the hotel parlour expecting only an interview. She expressed herself as in the best of spirits and said that she felt thankful for having an opportunity to tell the story of deceit and sorrow through *The World*. If there was anything she could do to complete the exposure she would be only too glad to do it, and leave no stone unturned in her effort to undo the wretched work she was led into when a thoughtless child. To demonstrate the utter absurdity of the claim made by mediums that she was possessed by a spiritual power in spite of her denials, she desired to give the *World* reporter some evidence of how the tricks were done.

"Now," said Mrs. Kane, "I will stand up near these folding-doors, and you may stand as near as you please and I will call up any 'spirit' that you wish and answer any question. One rap means 'No'; three raps mean 'Yes.' Are you ready?"

"Is Napoleon Bonaparte present?" the reporter asked, watching Mrs. Kane closely.

Three raps (yes).

"Does he know me? I mean, did he ever meet and converse with me?"

Three raps.

"That is strange, isn't it?" remarked Mrs. Kane, smiling. "In view of the fact that he must have died before you were born. Try again."

"Is Abraham Lincoln present?"

Three raps.

"Well, you see the 'spirits' are very obliging."

"Will Harrison be elected?"

One loud rap (no).

"Will President Cleveland get another term?

Three raps.

For half an hour Mrs. Kane continued the "spirit rappings" in all parts of the hotel parlour in the broad daylight. At times the knocking was faint and at other loud, and she had the power of making the sounds come from under chairs and tables at a short distance — a sort of expert ventriloquism of the feet. The closest watching gave no evidence of even the slightest muscular effort. She remained perfectly quiet to all appearances and produced the rappings with ease and rapidity.

It was plain to see how even the strongest skeptics failed to understand or detect the secret of the rappings and, after many attempts to fathom the mystery, settled down to the belief that they had really seen manifestations from the "spirit world."

Nothing Is Left

Simon Newcomb

Simon Newcomb (1835-1909) was numbered among of the most distinguished scientists of the day and the leading astronomer of his time. Born at Tatamagouche, near Pictou, N.B., he became a resident of the United States in 1853 and specialized in the application of mathematics to astronomical observation. For many years he was a professor at Johns Hopkins University, and so distinguished was his contribution to the subject of nautical astronomy that by an Act of Congress he was appointed Rear-Admiral in the U.S. Navy. Upon his death in Washington, D.C., he was accorded a military funeral.

Newcomb is recalled for more than his contribution to astronomy. Curiously, he is remembered as a false prophet. While he was an outstanding analytical thinker, he fared poorly as a predictor. No books on "misguided predictions" are complete without Newcomb's celebrated declaration about heavier-than-air flight. He dismissed such flights as "utterly impossible" — one year before the historic flight of the Wright Brothers at Kitty Hawk in 1903.

Newcomb served as the first president of the Astronomical and Astrophysical Society of America. He also served as the first president of the American Society for Psychical Research, founded in 1885. (The latter fact goes unmentioned in the 1750-word entry on Newcomb in the Eleventh Edition of the Encyclopedia Britannica.)

In the latter capacity he gave much thought to the subject of "the spirit world" — specifically the achievement of psychical re-

searchers. He found no achievement whatsoever. He organized his thinking and expressed his thoughts and feelings on the failure to achieve results in an essay called "Modern Occultism" which he contributed to the January 1909 issue of the journal Nineteenth Century. *It appeared six months before his death.*

The complete essay "Modern Occultism" is anthologized in A Skeptic's Handbook of Parapsychology *(Buffalo: Prometheus Books, 1985) edited by Paul Kurtz. Here only the last paragraph is reprinted. Earlier in the essay Newcomb noted with distaste "the statistical onesidedness of all evidence in favour of ... forms of supernatural mental action." He likened the available evidence to the action of a blindfolded boy reaching into a bag of corn which contains a million normal grains of corn as well as a single black grain. The boy repeatedly draws the black grain. Newcomb argued, "The whole question turns on the number of unrecorded failures."*

WE LIVE IN a world where in every country there are millions of people subject to illusions too numerous to be even classified. They arise from dreams, visions, errors of memory that can rarely be detected, and mistakes to which all men are liable. It is unavoidable that when any of these illusory phenomena are associated with a moving event at a distance, there will be an apparent coincidence that will seem more wonderful every time it is recalled in memory. There is no limit to devices by which ingenuity may make us see what is unreal. Every country has ingenious men by the thousands, and if a willingness to deceive overtly characterizes only a small fraction of them, that fraction may form so large a number of individuals, always ready to mystify the looker-on, that the result will be unnumbered phenomena apparently proving the various theories associated with occultism and spiritualism. Nothing has been brought out by the reaches of the Psychical Society and its able collaborators except what we should expect to find in the ordinary course of nature. The seeming wonders — and they are plentiful — are at best of the same class as the wonder when a dozen drawers of the black grain of corn out of a million are presented to us. We are asked to admit an attraction between their hands and the black grain. The proof is conclusive enough until we remember that this dozen is only a selection out of millions, the rest of whom have not drawn the black grain. The records do not tell us, and never can tell us, about the uncounted millions of people who have forgotten that they ever had a vision or any illusion, or who, having such, did not find it associated with any notable occurrence. Count them all in, and nothing is left on which to base any theory of occultism.

Some Strange Power Existent in Ourselves

L.M. Montgomery

L.M. Montgomery (1874-1942) is internationally known as the author of Anne of Green Gables, but the fame of that child's classic, which was first published in 1908, should not eclipse the fact that Lucy Maude Montgomery was a most remarkable person. In fact, she was an extra-ordinarily able, imaginative, and sensitive woman. These qualities are characteristic of her life and work, and evidence of their presence is found in every entry and on every page of The Selected Journals of L.M. Montgomery: Volume II: 1910-1921 (Toronto: Oxford University Press, 1987) edited by Mary Rubio and Elizabeth Waterston.

Montgomery was the wife of a Presbyterian minister and not a Spiritualist. Yet she experienced precognitive dreams and was repeatedly drawn to the operation of the Ouija board. She first encountered the board as a child in Prince Albert, Alta. She introduced it to her friends at Cavendish, P.E.I. Here is what she says about the board and the "strange power" it produces in an entry she made in her journal while visiting Park Corner, P.E.I.

Friday Night, July 19, 1918
Park Corner

LAST NIGHT, after I had got back from my walk, I said to Mary, "Let's call up Jane for a bit of fun tonight."

Thereby hangs a tale — or what is worse, an explanation! It is twenty-eight years since I first learned to "make a table rap." We used to do it out in Prince Albert for an evening's fun. When I returned home I introduced it among the Cavendish young fry and it was the fashionable amusement of the winter. Then we grew tired of it and dropped it. About ten years ago something started it up again and one winter we had lots of fun over it. I remember some rather remarkable evenings at Will Houston's, where we got a great many rather strange answers. But I soon gave up this form of amusement — at least in public — for two reasons. In the first place, it annoyed me to have people say that "I pushed the table"; in the second place ignorant gossip got busy and circulated weird tales of dealings with devils.

I have never for one moment believed in what is called "spiritualism." Nothing I have ever seen or read has convinced me for a moment that any communication from the dead is possible by such means. But I *do* believe that the phenomena thus produced is produced by some strange power existent in ourselves — in that mysterious part of it known as the subconscious mind — a power of which the law is utterly unknown to us. But that there is a law which governs it and that the operations produced by that law are perfectly natural could we but obtain the key to them I am firmly convinced.

Although I gave up making tables rap in public May and I kept it up in private for our own amusement — and we had many an afternoon's fun out of it. We both held our tongues religiously and it never leaked out, so that ignorance and malice did not get any chance to flesh their tongues on us.

We used a little square "fancy" table in May's parlor and for convenience sake we called the power that made it move "Jane." We also assumed, for the fun of it, that spirits *were* present and wanted to communicate with us. We got no end of messages from this source — and some of them I must admit were strange enough. For one thing, they always were true to type — quite characteristic of the people as we knew them in life, or as we conceived them to be, for we did not limit ourselves in time or space and the "spirit" of "Roaring Ack" Stewart talked to us through "Jane" as freely as that of Queen Elizabeth and St. Paul — the latter always couching his message in Biblical style! I do not pretend to understand it. There was one message in particular which I could never explain and which gave me a queer chill. There was a circle of us around the table that night and "Jane" was rapping out a message from Alec's father — old "Mr. Charles." It began "See to our Pensie's — ," at this juncture I, who was spelling out he message, felt quite sure that the next word would be "son" or "child." The others at the table all told me afterwards that they thought the same. But the next word was "grave" — "See to our Pensie's grave."

After the others had gone May and Alec told me what I had never before heard — that Pensie's husband had never put a head-stone up for her and that the grave was so overgrown with briar bushes that they could not be sure just where it was. Nobody at the table but Alec and May knew this and they had not thought of it. Nevertheless, I suppose the knowledge was in their subconscious minds....

It is a curious fact that when there are in the circle one or more people, who have never seen a table rap, even if they are not incredulous, it is a long time before it will begin. I have often sat for as long as three or four hours with a "green" circle before it would move. But once it has moved then ever after, if that same "circle" sit down the table will rap very quickly. In our old afternoons "Jane" would respond as soon as May and I laid our hands on the table; but it had been so long since we had tried it that I thought likely it would be proportionately long before the raps would begin. To my surprise, the minute we placed our hands in position the table almost *leapt up* — the impression made on both of us was that *something* was so amazingly glad to see us that it fairly bounded out in its joy.

We had an hour's fun out of "Jane." We did not call up any spirits from the vast deep but contented ourselves with asking comical questions and putting "Jane" through all her old stunts — such as walking around the room on two legs exactly like a human being, bowing, dancing, keeping time to music etc. etc. When we finished Alec got up off the sofa where he had been lying, said "Well, there's something in you, Maud, that isn't in other people" and went to bed.

This morning Stuart and I drove over to Park Corner with Alec, and Ham Macneill brought Chester and my trunk. As we drove up under the birches Frede was at the well, fat as a seal and looking like the spirit of laughter incarnate. We've been talking ever since and our tongues are not quite worn out yet. There is enough to talk of, goodness knows — if talking would do any good. Matters here are bad and complicated enough. I see no way out and am rather sick at heart over it all. But then I'm very tired.

In spite; of all, though, it is good to be here again. To adapt Alec, "There's something about Park Corner that isn't in other places"....

A Rather Strange Thing Happened

L.M. Montgomery

The Ouija board held many attractions for L.M. Montgomery (1874-1942), the prolific author of children's books.

The celebrated author Lucy Maude Montgomery was the wife of the Reverend Ewan Macdonald. She was the perfect Presbyterian minister's wife and a model of propriety. In the 1910's the Macdonald family occupied The Manse, the brick house attached to St. Paul's Church, in the small farming community of Leaskdale, Ont. However, regular trips to Toronto offered Montgomery relief from the constraints of small-town living and the ministerial life.

The highlight of one week in Toronto offered some excitement over the Ouija board, as is made clear in this passage from The Selected Journals of L.M. Montgomery: Volume II: 1910-1921 *(Toronto: Oxford University Press 1987), edited by Mary Rubio and Elizabeth Waterston.*

Sunday, April 13, 1919
Leaskdale, Ont.

...ON FRIDAY EVENING Laura, Ralph and I had a very interesting seance with the Ouija board. A wave of Ouijaism has flooded Toronto as a result of the publication of *The Twentieth Plane*. Honest dealers in Ouija boards have made small fortunes.

A rather strange thing happened. When we asked if any spirits were present the answer was — as usual — "Yes." "Frede" was present and wanted to speak to "Maude." This is the ordinary thing at seances like this. I was minded not to go on. I did not believe that Frede was there — and yet — I did hunger so for some communication from her. Why not try? So I crushed down a certain distaste and asked Ouija to give me the message.

Ouija thereupon began spelling out rapidly. In passing, I may remark on the curious fact that whenever *I* am present at a Ouija seance the Power that moves the pointer always spells *phonetically*. As I have not heard of this occurring when I am not present I must conclude that the reason is in me. But why? I have always detested the idea of phonetic spelling and have virulently opposed the idea all my life.

To resume: — Ouija spelled out,

"Has she cashed the second check?"

I was rather staggered. Certainly it was not the sort of message I had expected from Frede — or whatever power or personality was imitating Frede. Who was "she"? And I had no idea what "the second check" referred to. I asked of Ouija, *"Who is she?"* "Miss B.A. Hill" was the reply. Now, Miss Hill's initials are A.E. I did not know this at the time but I knew one of her initials was "A." Neither Laura nor Ralph knew of the existence of Miss Hill, so this answer *must* have come either from my subjective mind or from some outside intelligence. I said to Laura, "When I see Miss Hill I will ask her what it means." Instantly Ouija began to spell and spelled, "Trust a clear appearance, dear Maud." I then asked, "Shall I write Miss Hill or wait till I see her?"

Answer. "Better visit her. Her talk will convince you that I am right. Trust your uncle F.C."

Laura and Ralph laughed at the "uncle," thinking it nonsense. They did not know that in our family circle we have always called Fred — and she called herself — "Uncle Fred," as a little joke on her masculine nickname. But she *never* called herself, or was called, "Uncle F.C."

I then asked if when I saw Miss Hill, I should ask about that "second check" or wait until she introduced the subject herself.

Answer. "Just let her talk."

I asked. "Where shall I see her?"

Answer. Tomorrow at Uxbridge. She is on her way now."

Up to this time I had been feeling rather weirdly credulous. But now I knew this was not the truth. I knew perfectly well that Miss Hill would not be in Uxbridge the next day. However, I asked,

"Where shall I see her in Uxbridge?"

Answer. "Willis' drug store. Good-night dear Maud."

That ended Frede's communication. I did not — could not — believe it came from her. Yet it gave me a queer comfort — as if I really had been talking to her. I *knew* Miss Hill would not be in Willis' drug store. Yet when I reached Uxbridge Friday evening I induced Ewan to drive up to Willis' through the vile mud, alleging that I wanted to get some notepaper.

I did *not* find Miss Hill there!

Now *whence* did that message come? Why was part of it a lie? And is there any meaning or truth in that "second check"? Shall I ever know?

We had some other funny communications. The Aylesworth Ouija has, it seems, a great spite of Laura and always says something sarcastic to her. As soon as we stopped asking questions it started in of its own accord.

"Now Laura will dance. Tee-hee!"

Really, one could almost hear the sardonic chuckle. Laura said teasingly, "But Ouija, I have no music. I can't dance without music." "Oh, Maud will whistle," retorted Ouija.

Again we all asked Ouija to tell us our worst faults. Ouija promptly told Ralph and Laura theirs but all I could elicit was the mysterious remark,

"Ewan knows."

Ralph's father, Dr. Aylesworth, believes that the power behind Ouija is a demonism. He may be right. But evidently some demons have a sense of humor!

The Trails of Truth

Jenny O'Hara Pincock

Jenny O'Hara Pincock died in October 1948. It is not certain that she was a relation of Geoffrey O'Hara who was a namesake, a native of Chatham, Ont., and Tin Pan Alley composer of novelty songs like "K-K-K-Katy" and the once-popular "There Is Not Death." What is known is that Mrs. Pincock knew and loved the latter composition with its theme of survival after death.

Following the untimely demise in 1928 of her husband Robert Newton Pincock, a chiropractor, Mrs. Pincock held a series of thirty-six seances in the parlour of her home in St. Catharines. Each mediumistic session was three hours in duration and note-takers recorded the proceedings for posterity. The sessions or services were scheduled in an attempt to console the living, to communicate with the "discarnate," and to confirm the theory of "spirit-return." Mrs. Pincock felt that all these objects were accomplished, and she expressed this opinion in her published account of these sessions, which appeared as The Trails of Truth *(Los Angeles, Calif.: Austin Publishing Company, 1930).*

Here is her account of what brought it all about — Chapter 3 of her 396-page book.

MY HUSBAND and I had had but one experience with mediumship before he passed into the Great Beyond. This was in September 1927, and the following May he went.

We had stumbled on the subject, for we had no knowledge of spirit-return. He was a son of the parsonage, born and reared in an atmosphere of devout orthodox Christianity. Though of this mind, my husband was also an independent thinker, and freely used the brains with which he had been endowed. We often discussed the various theories and philosophies expounded from the pulpit, but in no spirit of conscious rebellion. His faith in a future existence was unwavering; mine was not. He had lost no one dear to him; I had. Both parents had gone — and it makes a difference. But when we dwelt on these thoughts by our own fireside, his love for me in my doubtings never faltered. His strong arm of sympathy and understanding never failed me. We prayed for light — and we received it.

It came from most unexpected quarters. But its coming was so complete, so dazzling, that we were well nigh stunned by its brilliancy. A friend of my husband, a man uncommonly astute (a graduate of Toronto University in Civil Engineering), walked into our home one day and confidently announced that he had just talked with his wife! She had "died" three years before. We listened to his story. Through him we secured many books on psychic subjects, and it was with his family that we, who were complete strangers to the medium, had our first experience. I am in possession of the account of this sitting in the handwriting of my husband. Being of a practical turn of mind he submitted the evidential points (which identified completely the intelligence with whom we conversed) to his lawyer and friend, Mr. F.H. Hetherington, M.A., of St. Catharines, Ontario.

Six weeks after my husband passed over I talked with him. Altogether I had ten such experiences with the medium, Mr. William Cartheuser, prior to the first one recorded in this book. The evidence was of such a startling nature that some of our friends, who had become interested, decided to bring Mr. Cartheuser to our city. This was done in September 1928.

One other personal explanation will be necessary before the reader is launched into a sea of amazing experiences of many witnesses. In July 1921 the author experienced a premature birth of about six weeks conception; in July 1923 one of six weeks conception; and in April 1927 another. "Jane" and "Bobby" have now been introduced. It is not my purpose to further extend this particular revelation. Others have written their findings. Those who run may read.

A few specific directions on the method of conducting seances under the mediumship of Mr. Cartheuser (well-known at the American Society of Psychical Research) may not be amiss. Water is always placed in the centre of the seance room at the request of the invisible operators. The flowers that are frequently mentioned are merely offerings of love from a sitter, or sitters, to these entities, and should not be confused with materializations, such as the materialization of hands. Musical instruments have also been frequently placed at the disposal of the "spirit" friends; for hereafter these invisible intelligences shall be known by that term.

Conversations reported throughout the following seance accounts have been left in their original wording, with slight changes only when the context needed greater clarity. This has been done that accuracy, intimacy and naturalness may be maintained.

I reverently and confidently submit these accounts to the public. I have nothing to fear from the storms that will eventually beat upon them. For we who have witnessed these things can afford to smile. "Once we believed, but now we *know*!

We have but added to our faith — knowledge.

Account of This Seance Under Mrs. X's Pen

Mrs. X.

So distraught was Jenny O'Hara Pincock following the death of her husband Robert Newton Pincock, a Newfoundlander who died in 1928, that the young widow arranged to hold in the parlour of her home at 47 Church St., St. Catharines, Ont., a series of seances that ultimately reached thirty-six in number. William Cartheuser, the medium who specialized in both trumpet and direct-voice communication, came from New York for a good many of these sessions. Minutes were scrupulously kept and special notes were made of the "evidential" material that "came across." The minutes were annotated and published by Mrs. Pincock as The Trails of Truth, a 396-page book issued in 1930 by the Austin Publishing Company in Los Angeles, California.

The publisher was Benjamin Fish Austin, a Ontario-born spiritualist and former Methodist minister, who contributed a foreword in which he stated that the book's value was incalculable. Referring to the work of all concerned, both living and dead, he expostulated: "Their united testimony is to the proof of the most stupendous fact, the most amazing truth, that can possibly enter the mind of man — a fact that alters the whole outlook of the individual upon life and destiny — a fact that is fundamental to any system of religion or morality and one of supreme personal import to every man everywhere."

It is not Mrs. Pincock's minutes of the seance held on 11 September 1928 that are reproduced here, although they do appear in her

114

book, but the description provided under the title "Account of This Seance under Mrs. X's Pen." The description was provided by one of two special guests at this seance who are referred to in the text as "Mrs. X., B.A.," and "Dr. X., Ph.D, M.A."

Mrs. X. and Dr. X have now been identified. According to David G. Pitt, in his masterly book E.J. Pratt: The Master Years *(1987), the guests on that occasion were Dr. and Mrs. E.J. Pratt. Pratt and Pincock were both Newfoundlanders who had moved to the Mainland. They had known each other as youths. At the time of this seance, Dr. Pratt was an instructor in Psychology, not yet the narrative poet of genius.*

The anonymously published account of the session was written by Viola Pratt, a sprightly and intelligent woman, who survived her husband (who died in 1964) by some twenty years. According to Pitt's biography of Pratt, the experience in St. Catharines and similar experiences at seances the Pratts subsequently held in their Toronto home brought about their "conversion" to spiritualism and gave them "full conviction of human immortality." Yet Pratt, as a Methodist minister, was mindful of his position; also, as a Professor of English at Victoria College, University of Toronto, so he was not about to shout from the rooftops (or even whisper in his parlour) his faith in "spirit-return." Pitt added: "But there is no question, though he was generally secretive about it, that the experience remained for him one of the pivotal events in his life."

THERE WERE FOUR OF US in the darkened room, Mr. Cartheuser (the medium), Mrs. Pincock, Dr. X. and I. In the centre of the room were vases of flowers, a large, low flower bowl, and three trumpets, one with a luminous band around it. We began by repeating in unison the Lord's Prayer, and the Twenty-third Psalm, and then we sang, Mrs. Pincock playing the piano for us. The air seemed full of whispers, and Mrs. Pincock said she felt hands on her hands and head, while a voice hummed the songs with us. As we were sitting waiting, the large bowl was put in Mrs. Pincock's hands, and a voice whispered to her, "No water." The bowl should have had water in it, and had been forgotten. Mr. Pincock filled it with water from a flower vase. Almost immediately a voice close to Dr. X. audibly whispered, "Codfish." (My husband is a New-foundlander.) This voice, which had been heard by us all during the beginning of the seance, Mrs. Pincock identified as her husband's.

Another voice then spoke close to my husband in a whisper, which we both recognized as that of his mother. She spoke first to her son and then to me, *pronouncing her words, and using the expressions as she had while on earth.* Dr. X. said to her, "Hello, old Socks." Another pause followed, then Dr. X. said, "Did you get that mother? Try to say what I want." The answer came, "Hello, old Boots." This was the usual greeting exchanged between these two, the test Dr. X. exacted for belief. Mrs. X. (the spirit) was overcome and cried after her effort.

She then patted us on the hands and heads. My husband told her that his sister was with him and she said, "Yes, but she is not so well." (She had, in fact, a very heavy cold.) Then she said, "Where's N----?" (her youngest daughter). I replied that she had returned from England and was back in New York. She remarked, "Yes, I know that; they lost the baby — a boy. He is here." On N----'s return she went to nurse a friend whose infant died. None but me knew of that episode, *and I had to verify the sex later.* She talked to us coherently and naturally, about our cottage, about our dinner on the train the previous evening, and then brought through some evidence concerning (what sounded like) 'Teresa Lake.' We had known a family of 'Lake's' many years before.

She asked my husband if he had finished his composition (he was writing all summer), also how his psychology was, and if he had thrown it in a heap. (He used to lecture in psychology.) She also talked to him about her *other sons.*

Then she went over to Mrs. Pincock and said, "Poor Jenny Pincock; people say she is delirious, that trouble has made her crazy, and somebody is trying to fool her! But, my child, do not work too hard at this. You shouldn't wear yourself out physically trying to convince stubborn people." She had a little joke with me, which Mrs. Pincock wanted to put down as evidence; and trying to prevent her from doing so, Mrs. X. (spirit) attempted to take the pencil out of her hand. When this failed, she went to the water, splashed and materialized again, then once more tried to get it. My husband said, "Here is a pencil, mother." He placed his hand so it would receive light from the luminous band on the trumpet and then he plainly saw nails and fingers on a hand which took his pencil (no arm entered beyond the materialized hand), moved over to the water again, and proceeded to mark his face with it. Before she left, I asked her if she had any message for another daughter. She answered, "Tell her there is no death."

Dr. Pincock then came and spoke to us, welcoming us to St. Catharines. He told us that "There is no Death" was sung at his funeral, and that Jenny had to prepare the minister (he gave his name) for the kind of ceremony they had. He talked to my husband about his new book, and when my husband tried to test him, they had some evidential jokes.

My husband's father then came, and talked to his son about this old home in England, mentioning the long walk the latter took to visit it. (My husband had walked seventeen miles.) Then he turned to me, and remarked he had followed us around all day at the Exhibition. He said we were carrying things in long envelopes, to take to the babies. These were the paper bags with samples we had collected. He asked if we got the soap. I thought he said "Soup," so he spelled it. (I had bought at the Exhibition some samples of soap.) He then inquired why a shoe had been taken off, in the rest-room at the Exhibition. He said, "You took something out of it. I could not see what it was." I *later discovered* that one member of our party had gone to the rest room to telephone, and had extracted a five-cent piece from her shoe for that purpose. He also asked who the preacher was who spoke to us, and if he bless us (with a laugh). We spoke to only one man at the fair, an acquaintance of another member of the party. *I found out after we returned home* that he was a minister.

My husband and I asked him if he had been with us at our summer home. He said he was, and in proof mentioned three facts; a yellow and black dog which was a nuisance up there, a Mrs. Bailey who had something to eat with us, and "Hannah," about whom he laughed. There was a dog of that description there, also a Mrs. Bailey, known only to me, and "Hannah" was a fictitious character in a series of stories told by my sister-in-law to the children. She and I joked about the "Hannah" stories, but no one else in the room knew about them. He told me that I had my head in my hands (which was true), and that he could see my face as in a fog. He mentioned the customs officer on the train, told us we were staying in a hotel on the third floor, that he saw us at a front window, that one of us picked up a newspaper and the other a book, all of which was true. Then he turned to my husband and told him he had just brought home a new suit which took two weeks to make (it was tailored to order), navy blue, with stripes. He said to me, "You criticized the stripes" (which I did). He mentioned many other trivial things, described our dining room furniture, breakfast dishes, etc. — as he said "to show I know what is going on!" He spoke of the wonderful experience this was, and left us with his blessing.

Dr. Pincock spoke through the trumpet to me and in direct voice to Mrs. Pincock, and gave us all a flower. These were always pressed directly in our hands.

My mother next spoke through the trumpet, saying they had to coax her to come — she felt too shy. I asked her who were with her, and she replied, "Your grandma and father, Aggie (a great friend of hers), and Mrs. Woodger (a former friend of whom I had not thought for years)." She mentioned Pennsylvania and Pittsburgh University and said, "No! no!" when we suggested she was referring to Dr. Anderson. The telephone rang outside, and she said, "Listen to the phone, it is interesting; he wants a seance." It was some man calling up about a sitting. The mother hummed one verse of "My Old Kentucky Home." She spoke rationally of the cause of her sudden passing, and said she was in her house till the last thing was out. She remarked we could not be agnostic any more now. She mentioned a birthday of one of her grandchildren, October 16th (it was the 15th), and said to send her very best wishes. (It was characteristic of mother never to forget a birthday remembrance, though frequently she was out as to the exact date.) She said she and mother had many a chat over the past, and ate seedless fruit together.

My father then spoke. "Hello, can you see my whiskers?" He said this was the first time he had been able to get through, although he had tried before. He knew mother was coming over, in fact had a party arranged for her, and that all passings are recorded, but they are not allowed to tell. He said it was just like the change from the caterpillar to the butterfly. He mentioned our house, the street, and that the house needed painting. (We are having it painted now.) He sent his blessing to his children.

Dr. Anderson then came in, and spoke in a very loud voice of this great revelation, and how it lifted the horror from death. The teaching of Jesus was true when He said, "In my Father's house are many Mansions." He said that God does not punish sin, but our own actions. He told the accurate time, and closed the sitting with a brief prayer.

The Philip Phenomenon

Iris M. Owen

The Philip Phenomenon *is assuredly the single most fascinating development in the field of parapsychology over the last few decades.*

The Toronto Society for Psychical Research was founded in 1970. Its model was the original Society for Psychical Research, established in London in 1882, and its counterpart, the American Society for Psychical Research, which was founded three years later. Some members of the Toronto SPR directed their efforts to the study of the conventions of the séance. It should be noted that these members were not mediums, although a number of them felt themselves to be mediumistic. They made no attempt to communicate with distant spirits or with the spirits of the deceased. Instead, they decided to experiment. They asked themselves the following question: Is it possible, through the use of raps — one for "yes," two for "no" — to communicate not with a spirit entity but with the idea of a spirit? After some months they were able to give an affirmation answer to that question: (Rap) "Yes."

The group fabricated a spirit out of whole cloth. In the time-honoured manner of the historical novelist, they created a credible character. They imagined a young Cavalier at the time of the English Civil War, named him Philip, and established him in Diddington Manor, a real country estate in Warwickshire. It was explained that Philip was born in 1624, at twenty he married the beautiful but imperious Dorothea, at thirty he fell in love with the sensuous Margo, and he died in 1654. Such are the bare bones of the authorized biography. Most intriguing is the fact that when the group began to question Philip through raps, the spirit substantiated the "cover" story and then began to embellish and revise it. New facets of his life began to emerge. Some facts were consistent with what is known of English history; some were contrary to the historical record. The group had contacted a spirit — at times a truthful spirit, but at other times a lying spirit!

The full account of this important experiment in the history of parapsychology has been well told by Iris M. Owen, a leading participant. Owen is English-born, a social-worker, and the wife of A.R.G. (George) Owen, a former Cambridge fellow, a lecturer in mathematics, and an authority on poltergeistery. Iris M. Owen (with Margaret Sparrow) wrote Conjuring Up Philip: An Adventure in Psychokinesis *(Toronto: Fitzhenry & Whiteside, 1976), from which the excerpt which follows is reproduced.*

The Philip Experiment offers proof of nothing, but it does dramatically demonstrate the dynamics of the séance situation — with its physical and mental mediumship and its reputed "spirit-communication." This episode in parapsychological history offers promise of a better understanding of the dynamics of group interaction, of the psychical consequences of belief, if not of contact with the "spirit-world."

Members of the Toronto SPR were investigators and researchers in fields of phenomena other than that of the Philip Phenomenon, and many of the members were also active in the New Horizons Research Foundation, which was founded by George Owen at the same time as the Toronto SPR. Both associations ceased to exist in 1978, when George and Iris Owen withdrew from active work in the field. Yet the accomplishments of the Toronto SPR and the New Horizons Research Foundation introduce a new chapter in the textbook of parapsychology and illuminate, if obliquely, the nature of the spirit of mankind.

IT WAS NOT SURPRISING that each member of the group became quite adept at carrying on a conversation as if with an imaginary guest. There was rarely confusion. Sometimes someone would forget that Philip could answer only yes or no, and a question would be asked that required a different type of answer. When this mistake was made Philip would invariably produce scratching noises. On one occasion, during a good session, one of the group jokingly asked Philip to give a rap under each person's hand at the table. Philip took the request literally, and each member felt a loud rap under his or her hand at the same moment in time.

Another typical meeting, which was taped and recorded, went like this.

The group met, stopping on their way to the table to eat a candy. They placed one on the table for Philip.

"Here is your candy, Philip. Would you like a song?"

(Rap) "Yes."

Andy: "What shall we sing? 'Lillibulero' and 'Greensleeves'? Perhaps he doesn't like the Lloyd George song because we sing it to the tune of 'Onward Christian Soldiers,' and that was one of the songs sung by Oliver Cromwell's Puritan army."

(Rap) "Yes."

Dorothy: "There you are, I knew he didn't like Lloyd George."

Someone else: "We can keep it to threaten him with if he won't talk to us."

To some extent this is how this particular song was used in subsequent sessions. It usually provoked a violent response in table movement. So 'Lillibulero' and 'Greensleeves' were sung, and the conversation was resumed. It was decided to change the conversation completely and to ask Philip about his personal likes and dislikes.

"Do you like horses?"

(Rap) "Yes."

"I expect you had a favourite horse?"

(Rap) "Yes."

"I bet it was a white one, was it, Philip?"

(Rap) "Yes."

"Did you have any mistresses?"

(Loud rap) "Yes."

The group went on to suggest, and to elicit from Philip that he had had a good time in London, and he was asked if he enjoyed going to the chocolate houses and meeting the ladies there. As an enthusiastic yes was elicited by this line of questioning, the group went on to tease him about his love of chocolate houses. As an historical fact, however, chocolate was not known then, and chocolate houses were not introduced into London society until more than a century after the date of Philip's "death."

"Did you get drunk sometimes?"

(Rap) "Yes."

"But not too often?"

(Rap, rap) "No."

Philip was not a drunkard, and he did not get into fights.

"Did people fight duels in your day?"

(Rap, rap) "No." When Cromwell came to power the fighting of duels was banned.

"Was life much gayer before Cromwell came to power?"

(Rap) "Yes."

As everyone started to discuss the differences between life in London during Charles' and Cromwell's rules, raps continued to come from the table as various points were agreed upon. Philip was asked if he had a position at court, and the answer was yes. But when he was asked, "Did Dorothea go to court with you?" there were knocks and scratchings, which seemed to indicate that this was a subject that Philip did not want mentioned. However, on this occasions the various members of the group persisted in asking questions about Dorothea, assuring Philip that they were his friends, and that they needed to know all about him.

"Were you forced to marry Dorothea?" he was asked.

(Rap) "Yes."

"Did her parents force this marriage upon you? Did they need the financial help your money could give?"

(Rap) "Yes."

"Was she a cruel person?"

(Rap) "Yes."

As questions and comments about Dorothea came thick and fast from the group, a picture of her emerged. She was a beautiful but cold woman, physically and mentally cruel, whom he had married to please his father and her parents, who needed the money he brought to the marriage. He had never loved her. She refused to bear him children, and they lived separate lives. Marriages of this kind were approved by the court as was the custom in those days, but it never became clear why Philip should have been prepared to enter into such a one-sided bargain; however, he did. Dorothea was the oldest in the family, she had brothers and a sister, but she was spoiled and indulged by her parents.

At this point Philip was again questioned about his religion, and he answered yes to a question as to whether he was born an Anglo-Catholic.

At this point everyone paused for some conversation and to sing songs. At most sittings there would have been much more singing and joke telling, but conditions seemed to be good on this particular night. The raps came continually, and it was evident that the group had plenty of energy.

Questioned further about Margo, Philip said, to everyone's surprise, that she had not lived in the gatehouse, but in his quarters in the house.

"Was it in the stables?"

(Rap, rap) "No."

"Perhaps they would have called them something else in this day?" someone suggested. "Perhaps she lived in the main house."

"Perhaps she lived in his quarters," Bernice speculated.

(Rap) "Yes."

So Margo had lived in the main house.

"Did you go to the theatre?"

(Rap) "Yes."

"Did you see plays by Shakespeare and Marlowe?"

(Rap) "Yes."

"Did you walk over London Bridge?"

(Rap) "Yes."

"I wonder what he would think now of London Bridge being sold to America, and being assembled somewhere out in the desert?" (This from Dorothy.) A series of scratchings was the only answer they got to this question.

"They had houses on it in this time." (This from Iris.)

(Rap) "Yes."

"Did you cross the bridge many times?"

(Rap) "Yes."

"They had a lot of illness in this time — plague, smallpox — all sorts of illness."

"Did anyone in your family die of plague?" (This was from Andy.)

(Rap) "Yes."

"I wonder who? Dorothy didn't die till after he did — after he threw himself from the battlements. Could it have been her parents?"

(Rap, rap) "No."

"Was it his parents?"

(Rap) "Yes."

When asked about Charles I's pets, Philip asserted that the king did not like horses or dogs, but that he loved cats. This is at variance with the historical facts, but the questioner was an ardent cat lover. Questioned further, Philip said he himself didn't like cats; he preferred dogs.

"Did you use dogs when hunting?"

(Rap) "Yes."

Questioned as to whether they hunted boar or deer, Philip replied yes to deer. Not only did he hunt deer, but he had deer-hounds. He also kept peregrines. Asked if he used guns for hunting, the answer was yes, but when after birds he used human beaters to retrieve, not dogs. Yes was the reply.

Someone asked if he had had smallpox, and the answer was no. Dorothy followed up by suggesting — "But I beg you wished Dorothea had it?" To this question, asked half in jest, there came a series of rolling knocks. When asked directly if Dorothea ever had smallpox, the answer was no.

He was asked if he liked drinking, as he had shown an obvious preference for drinking songs, and always beat time vigorously to them. A loud rap was his reply.

At this time the reader should be convinced that in the vast majority of cases, the answers Philip gave to questions asked him were in accordance with the responses that the questioners expected to receive from him. Or, to put the matter in reverse, the questioner was usually able to elicit the answers from Philip that he expected. Rather than bore the reader with a long description of the questions and answers given, the following summary of Philip's life and times were filled in by the group. There were, however, some anomalies....

4. Psychic Mysteries

The House of My Dreams

Harry Stevens

Harry Stevens, a native of Cameron, Ont., had a strange experience during the Second World War. In Europe he came upon "the house of my dreams," the house he had dreamed about as a child in Canada!

He recalled the experience for George Gamester, the columnist with the Toronto Star, *who invited readers to contribute their "eerie tales" to his column. Gamester published Stevens's account in his column on 30 June 1989.*

The necessarily abbreviated newspaper account is reproduced here. Following it, in the author's own words, is a longer version of that episode, taken from a letter written by the author to the present editor, dated 14 July 1989.

1.

AS A CHILD, HARRY had a recurring dream about a house where he would go to play....

There was a specific room in the back of the house, overlooking a vineyard. It was my favourite because it had a secret chamber where I could hide and play.

Years later, during World War II, my unit took a rest stop in an Italian village. There, across the road, was the house of my dreams.

I entered, and found everything in the abandoned house was as I had "seen" it. Only one thing was missing: the secret room.

So I inquired — and learned the family which had lived there had for a time kept their valuables in a hidden chamber before fleeing the war.

I returned to the house, found where the wall had been sealed, and poked a hole in the partition.

There it was! The secret room of my dreams.

2.

When I was a young Canadian lad of about eight, or twelve, years old, I had frequent dreams, some good and some bad. But there was one dream that kept recurring. The dream came back so many times that it seemed real to me at the time. Even now, many years later (I am now sixty-six years old), I can still remember the dream as a very pleasant experience, and I can remember the appearance of the house in my dream, both inside and outside.

As I approached, I could see it was a very large house, two-storeys in height and quite wide. Then, as I entered the front door, I stepped into a large sitting room with a high, cathedral-type ceiling which ran right up to the roof. Then there was a stairway on the left which rose to a balcony that ran all round the inside, with doors leading off into various rooms.

But there was one room at the back of the house into which I was always sent to play. In this room, I had a secret compartment where I could hide all my valuable toys, so that other kids could not play with them or take them from me. Also, this room had a large window looking out over a vineyard and an orchard of some unknown kind of trees.

Then, many years later, when I was about nineteen or twenty years old, I was in the Canadian Army in Italy. We were marching along a country road after the Germans had retreated to the north. Our unit commander called for a rest break (or a "smoke break," as we called it then). So I sat down at the side of the road beside a buddy, and just as I was lighting my cigarette, I looked across the road at a house, and stared at the house of my boyhood dreams. A cold chill ran up my spine.

I told my buddy about those dreams of long ago, and then talked him into going inside with me to investigate. I told him, in advance, just exactly what I expected to find and, sure enough, everything was just as it was in my dreams, even to the vineyard. Outside that backroom window there was a grove of olive trees, the orchard in my dreams.

Everything was there except the secret panel where I hid my toys in my dream. I was so disturbed by this one thing being different that I was prompted to check the room's dimensions from the door to the wall and then do the same in the room next door. Thereby I discovered an area of four to six feet that was unaccounted for in the room size. I then took my bayonette and punched a hole in the plaster wall, exposing a hidden compartment where the Italian family (before retreating from the war zone) had hidden all their worldly treasures, things that they could not carry while retreating, things like linens, silverware, dishes, etc.

Now the mysterious questions.

1. I had those dreams long before the war, so how did I know there would be a secret room?

2. Why did I dream the same dream over and over, when there was nothing my present life to relate the dream to?

3. What caused me to remember those dreams so vividly, when most dreams are forgotten as soon as a person wakes up?

4. Had I lived in that house in some previous life, before being reincarnated to a Canadian life?

5. Or was there someone sending me messages through mental telepathy?

6. What quirk of fate caused our unit to stop in exactly the right spot to have me placed exactly opposite the house?

7. Has some mysterious soul from the past been put to rest by my finding that house?

Another mystery that I forgot to mention was that while in Italy I had no trouble talking Italian, and since I found the house I have never had the dream again, and I have forgotten most of the Italian language that I knew then.

My Encounter with a Gifted Clairvoyant

W. Edward Mann

The "gifted clairvoyant" who is described in this article is James Wilkie. Wilkie was born in Scotland. His psychic abilities or "gifts" must have seemed impressive, for they made an indelible impression on at least two qualified observers. One of these observers is the sociologist W. Edward Mann, the author of this article. The other observer is Allen Spraggett who co-authored with Wilkie a book titled The Gift Within: Experiences of a Spiritual Medium *(1970).*

W. Edward Mann has enjoyed a distinguished career. He was the first student of sociology to receive a doctorate in that discipline from the University of Toronto. For many years he was one of the mainstays of the Department of Sociology at Atkinson College in York University. He has so many facets and talents that he has been described as "a multi Mann." He was ordained an Anglican priest and he has worked as a lay counsellor. Among his numerous scholarly articles and books there is one about alternative energy sources called Vital Energy and Health: Dr. Wilhelm Reich's Revolutionary Discoveries and Supporting Evidence *(1989).*

Mann first met Wilkie in 1957, the year that this article was written. Since then Mann has devoted much of his time and attention to studying, investigating, and writing about the paranormal. Wilkie eventually moved from Toronto to the West Coast where he continued his work.

TODAY, INCREASING interest is being shown by lay people and scientists in the whole area of ESP or extrasensory perception. Most people first approach this subject, and in fact the whole field of the psychic, with strong misgivings and doubts, if not with vigorous ridicule. It is surprising, however, how many persons have changed their minds after going through, often unexpectedly, unusual experiences.

Prior to my meeting with James Wilkie, a young man from Glasgow, whom I met by purest accident, I, too, was skeptical and not without misgivings about seances, etc. However, some of these doubts began to give way, under the impact of James's unusual gifts.

Before you close your mind to this subject, let me tell you of my experience with James in what was a strictly unexpected and non-professional "sitting."

In the words of the King in Alice's Wonderland, I suppose I should begin at the beginning, and if this be so, I must confess that James was not the first clairvoyant I had ever met; but he *was* the first who gave me his undivided attention for a considerable period of time. He also "produced" some rather disturbing information.

My first introduction to clairvoyance had taken place two years previously at a rather high-level seminar on faith healing and psychic phenomena when several famous American clairvoyants were present. I managed to talk briefly to each of them between sessions of the seminar, and also had an eerie experience of seeing a certain medium, world famous and highly investigated, go into a trance in broad daylight. However, all she "produced" was a long and learned speech, seemingly given by her "control," that told nothing which could not have come from her own mind. Subsequent to this seminar, which greatly piqued my curiosity concerning psychic persons, I had run into several people with limited clairvoyant gifts, but nobody who ever really impressed me, or who had any sort of professional status. James was different....

I met James at the home of a friend and our encounter was entirely unexpected on both sides. I had, in fact, gone there in the hopes of meeting a physical medium — one who can produce ectoplasm — but this man had left the house early, and shortly after I arrived, another guest arrived completely unexpectedly, who was introduced to me as James Wilkie.

James is a man whom you might pass any day on the street. He has an athletic spring to his walk but a generally undistinguished appearance: slight, dark, with curly black hair, and a respectful, reserved manner. The only unusual thing about him is his remarkably broad Scottish accent, which is as thick as any to be found in the heart of the Highlands. At first I had to strain greatly to follow his speech, but as I became more and more interested in what he had to say, I gradually managed to penetrate his brogue.

A few years ago, on a blind impulse, James left Scotland for Canada. After arriving in Toronto he held a variety of undistinguished jobs. Soon after getting settled, he visited the local spiritualist churches and at once found himself asked to speak and to give clairvoyance at the Sunday evening meetings. In Scotland he had done this kind of thing many times, and he spoke glowingly to me of his Spiritualist Church in Glasgow, which he claimed was "the biggest church in the whole city." However, after his many satisfying experiences in the "old country," James found much to criticize in meetings with Toronto spiritualists. Apparently he did not hesitate to tell them so to their faces. His popularity quickly waned, on this account, and requests to speak became fewer and fewer.

As he rambled on about his early days in Toronto, my new friend spoke of a chance meeting with a certain clergyman, and of the friendship that resulted in spite of the severe disapproval of spiritualists among the clergyman's superiors. The two men had met by accident at a concert of classical music, and, over a cup of coffee after the performance, struck up a casual acquaintance. When the young clergyman learned that his new acquaintance was a clairvoyant and medium, rather than displaying the official coolness of his particular church, he arranged to attend a meeting where James was to speak.

At this meeting the young minister was quite impressed and as the friendship deepened between them, he asked James to bring him a message from his father, who had not long died. Initial attempts at "sittings" for this purpose were fruitless, and James was almost despairing of giving the clergyman real proof of his powers, when it suddenly happened. The occasion was a Sunday evening, quite late, when James felt prompted to telephone the minister from his room. He had only begun to talk with his friend when he saw a spirit in the room, and as he described it to the clergyman, the latter cried excitedly, "That is my father! What does he say?"

The message was given and the clergyman was not apparently really convinced of the reality of mediumship. But feeling guilty about his behaviour, he told James that he would have to tell his superiors that he had been meeting with a medium. It was several days later that James had a hurried call from his friend announcing that he was being abruptly moved to another city, undoubtedly as the result of his confession. However, to express his appreciation he sent James an expensive present which the clairvoyant still treasures as a token of this unusual friendship.

The evening now grew late as we sat listening to this and other stories. I finally screwed up nerve and decided to ask him for a "sitting." This is the term used by mediums when they practise clairvoyance for someone without the usual procedures of a seance. When I suggested the sitting, James at once refused to guarantee that anything would happen but agreed to try. I learned later that this kind of refusal is invariable with good mediums, since the inspirational nature of clairvoyance means that results can never be commanded or guaranteed. At the same time, in a private sitting such as mine, where no money passes hands, the medium is under no compulsion to get results, and thus if something comes through it is more likely to be genuine.

Now, let me make it perfectly clear that, having just met him, James had no prior chance to question anyone about me, and also that I had given almost no information about myself during the earlier part of the evening. He had done almost all the talking. Furthermore, as he prepared to begin, I said to myself, "Don't give him any clues at all, but play it mum; don't even say, 'That's right,' or let him know whenever he gets 'warm.'" I kept to these simple rules throughout the sitting.

From previous experiences I rather expected James to go into a trance, or at least a partial trance, but instead he simply concentrated for perhaps fifteen or twenty seconds, his hand over his eyes, seeming to withdraw into himself, and then he began to talk. For the rest of the time his eyes were open, and he gestured and moved about in a perfectly normal manner.

This very casual beginning threw me off at first, and I didn't listen too carefully to what he was saying, not being sure that the sitting had actually begun. In fact, all that I can recall about the early part of the sitting were references he made to growing success in my writing during the year and to changes in my line of work. Both these prophecies were proved true; my writing during the year was successful beyond my dreams at that time, and in my vocation I had more complications than ever before.

As I sat half-thinking about these things, I heard James speak of my home. I listened carefully this time. "I see a two-storey house near some woods. It is a nice home." These statements were quite true and I became excited, but remembering my self-imposed rules, I only said, "Hmm." He continued, "You ought to set aside a room for a healing sanctuary for your prayers." He added, "This would be of great help in your future work." At the time I was not attempting any spiritual healing, and I was puzzled at this advice, yet the idea had appeal. Later events showed that the proposal had much merit.

James had been moving about the room casually, hands thrust in his pockets. He stopped pacing and turned to look directly at me. His manner changed and sitting down he said, "You have many helpers on the other side. One is a brother of your father, who died quiet young, perhaps in boyhood. He is interested in you, and he is a doorkeeper up there, bringing in other helpers." I could remember no uncle who had died early, but later on, checking with my father, I discovered that there was an uncle who died in England in his early twenties who had apparently had a temperament like mine. My father also confirmed another statement made by James, that my physical appearance was like that of his father, a fact I had not known until that day.

At another point James came to something that checked out amazingly. "There is a man who has spent some time in India, he is a minister and has been head over something in the teaching field. He is a friend, and will be getting in touch with you within a month; something that you have written has impressed him strongly, and he will want to contact you to suggest certain lines of action, apparently in the field of spiritual healing." At once I cast around in my mind for anyone this might be, and thought of several people, but subsequent events proved that it was none of these. Some weeks later, a friend did approach me about having discussions on spiritual healing. The man is a minister and had previously occupied a teaching post in a boy's school in India, something he had never before divulged to me.

James was intriguing me with his tendency to prophesy, and so I decided to ask him a question about my son who was then only a few months' old, and with regard to whom I had had one prophetic vision myself. I said, "What do you see for my son?" He replied, "I see a boy who is happy, with a deep, independent mind, a boy ahead of his age. He needs special training." Other comments are too personal to mention, but what happened next is of crucial interest. As he spoke about my son in this manner, an old friend, long dead, apparently appeared to him.

"There is a chap here who says his name is Jimmy. He says he knew you when you lived in residence at college. He was a brilliant student. Can you recall who this would be?" At first, I was stumped. I thought back to my most recent years of college residence, taking theology, and could think of no college friend who had subsequently died. Suddenly I went back to a year of college residence during the war, and to a close friend called James or Jimmy, more often the latter than the former. "Yes, I could certainly remember him." James went on, "He says he went suddenly; there was an explosion, a kind of accident, and his head was affected the worst." This was all true. Jimmy had been killed in action shortly after D-Day in France. I asked James to describe Jimmy for me. "He is tall, taller than you, dark, and has a slight stoop. He speaks with good diction and great clarity. His speech is one of the most distinguishing marks." This again was true. Jimmy had been about six feet tall, and always spoke with exceptional diction, reminding me of an Oxford don, though he had not been there.

I listened carefully to what James would say next. "Jimmy says that he saw you writing today, and you stopped several times, puzzled as to how to go on. He was much interested in your article, and says that you should try again tomorrow. Say prayers first, and the conclusion that you want to be strong, perhaps even dramatic, will come." It was true. I was working on an article, an important article on the subject of politics, a matter that would have been close to the heart of my old friend Jimmy. And as I wrote, the words *had* grown heavy, and fought the page so that I had difficulty in finding a proper conclusion. In the past, Jimmy and I had often been drawn together by just such topics as this, and it was also likely that he would counsel prayer, as he had been training for the ministry before his death. Although this was a small matter, to me this piece of advice was "evidential," as they say in psychical literature.

To that point in the sitting very little had been revealed that could be thoroughly verified, but the next piece of information erased all doubts from my mind about the reality of James's powers. He said, "Jimmy says you helped me materially once, and he is very grateful." What could this mean? I searched my memory for a clue, and then it came to me. After his death, along with another close friend, I had organized a collection for the university education of Jimmy's son, then a mere boy, and we had put the money collected into a trust fund. This all happened back in 1944, and had long since been forgotten. I described this to James with wonder in my eyes, and he replied, "Yes, that is the help he speaks of. He says that he is very grateful, and that he appears around you every so often."

I asked then, "What is Jimmy doing now?" James replied, in a quiet voice: "He says that he is a teacher over there, in the field of philosophy, that he is happy, and is learning still, but that there is yet much to learn." This closing piece of information also seemed evidential, for not only did it sound like Jimmy's outlook, but also it touched on his main interest, which had been the study of philosophy.

A skeptic may be able to punch holes in all this material, and if he can, well and good. But to me, this encounter with a gifted clairvoyant gave me a new respect for people with psychic gifts.

The Precognitive Dream

Candace Cael Carman

Candace Cael Carman is a poet and artist who was born in 1952 in East St. Paul, Man. She studied Religion and Philosophy at the University of Winnipeg and trained in music and visual art. Her art work is held in collections throughout North America, Europe, and the Middle East. Two volumes of her poems have been published by Fiddlehead Press: Pale Lady (1980) and The Songs of Bathsheba (1981). *She lives in Toronto and is a member of the League of Canadian Poets and PEN International.*

"The Precognitive Dream," a short memoir written by Candace Cael Carman, is her recollection of a youthful experience. As such it owes everything to memory and experience, nothing to the literary imagination. Yet reading it, one is aware of the hallmarks of the born writer, especially the ease with which the writer is able to convey personality and excitement.

NINE IN THE evening and I had had it. My eyes had been shutting and my head falling towards the soup at supper time. Now it was a lost cause. Those eyelids would not stay propped open. Grade Eleven was rough, much rougher than I had imagined it could be. Up early, out late, the usual teenage wheel of torture, did not make life any easier. Tonight would have to be an early-to-bed night whether I wanted it to be or not.

Sitting at the kitchen table, I invented complicated strategies to get me from here to there — there being my bedroom which was directly off the living room — with the least amount of hassle. My parents sat in the blue haze of evening television. *Star Trek* was just winding up and beaming up all its characters to the great starship *Enterprise*. This particular evening, "Beam me up, Scotty!" had rankled my nerves and I had retired to the kitchen.

As the commercials came on, my parents broke for coffee and a visit to the washroom. Ideal exit time. I mumbled goodnight and crossed the carpeted space to my bedroom in six swift steps. No hassles. Remarkable. I closed my door on my mother saying, "Goodnight, honey," and then speaking to my father she said, "Hope she's okay, she's been looking really tired."

My bedroom was small and utterly crammed with books and odds and ends. I had taken great care in decorating my space. Psychedelic posters hung everywhere including from the ceiling which was done in the trendiest supermarket aluminum foil. Candles, bones, rocks, and fossils covered any open horizontal space. From the back of my door, the Beatles' faces looked out at me: gold currency in the world of up-and-coming freaks. I said my evening sacrilegious prayer, "John, Paul, George, and Ringo, / Bless this night and make me tingle," and switched on the reel-to-reel. The Cream poured out "White Room."

Just before I undressed for bed, I went over to my bedroom windows. They looked out past an expanse of lawn and trees to the highway. It was an old road, one of the two oldest roads in the area. It followed the original Red River Trail which curved around the old Red River on its eastern side. The second oldest road, on the western side, mirrored the Red's movements. Old River Road clung to the bends of the Red like a skin. It was not a road like the highway; its traffic was limited to sightseers and old cemetery buffs.

Our highway was a high-volume road. Esso trucks hurtled past day and night from the nearby refinery: four lanes of multi-layered, top-grade asphalt to carry Esso's immense beasts. It was almost always noisy, even though we were at some remove from the road. But tonight it was still. The trees stood like stilettos, their shadows gradually elongating in the deepening night. The sky was clear and the air crackled and hummed with an intense silence broken only by the grinding of ice in the Red River an eighth of a mile away.

Spring breakup was just beginning. I moved into bed, pulled the covers over my head, and sleep promptly took me.

I awakened abruptly, soaked with a fearsome sweat. It was absolutely black out. I had no idea what time it was or for that matter anything else. Propelling myself out of bed, I dashed into the living room. My mother was still awake having a last cup of coffee in the kitchen. I stood in the middle of the living room surrounded by the silent television's blue glow and shrieked at my mother that she had to do something, had to do something about it right now. She had to stop it from happening. Call the police, somebody, something, there was still time.

She had no idea what I was talking about. My voice edged higher and higher as I told her what I had just seen. It had been very dark. The road was gravelly, bumpy. The River was sounding loud in my ears. There was a car, not a new one but an older model, souped up, standing on this road. Inside were several young men and two young women. The women, actually girls, were younger than I and very afraid. They did not want to be there and were being hurt. I felt their mounting panic, felt the push, the thrusts, the strikes. The skin slid on the ice-edged gravel and hit the brush in the snowy ditch. The young men drove away. I glimpsed the old Stones of St. Andrew's and the sound of the river grinding and rising was loud in my ears. I described the car to her as best I could and urged her to contact the police.

My mother, a practical woman at the worst of times, sat me down and tried to get me to use reason. "It was just a dream, a very realistic dream, a nightmare. Of course, it was horrible. That's what a nightmare is all about. But it's not real. You've been too tired lately. You've got to ease up, don't get involved in so many things. Yes, dreams are like that. They are very real while you're dreaming them. But you're awake now, honey. It's only midnight. You only slept for about two hours. You probably picked up on some part of a t.v. program Dad and I were watching. I bet you that that's what happened. No., I am not going to call the police. What would I possibly say to them? My daughter had a dream that she says needs investigating? Go back to bed. Sleep, sleep, all of this will seem fuzzy to you by tomorrow morning. Don't worry. Nothing happened. It was just a bad dream."

Seven in the morning and my mother is knocking at my door to make sure I get up for school. I feel stiff all over as if I had run the Marathon. Suddenly, the dream floods back in absolute vividness. I want distraction. I need distraction. I turn on the radio to the local underground rock station in time to catch the last part of the news. The information is just now being released by the police, although names are being withheld, about the violent rape shortly after midnight of two girls in a car up on Old River Road.

I close my eyes.

The Double Dream

Audrey Soltys

"*The Double Dream*" *reads like a short fantastic tale from the pen of Jorge Luis Borges or the typewriter of Julio Cortázar. Yet it is not a work of fiction at all, but the faithful account of an experience that occurred to Audrey Soltys.*

Mrs. Soltys wrote up her experience for George Gamester, the noted columnist with the Toronto Star, *who devoted a series of columns to just such accounts. He called the series "Tell Us Your Eerie Tales," and published "The Double Dream" on 7 July 1989.*

Mrs. Soltys is a graduate of the University of Manchester in England. She has travelled around the world with her husband M. A. Soltys, a microbiologist, and their children. She now lives in Guelph, On. In a letter she sent to me on 27 June 1989, she explained the following:

The incident happened in Melaka (Malacca) in 1975. I can't recall the season as Malaysia has an average temperature of about 32° year round, hot and humid. Our friends were looking in town at some apartments, which were too small, and at some houses, which were too big, which was why they went the next day to a different neighbourhood....

That was an old area in the country. The houses on stilts were of wood burnished to a golden brown. The area under and around the house was planted with fruit trees and flowering bushes, and the ground was raked free of leaves and weeds.

Then she added the following postscript:

> I forgot to mention the sequel. The daughter of the old man came to see us. Apparently since his wife had died, he spent most nights and mealtimes with them, the daughter and family. The final arrangement was that they rented the house for two years, then left for study-leave in Australia. The old man tended to his garden every day, but only extended conventional greetings. There is a charming custom in Malaysia that when the father retires, the family (sometimes numbering ten or so) contribute automatically to the household.

WHILE STAYING in Malaysia, we became friends with a young couple named Omar and Sharifah who were looking for a house.

One day, when we were going through an older, more traditional area outside the town, Sharifah clutched her husband's arm and said: "Look at that sweet little house. I dreamed last night of a house exactly like that."

As we approached, we saw an old man sweeping the walk. The moment he spotted us, he rushed inside.

Omar knocked at the door and told the man: "Don't be afraid."

The old man replied: "I'm not afraid of *you*. It's that woman. Last night I dreamed she came to steal my house."

The Spirit of the
Hanging Judge

Jean Kozocari

I first heard about the Spirit of the Hanging Judge from Robin Skelton, the poet and witch of Vancouver Island. I was naturally interested so I pressed Robin for more details. He urged me to contact Jean Kozocari, Victoria's well-known practitioner of wicca, whom he said "knows all about the Spirit of the Hanging Judge — and a great many other things as well."

I was in the midst of researching and writing Mysterious Canada *when I wrote to Jean Kozocari. Frankly, I was anxious about the Hanging Judge. Not once in all my research had I encountered a reference to this ghost or spirit, not even to an apparition of this man. Was this another West Coast tradition which I, someone from Central Canada, was destined never to learn about? Naturally I was familiar with Sir Matthew Begbie (1819-1894), the so-called Hanging Judge, the pioneer law-giver whose fair but tough judgements struck terror in the hearts of pioneer wrong-doers in the Cariboo. But I was planning to publish a comprehensive book about the supernatural and the paranormal in Canada, so the book, to be as complete as possible, had to make reference to Sir Matthew's ghost — assuming that he had materialized or in some sense "returned."*

Then I heard from Ms. Kozocari. I literally heard from her, for she was kind enough to send to me not a brief letter but a long cassette audio tape. When I played it I could hear her clearly and confidently recounting the details of her encounter with the Spirit of the Hanging Judge. The text which follows is a transcript of that audio tape.

Others describe Ms. Kozocari as "a practising witch." (There must also be non-practising witches.) She describes herself as "a teacher of the occult, an authority on the paranormal, and a practitioner of magic." Although she is not a person to offer biographical particulars, she did vouchsafe the fact that she was in her forties at the time of the incidents described and that she descends from a long line of witches.

IN 1980 WE WERE INVITED to investigate a haunted house. We found the house to be a Fifties bungalow built on the side of a hill in Saanich, which is just outside Victoria, B.C. It was a comfortable house, a very beautiful one. The people as newlyweds had drawn up a plan for their dream house, and this house fit every criterion they had. Years later they found and bought it. They owned it for more than three years. And although they were paying two mortgages, they were never able to live there in comfort.

Strange things happened. Workmen made commitments and never showed up. There were floods although the house was built on top of a hill. There were plagues of rats, and when the rats died in the building, there were plagues of flies. No matter what they did, always something came up to make the house unlivable. The woman suffered severe personality changes there. The man found that an incredible lethargy came over him whenever he tried to do work on the hill.

We arrived on Father's Day, and on the way out the two mediums whom I took with me, although best of friends and always pleasant and congenial, fought constantly all the way out. When we arrived at the house, we went in, walked through it, and investigated it. There were several places that were very uncomfortable, including one room in the basement that had been built over a large protruding rock so that the rock became part of the room. Over the three years that we investigated the house, this rock frequently oozed a very strange, oily substance that had the consistency of thick motor oil that was shiny and aluminum-looking. We would find it on clothing, on dowsing instruments, all over us, all over the people who came in and out of the house.

The haunting resisted exorcism. We had all sorts of meetings. We had dowsers come in to see if there were water deposits under the earth. One afternoon my eight-year-old son was having tea with us in the living-room of the house. As he was sitting there, drinking tea, a beautiful glass picture-frame lifted up off a bookshelf, did a complete somersault in the air, and landed in his lap! There was absolutely no way that it could have fallen — four feet high! — into the air, and in a complete circle, before it landed on the floor. He very carefully set his tea cup down and leaped into his sister's lap. He's now twenty, and we were talking about it last night. It is one of the lasting memories of his childhood, much outweighing Christmas and Halloween.

One of the unexplained phenomena was that the owners of the house had fastened glass mirrors to the wall and then built bookshelves in front of them. Slowly over the weeks the letter M appeared. It was scratched into the silvering on the back of the mirror in a place where no one could have got at it. At the time we didn't see any great significance to the letter M.

All our efforts failed in the house. All we were able to do was clean it up temporarily, then something else would happen. We began a research on the property. The house was reasonably modern, but in researching it back to its first owner, we found that the property had been the property of Sir Matthew Begbie, the Hanging Judge. We found that, although he had never lived there, built a shed, built a building, or did anything else on the land, he used to ride out on his horse, taking his lunch with him. He was seen from the distance sitting on the large rock (the one that now protruded through the basement) and meditating. He would spend hours just staring off into space.

This made a lot of sense to us because for some reason or other ropes accumulated in the basement of the house. The lean-to shed where they put their car had the modified shape of a gallows. But of course until we had the clue that this was Sir Matthew Begbie's property, we were never able to contact Sir Matthew Begbie.

At this time the owners were offered an enormous sum of money for the house. They sold it and threatened me: "Please, don't tell anyone that the house is haunted!" They were terrified that the deal would not go through.

On the last day they were in the house, I went there with a photographer who sometimes has the ability to photograph "extras" — shapes, sizes, or ghosts. We use an old-fashioned Polaroid camera, the kind with the pictures that separate. You have a negative and a positive with a gummy substance on it. She put the filmpack into the camera and walked around, taking pictures of the house. However, we were unable to get a photograph of the corner of the house that extends over the rock. That corresponded to the dining-room. It was always missing from the picture. If we took it in the middle of the picture, the rest of the picture would be fine, but there would be a white column down the middle. If we took it from the side, that part of the house never photographed. We went to two drugstores and got two different packs of film, thinking that perhaps there was a problem with the film. The packs were not labelled consecutively, so we knew they were from different batches. However, we were unable to take pictures of the dining-room. Everything else — the front of the house, the back of the house, the trees, the rock garden, the pond — were fine. It was only the one part of the house that refused to be photographed.

As we were driving away, the owners were standing, waving to us, and the photographer had one more negative. So she put the camera out the window and took a quick picture. As we drove down the driveway, she pulled out the film and held it for the proper time, then pulled it apart. The image turned out to be badly underexposed. We placed the negative, which was sticky, on the dashboard of the car and promptly forgot about it. (That sounds awful, but I am a slob about my car!)

One evening several weeks later we were sitting talking, and someone said, "Well, the negative is out in the car." So someone went out and got it and placed it on the table. On the negative was a picture of Sir Matthew Begbie. All of us had seen the photographs of him that appear in books and articles. In these he wears a broad-brimmed, cow-boyish hat, he has a dark beard and looks very elegant. So we were able to recognize him immediately, despite the fact that in our picture he had no hat on and his beard and hair were white and curly. It was not until three years later that I found a picture of him in his older years. Indeed, his beard and hair were white and curly. The Polaroid photograph is very old now. I put a strip of plastic across it to preserve it as much as I could. But for anyone who has ever seen a picture of Sir Matthew Begbie, it is quite obvious that Sir Matthew was there with the owners of the house saying goodbye to us — obviously quite relieved that we were leaving him and his property in peace.

One of the awkward things about investigating ghosts and haunted houses is that you can't, really, ten years later, go back and knock on the door and say, "Hello, I was here ten years ago, and this house was haunted. Do you still have a ghost?" Somehow, if I were a little bit pushier, maybe I could do that. But, at present, it's just not part of my reality.

That is Sir Matthew's story. While he is certainly not the offending ghost, it is obvious that his very strong presence at the house made it possible for other and later things to manifest. And we did find out in researching that practically everybody who had lived in the house had had problems with it. The previous owners had been a Navy gentleman and his wife. He had retired early and decided to become a minister. He studied there, rehearsing and memorizing passages form the Bible and hymns and prayers and so on. His wife, on the other hand, was totally devoted to the Maharishi Mahesh Yogi. She was deeply into meditation, and at the same time would be practising meditation and her mantras. So perhaps all this mental, spiritual activity, added to the already overpowering presence of Sir Matthew Begbie, made this haunting indeed most violent.

I Don't Question This Ability I Have

Najla Mady

Najla Mady is a psychic who was born in Rouyn, Que. Since the 1950s she has made her home in the Niagara Peninsula, latterly in St. Catharines. Listeners and viewers in the area know her well, for she has made frequent guest appearances on Radio station CKTB and Cable 10 Television. She is credited with predicting the assassination of Egyptian President Anwar Sadat the day before the fatal shooting.

Najla Mady is the author and publisher of Simply Psychic, *a 54-page booklet issued in 1983. It recounts in a positive manner a number of the author's experiences in helping people. This booklet is the source of the passages which follow.*

I FIND LIFE INTRIGUING and am constantly amazed by it.

It surprises people that what I can do for them I cannot do for myself, but this is how a psychic's gift works. If we could use it for ourselves, there would be some very wealthy psychics; if we could pick lucky lottery numbers, there would be many wealthy people. A psychic reading will not make a great deal of difference in your life; what it can do is take away the element of surprise.

When a person comes to me for a reading, I will tell that person what has brought him or her to me, whatever problem is on his or her mind. I will go into his or her past events, often giving dates and naming names as I go along. It is not unusual for me to pick up a medical problem. To do a reading, I need a client's name and age. During a reading I will pick up bits of information pertaining to relatives or friends, such as events going on in their lives.

To be psychic is to be able to do readings for people no matter what parts of the world they live in. I do readings by mail and by telephone for people as far away as Australia, Malaysia, West Germany, Saudi Arabia, India, Greece, Hong Kong, and Great Britain, as well as in the United States and Canada. By word of mouth, a reputation is born; that is what has led me to write this book. The interest is great and I feel I should share the knowledge.

Many people have asked me if it is uncomfortable to have a psychic ability. No, it is not. The only time I use my ability is when I am asked to use it. I don't approach people and spiel off what I think the future holds for them. I don't try to "pick up" on a person unless I am asked.

Although we each have an ability to respond to psychic phenomena, you cannot study how to be a psychic. You cannot even develop it. You either are psychic or you are not. Likewise I am against those courses that direct people inward to find a "guide" that will help them live their lives. I have had to de-program people who have had as many as seven "guides" they believe existed inside their minds telling them how to live their lives. I think this is extremely dangerous. I speak against this every chance I get. Those people suggest that a "guide," once adopted, can manifest itself in a person's mind and guide him through his life. It is wise to steer clear of such erroneous teachings....

I regard having psychic ability as another person would regard his own talent for doing carpentry or playing the piano; although it takes self-discipline, and responsible application, the talent just is. I don't worry about it, nor am I terribly impressed by it either.

I received a call one day from a rather anxious mother asking me if I would come over to her home. She reported "really strange things happening" in her house.

I replied, "You have a poltergeist. There are cupboard doors opening and closing, you're finding objects missing and they are turning   up   in   other   places.''

She said, "My God, you're right!"

I had picked up the problem over the phone, which is not unusual for me to do. I went to the home, and as I entered the house, I said, "Please don't say anything. Just let me walk around the house. Follow me and observe what happens. I don't want you to tell me what has been going on. I'll tell you, and correct me if you disagree."

As I stood there my eyes immediately went to the right, where a massive old piano-like organ stood. "I don't like that piano," I told her, "it does not belong to this house. The day you brought it here is the day your problems began."

(It's not unusual for me to walk into a home and "pick up" on other than what I was called in for, as I have no control over what I "pick up.")

"It belongs to my sister," the mother confessed. "She brought it here when she left her apartment to move in with me." She agreed, "The occurrences all began around that time."

I walked away from the piano and into the kitchen. Here the cupboard doors had been opening and closing and objects had been found in the corners where they had been moved by a non-human force.

(The strong emotional feelings that some children have when they are going through puberty are intense. If those feelings are combined with hostility and anger, they can boom out like a laser beam and actually move objects. It is the same energy an angry adult feels. It builds up so strongly a person feels like taking a crack with all his might at whatever is at hand to find some release. With the energy of a poltergeist, the force is actually doing it for the child. The child is not aware of it, however; the activity is occurring on a non-conscious level. The child is the poltergeist!

(A poltergeist usually lasts a year at the most. It will leave as suddenly as it came, unless there is another child of puberty age in the family who is also finding adolescence traumatic. It would then happen through the child. There are cases in which each child in a family in turn has been afflicted by this phenomenon. Oddly enough, once it's all over with, the child tends to just forget it. There don't seem to be any lasting effects.)

I walked through the hall and then upstairs. I was heading for one particular bedroom, and stood over a single bed. It was there I got a most terrible feeling.

"There is a presence here and your daughter has seen it," I told the mother. I then stood in the doorway and began absorbing the force that had been so disruptive.

I don't understand the absorption phenomenon, but for some reason I can serve as a conductor through which a negative force or disruptive spirit can be eliminated. I can only describe what happens and leave it up to those for whom I have performed such an absorption to attest to the fact and the results of my efforts.

A rather large floral arrangement on the woman's hope chest began swaying back and forth, and the air turned very cold.

As an absorption progresses, I concentrate with as much intensity as I can summon; then I wait until a heavy feeling starts to lift from me. I know the absorption is complete when the heavy feeling inside of me subsides, when the air starts to turn warm again, and when nothing else moves. It is exhausting, however; when it happens, I can't work the rest of the day, nor the day after that.

But the force in her home was removed. The whole process had taken approximately thirty minutes.

Although I am conductor through which a native force or spirit is released, I am not the kind of "medium" (I don't even like the word) who theatrically gets people together in a seance and contacts the dead. There is no purpose in such an endeavour. Those people who are dead are comfortable being so and should remain that way. There is no good reason to disturb them. People who selfishly insist on making contact with a dead loved one make it difficult for that loved one to pass on peacefully. I am a conductor, but I don't find it necessary to use dramatics, nor will I call up the dead.

I am always drawn to where a spirit is. If there is a spirit in a house, I will walk right to the spot where it manifests itself.

An extremely unusual case occurred in Niagara-on-the-Lake at the home of a friend of mine. Patricia called me and said, "For a long time something's been going on in my house, but now it's bothering my son David. He's not sleeping at night. He sees something in his bedroom. I have seen it too. Will you come? My older children have seen children playing in the house as well, but they're not bothered. The one in his room is troubling David, however."

When I arrived I discovered six or seven spirits living in that house. But one was much more complex and hostile than all the others.

I told Patricia and Michael, her companion, to follow me, to observe what was happening. When I am concentrating I am not always aware of all the things going on around me. Again, I asked them not to tell me what had occurred in the home; I would learn about it as I proceeded through the house.

I immediately walked through the living-room and up the stairs to David's bedroom. There I started to describe what had been happening. There had been apparitions at night from an ambiguous spirit. In a way, the spirit was friendly and trying to play with David, but in another way the spirit was trying to frighten him. I felt the spirit was a person who had never had the chance to be a child during his own lifetime — that his own life had been cut short and that he was envious and resentful of David's youth.

When I entered the bedroom, the air turned cold, the bedspread and drapes started to move, and an extremely cold current of air enveloped me. Digging my heels into the floor, I stood firm as the spirit moved through me. The air around me started to warm, so I felt I had put the spirit to rest. This process took about ten minutes.

As we started to go back downstairs, I realized I had only partially completed my work, for I began to pick up another spirit in another part of the house. I felt friction. Then, all of a sudden, Michael, Patricia, and I could feel a force behind us on the stairs, pushing us all down, as if to hurry us out of the way.

What followed next was one of the worst experiences I've ever had. If ever I was frightened, this was the time.

The pushing concerned me, but I was so exhausted I needed to rest, so I walked towards the chesterfield in the family-room and lay down. I listened as Michael and Patricia described what had occurred. They quietly described with incredulity things moving on the wall behind me, the air turning cold, and the hem of my dress swishing back and forth. Suddenly I bolted up and said, "Patricia, I must go into your living-room. Something is there!

They followed as I walked straight to the corner, where a large plant stood. It was there that I started to feel the most stubborn, hostile force I had ever felt. The plant was shrouded in a most bitter, angry field of negative energy. Never before had I experienced so much force.

The spirit had transferred itself into a living, growing thing. I didn't feel anything evil, merely angry. The air around the plant began to turn ice cold, colder than anything I had ever experienced before, and I thought, "Oh, my God, I don't know if I can do this." It was so strong!

I took a very stern stance and said I was going to absorb that spirit no matter what. Now I was beginning to get angry myself — to think the spirit was so stubborn, so hostile, and so determined to stay and continue to bother the children!

I stood directly in front of the plant. The feeling inside of me was extremely heavy, yet I felt I was starting to absorb the spirit. It started to lift, but there was something wrong this time.

For the first time ever, I didn't feel it was lifting on its way to rest. It was lifting because it was so much stronger than I was. (I even felt it might "escape" me entirely.) So I just stood there, as firmly and as defiantly as I could, and willed it to me.

Then I started to feel it. The hem of my skirt began swaying back and forth, and my one foot began to move involuntarily, inching away from its place beside my other foot, putting me off balance, distracting me. With all my strength, I concentrated my will to remove the force that was now concentrated around my ankle. I stood still, arms raised, fighting for every bit of energy I could muster to combat its force. It was my will against the spirit's will.

As I stood there, concentrating on the plant itself, I saw it!

At first it was just a shimmer of its leaves. Then, as if relenting, one by one its leaves began to droop and shrivel. As this happened, I began to feel lightness and warmth around me.

I had absorbed the spirit. The spirit had "died" and, with it, the plant.

By this time I could barely walk, I was so weak; Patricia and Michael helped me into the living-room where I lay down. Then they both noticed a most startling thing. There, on my ankle, were white indentations — thumbprints where something had grabbed me and tried to knock me off my feet. Michael rubbed my ankle until it returned to normal.

I told them to bury the plant as soon as possible, which they did. I learned later from Patricia that at one time a young boy had lived in their house and had died of leukemia at nine years of age. Although Patricia speaks freely about the episode, she is concerned about the young boy's parents who still live in Niagara-on-the-Lake and remain grief-stricken by their son's tragic death. For that reason she doesn't speak very often about the occurrence in her home on that day. Her children have not been troubled, so there is no reason to ever mention it again.

I am an instrument, a conductor, through which a disturbed spirit may find release and eventual rest. It doesn't stay contained in me. I absorb it and then release it. It is as if such spirits don't know their way to "the other side," and I show them the way, which direction to take, which channel to enter.

I don't question this ability of mine. I only know I am able to do it, and when it concerns the well-being of children, I thank God I have it. Otherwise, the disturbances would go on indefinitely.

The End Result is Hardly Convincing

James Randi

James Randi, who performs as "The Amazing Randi," follows in the footsteps of the late Harry Houdini. Like the master magician, Randi is an escape artist, second to none; also like the master magician, Randi is a tireless debunker of psychic pretensions.

James Randi, who was born in Toronto, made his debut as a conjuror in Montreal. Florida is now his home base, but he travels widely, performing magical acts and lecturing on the practices of self-proclaimed psychics and faith-healers and on the gullibility of parapsychologists. Along with Paul Kurtz, Ray Hyman, Henry Gordon, and others, he is a founding fellow the Committee for the Scientific Investigation of Claims of the Paranormal. There is a reference to CSICOP in Randi's article which follows.

This article originally appeared in The Skeptical Inquirer, *the journal published by CSICOP, where it was called "Cold Reading Revisited." It is reprinted from* Paranormal Borderlands of Science *(Buffalo: Prometheus Books, 1981) edited by Kendrick Frazier. As Dr. Hyman explained in the classic article he devoted to the phenomenon, a "psychic" will do a cold reading when a hot reading is impossible. A hot reading is one which introduces information gathered from organized research prior to the reading. A cold reading is one done "from scratch," so to speak, with the psychic closely observing the subject and watching for signs of corroboration and even the unconscious volunteering of additional information.*

Geraldine Smith is a psychic — or as Randi puts it a "psychic" — from Brampton, Ont. She makes guest appearances on Toronto-area radio shows and television programs.

TWO YEARS AGO in the pages of this journal, *The Skeptical Inquirer* (Spring/Summer 1977), Ray Hyman gave a quite definitive account of the art of "cold reading" as practised by those with psychic pretensions. Dr. Hyman, as a psychologist and an advanced student of "mentalist" techniques, outlined the often surprising subtleties that are employed to convince the unwary that marvelous forces are at work. More recently (Fall 1978) Ronald A. Schwartz showed how stage performer Peter Hurkos applied some of the same techniques.

Recently Dr. Paul Kurtz and I were invited to appear on Canadian TV with one Geraldine Smith, a renowned "psychic" in Toronto. She had been extensively and convincingly written up in the Canadian papers as a powerful worker, and we were looking forward to being astonished. I had brought along an object that I thought would have strong "vibrations" for a genuine psychic, and the host of "Point Blank," Warner Troyer, had an article of his own to try for results.

We reproduce here the text of Miss Smith's "reading" for each article and suggest that students of cold readings note carefully the techniques used. The end result is hardly convincing, but that is due to the fact that the owner of each object was careful not to provide any feedback to Smith at any time. The words are transcribed directly from a tape recording provided by the people at Global TV in Toronto. We thank them for their courtesy.

The host decided to try a silver chain bracelet.

Host: Tell me something about the owner of that [handing her a "Medic Alert" bracelet].

Smith: Okay.

Host: A little bracelet. Other than the fact that they need a Medic Alert bracelet.

Smith: [laughs] Okay. First of all I'm getting a very strong gold. Now one thing I should let everybody know is, I also work with what is called "auras," and I've tuned myself into picking up vibrations, colours, from the article that the person has worn — had for some time. Now, first colour is gold, and that is an extremely sensitive colour. It's also, of course, allergy colour too. It's the colour of super, super, super nervousness. This person I'm feeling physically, upper, lower back area problems. I'm also seeing some upper stomach area things going on. Do you know this person?

Host: Uh-huh.

Smith: Personally?

Host: Uh-huh.

Smith: All right, there's something in this area here [points to chest]. You see, as soon as I pick up an article, I will physically feel different areas that perhaps have been affected by the person. Feeling this area [indicates chest], feeling this area [indicates forehead], headaches, eyestrain, something like that. Upper and lower back areas. It's also the intuitive colour. I would also, I'd have to say that the person who owns it is extremely intuitive, probably clair-sentient, which is very clear on the gut-feeling type areas. I'm seeing — there's a separation around this person. Are they in this area now? Because I see them, like, not here.

Host: Physically not here?

Smith: Physically not here. No.

Host: Uh-huh. Well!

Smith: Which — which would make me wonder if the person is [laughs] either dead or if there's been some very, very bad health problems with them, because I'm just *really* feeling sluggish myself. Interesting. I'm seeing the month of January here — which is now — but there would have to be something strong with the person with January as well.

Host: Okay. What colour is *my* aura?

Smith: You've got blue, you've got gold, you've got green.

Host: What do these things *mean*? What's an aura?

Smith: An aura is — I perceive it as a colour. A colour energy vibration that surrounds the person's body. It tells me mental, physical, spiritual — ah — general personality. Green is the colour of the communicator. Anybody in the communications area has to have green in their aura. In other words, in any area.

Host: So you can tell me that without looking, huh?

Smith: Yeah. In other words, yeah. In other words, you've got to have good communication in all areas. The one thing I would emphasize very strongly right now is that the green is a little bit blocked in the mental area of your aura, so that means you have been very frustrated in the area of communication on a personal level. It's almost as if you've been talking to the wall. I'm seeing a lot of [laughs], a lot of vibrating there. And it's more in a personal area rather than in — you know — a work, business situation.

Host: Okay.

The host, who had been very careful not to top his hand, following my admonitions to that effect before the program, was the owner of that Medic Alert bracelet. He had not tried to conceal the fact, though he picked it up from a small table to hand it to the psychic. She assumed that it belonged to another person who gave her "reading" with that assumption. Note that she did not tell us the age, sex, or relationship of this mythical person. She tried to "pump" the host by asking whether he knew the person and whether the person was physically there or not. Warner carefully gave answers. Yes, he knew the person. And he answered her question about the whereabouts with another question. I'm proud of him.

Jumping the gun, she guessed the person was absent, and then covered all bases with a classic generalization/cop-out — "...which would make me wonder if the person is either dead or if there's been some very, very bad health problems." Note that she was only "made to wonder," not know, and as phrased, it was also a question that might prompt an answer but failed to do so.

The host was neither dead nor absent. His back, he assured her, was excellent, nothing was wrong in the chest area, and when she tried to add a neck/upper-shoulder area quickly to the reading as he revealed his good state of health, he denied that as well. But she mumbled an encouraging "excellent...fine" as he outlined his condition to cover the fact that she was dead wrong. He is neither nervous nor allergic and has no stomach problems. Headaches and eyestrain, he assured us, do not bother him either.

But I must report that our host tumbled for one of the most common tricks of such readings. You see, the victim is allowed and encouraged to read more into the recitation than is already there. Smith had said, "I'm seeing the month of January here," and during his denial of the accuracy of her reading, he admitted that she had determined that his birthday was in January! But she had said nothing about a birthday, particularly his birthday, since she didn't even know the bracelet belonged to him! When confronted with all this evidence, Ms. Smith explained: "The thing is, that, to me, in a reading, means quick removal from a situation, which means either leaving this place, leaving the country — quick removal." Perhaps the lady was expressing her own desires of the moment. It certainly didn't make any sense to me.

Looking at Paul Kurtz and myself, she tried another tack. "Understand, I can totally see what the two of you are saying. The thing that I take a little bit further down the line is — my readings — as much as many things can be applied to many people, aren't there a lot of similarities in life? [There was a short stunned pause here, as we all tried to think what she could possibly be trying to say.] You know, we get married or we don't, we're male or we're female, we have children or we don't."

Ms. Smith was a little bit subdued, but smiled bravely after this confrontation. She was yet to be tested with an object that I had brought along specifically for the purpose. It was an object that I had a complete history of, and it was something I had owned for some time. In terms of a psychometry reading, it should have been excellent material. I will reverse the regular procedure in that I will tell you in advance all about the object, and then give you her entire word-for-word "reading" of it. You will then be in the position I was and be able to do your own analysis of her accuracy.

The object was a small bisque-fired ceramic, black in colour, of Peruvian origin. It measured seen inches long and was in the form of a bird, with a spout coming from the top. It was a fake — a replica — of a genuine Mochica grave object and had been made by a friend in Lima who is Peruvian by birth but Chinese in ancestry. He is a short man, five-foot-seven or so, heavy, straight black hair, twenty-eight years of age, with totally Chinese features to all appearances. He is single, or was at the time the reading was made. He speaks only Spanish. His business is making accurate replicas of original Peruvian art and repairing ceramics. The ceramic was given to me by him because it had been broken, and I repaired it myself when I returned to the United States. I have a large collection of similar pieces, both genuine originals and good replicas. I had brought this one with me to avoid breaking a valuable original, and to get around the tendency of psychics to expound on non-existent people long extinct, who they can safely claim were associated with such an article. I knew the whole history of the object, from molding to breaking and beyond.

Geraldine Smith took a deep breath and started on her "reading" of this article, while I carefully sat there unblinkingly.

Smith: Okay. The first thing that — actually I'm very quickly being taken over maps, and I'm turning in very strongly to Mexico, United States — general area there. I'm, seeing three very strong personalities, two females and a male, and I'll describe them all for you. First of all, the man I'm seeing is approximately five-foot-eight, five-foot-nine. To me, that's short for a male. Very deep brown hair, but receding at the temples. Glasses, quick thick. obviously very bad eyes, because the focus I'm seeing is very, very strong. I'm seeing kind of a round-neck shirt. It's not the type you have on now. I guess it would be more along the line that he is wearing [she pointed at two of us]. Then I'm going to the two ladies. Oh, I didn't give you an age on the man. He would have to be forty-five to fifty. Something like that. The ladies I'm seeing, one would be, hmmm, five-foot. Very short. Four-nine, five-foot. The other lady is quite a bit taller. One is very, very, very heavy-set, and shortish curlyish hair, but fluffy. And the other one, the shorter one, is just, well, there's nothing really big about her. I'm seeing these three people very much in connection with this. Do you recognize them at all?

Randi: Now you're asking me something. You're supposed to be telling me.

Smith: I mean, do you recognize them?

Randi: Do you want now the history of the object? Is the reading finished?

Some things about this exchange will be obvious. She took a guess at an Indian origin, but missed. It could have been North

American Indian or Mexican to the uninitiated, but it was not. She threw in three people for a try-on, and I'm still trying to fit in the two women, but I can't. The man's eyesight is excellent — he does not wear glasses. As for height, she's great on that, and the fellow does wear turtleneck sweaters frequently. His hair is very definitely not receding — quite the contrary. The age she gave is at least seventeen years off.

Now, you should know two other things about this test. First, I told Geraldine Smith very clearly that this was not to be considered a formal test. My reasons should be obvious. It was quite possible for her to have looked into my background and discovered my interest in Peruvian archaeology. She could have visited a museum and come up with the origin of the object easily. Second, she agreed to consider a formal test by the CSICOP, to be conducted regardless of the outcome of this demonstration. We have not heard from her since that time.

Soltys and the Gypsies

M.A. Soltys

The account which appears here reads more like the curriculum vitae of a professional scientist and academic than it does the personal account of an extraordinary experience. Yet the academic details of Professor Soltys' life provide a sense of drama in light of the predictions of the two Gypsy women.

The account comes from a letter dated 27 June 1989 and was sent to the present editor by the Professor's wife, Audrey Soltys. The "follow-up" was added by Mrs. Soltys, whose own experience appears elsewhere in this collection.

BEFORE WORLD WAR II, when I was working as a scientist in the Research Institute in Pulawy in Poland, several of us, men and women scientists, used to meet on Sunday mornings in a café bar for coffee or ice cream.

During one of these meetings, a Gypsy woman entered, came directly to me, and told me that I would live abroad in a country surrounded by the sea, and would travel widely and become well-known. She said I would marry while I was abroad, and (pointing to the girls) added, "You won't make bread from this flour." I told her to tell the girls their fortunes, but she said I was the only one with an interesting future.

A year later, when I was in the western part of Poland as an Army Reserve Office in summer training, I was stopped in the street by a different Gypsy woman who told me the same thing, adding that I would have a long life.

When the war started, to escape from the Germans and Russians who invaded Poland, I crossed the frontier with my unit to Romania, and later to France. After the occupation of France, I escaped to Britain. After taking my Ph.D. in Medicine I was awarded a postdoctoral fellowship in Cambridge, and then worked as a lecturer in Microbiology in Glasgow and later in Liverpool where I met and married the woman who became my wife. From Liverpool I went as the Director of a Research Institute on Trypanosomiasis in Uganda, where we spent three years. While in Africa I was invited by the University of Cambridge, where I spent twelve years as a University Don attached to King's College. While in Cambridge on sabbatical leaves, I was invited as a visiting professor for a year to Utrecht, Holland, and later to the Sudan. When one of my graduate students became the Vice-chancellor or Khartoum University, he wanted me to replace him for a year as Professor of Microbiology. In 1966, I was invited to take a permanent post by the University of Guelph, where we stayed until I retired. From Guelph, I gave various lectures and seminars at various universities in the United States and Central America, and spent some time as a Visiting Professor at James Cook Univeristy in Townsville, Australia, and the University of Palmerston North, in New Zealand. After my retirement I was asked by CIDA to help Malaysia to organize their Veterinary School. After four years there I returned to Canada, and was approached to teach Microbiology at a private American University in Dominica, where we spent a year.

During my academic career, I have written three books and over one hundred scientific papers. As an expert on Trypanosomiasis (sleeping sickness), I was invited to serve on the World Health Organization in Geneva. Having just celebrated my eighty-second birthday, and been given a clean bill of health by my doctor, I can honestly say that the predictions have been justified.

Follow-up to the above by his wife, Audrey Soltys:

We were in Warsaw in 1978, walking down the busiest main street with fairly heavy summer traffic and crowded sidewalks, when I noticed, on the other side of the street, some Gypsies approaching people. One of them looked in our direction, and started to cross the street, in and out of the traffic, seemingly coming towards us. We were surrounded by other people, and were not conspicuously dressed, but as she crossed, she was keeping us in sight. I asked my husband if we could go into one of the amber shops, and we watched through the window as she looked anxiously up and down the street without approaching anybody else. After some time she crossed the street and rejoined her companions. I wish today I had not so reacted, but it seemed very strange to me. She was much too young to have been one of the Gypsies who had approached my husband years earlier.

5. Natural Mysteries

The Phenomenon of 1819

Correspondent,
Scientific American

Montreal was the centre of the "dark day" that is known to meteorologists and historians as the Phenomenon of 1819.

A "dark day" is an eerie phenomenon that occurs from time to time. To the meteorologist such a day is one during which daylight is replaced by darkness. The sky grows dark with heavy clouds and mid-day looks like midnight. Many descriptions of the effect stress its freakish appearance and the fear and terror it occasions in the hearts of those who witness it. There are natural causes at the root of the phenomenon, some of them simple, some of them complex.

The difference between Montreal's "dark day" of 1819 and many other "dark days" is that the phenomenon in Montreal was accompanied by untypical electrical and luminous effects. The account here, although an anonymous one, is based on a first-person description. It was published more than seventy years after the phenomenon. It appeared as "The Dark Day in Canada" in the 21 May 1881 issue of the Scientific American. It is reprinted from Handbook of Unusual Natural Phenomena (Glen Arm, Md.: The Sourcebook Project, 1978) compiled by William R. Corliss.

ON THE MORNING of Sunday, November 8, 1819, the sun rose upon a cloudy sky, which assumed, as the light grew upon it, a strange greenish tint, varying in places to an inky blackness. After a short time the whole sky became terribly dark, dense black clouds filling the atmosphere, and there followed a heavy shower of rain, which appeared to be something of the nature of soapsuds, and was found to have deposited after settling a substance in all its qualities resembling soot. Late in the afternoon the sky cleared to its natural aspect, and the next day was fine and frosty. On the morning of Tuesday, the 10th, heavy clouds again covered the sky, and changed rapidly from a deep green to a pitchy black, and the sun, which occasionally seen through them, was sometimes of a dark brown or an unearthly yellow colour, and again bright orange, and even blood red. The clouds constantly deepened in colour and intensity, and later on a heavy vapour seemed to descend to the earth, and the day became almost as dark as night, the gloom increasing and diminishing most fitfully. At noon lights had to be burned in the courthouse, the banks, and public offices of that city. Everybody was more or less alarmed, and many were the conjectures as to the cause of the remarkable occurrence. The most sensible thought that immense woods or prairies were on fire somewhere to the west; others said that a great volcano must have broken out in the Province; still others asserted that our mountain was an extinct crater about to resume operations and to make of the city a second Pompeii; the superstitious quoted an old Indian prophecy that one day the Island of Montreal was to be destroyed by an earthquake, and some even cried that the world was about to come to an end.

About the middle of the afternoon a great body of clouds seemed to rush suddenly over the city, and the darkness became that of night. A pause and hush for a moment or two succeeded, and then one of the most glaring flashes of lightning ever beheld flamed over the country, accompanied by a clap of thunder which seemed to shake the city to its foundations. Another pause followed, and then came a light shower of rain of the same soapy and sooty nature as that of two days before. After that it appeared to grow brighter, but an hour later it was as dark as ever. Another rush of clouds came, and another vivid flash of lightning, which was seen to strike the spire of the old French parish church and to play curiously about the large iron cross at its summit before descending to the ground. A moment later came the climax of the day. Every bell in the city suddenly range out the alarm of fire, and the affrighted citizens rushed out from their houses into the streets and made their way in the gloom toward the church, until Place d'Armes was crowded with people, their nerves all unstrung by the awful events of the day, gazing at, but scarcely daring to approach the strange sight before them. The sky above and around was as black as ink, but right in one spot in mid-air above them was the summit of the spire, with the lightning playing about it shining like a sun. Directly the great iron cross, together with the ball at its foot, fell to the ground with a crash, and was shivered to pieces. But the darkest hour comes just before the dawn. The glow above gradually subsided and died out, the people grew less fearful and returned to their homes, the real night came on, and when next morning dawned everything was bright and clear, and the world was as natural as before. The phenomenon was noticed in a greater or less degree from Quebec to Kingston, and far into the States, but Montreal seemed its centre. It has never yet been explained.

A Meteoric Shower

Canniff Haight

No one who has ever observed a celestial display like
a shower of meteors is ever likely to forget it.

Canniff Haight (1825-1901) was a lad of eight and living with his
parents in Adolphustown, in the Bay of Quinte area of Upper
Canada, now Ontario, when he witnessed a meteoric shower. The
appearance of those celestial objects crossing the night sky
remained with him through the years.

Haight is remembered today for his detailed books about
pioneer life in Upper Canada. When Haight began to pen his
memoirs, he found that the spectacular display, visible in the night
sky over Adolphustown in 1833, was as vivid as ever, despite the
passage of time. Here is how he recalled the sight in Country Life in
Canada Fifty Years Ago (1885, 1971).

...ALTHOUGH FORTY-FIVE YEARS have elapsed, the terrifying scene
is as firmly fixed in my memory as thought it had happened but an
hour ago. I refer to the meteoric shower of the 13th of November,
1833. My father had been from home, and on his return, about
midnight, his attention was arrested by the frequent fall of meteors,
or stars, to use the common phrase. The number rapidly increased;
and the sight was go grand and beautiful that he came in and woke
us all up, and then walked up the road and roused some of the
neighbours. Such a display of heaven's fireworks was never seen

before. If the air had been filled with rockets they would have been but match strokes compared to the incessant play of brilliant dazzling meteors that flashed across the sky, furrowing it so thickly with golden lines that the whole heaven seemed ablaze, until the morning's sun shut out the scene. One meteor of large size remained somewhat stationary in the zenith, emitting streams of light. I stood like a statue, and gazed with fear and awe up to the glittering sky. Millions of stars seemed to be dashing across the blue dome of heaven. In fact I thought the whole starry firmament was tumbling down to earth. The neighbours were terror-struck: the more enlightened of them were awed at contemplating so vivid a picture of the Apocalyptic image — that of the stars of heaven falling to the earth, even as a fig-tree casteth her untimely figs, when she is shaken by a mighty wind; while the cries of others, on a calm night like that, might have been heard for miles around.

The Mirage of Toronto

Sir Charles Lyell

The British geologist Sir Charles Lyell (1797-1875) was so respected during his lifetime that his remains may be found in Westminster Abbey where they lie "among kings." For professional reasons he made extended visits to North America in 1837 and in 1842. At Niagara Falls he estimated the recession of the cataract, and in Nova Scotia he undertook a study of coal-formations.

Lyell described "the mirage of Toronto" in the second volume of his Travels in North America with Geological Observations on the United States, Canada, and Nova Scotia *(London: John Murray, 1845). Today, from Queenston Heights, which is situated on the Niagara River above the Falls, one may see in the distance, perpendicular to the horizon, Toronto's CN Tower. But the CN Tower was not in place in 1842 when Lyell visited Queenston Heights and boarded a steamer which took him from the Niagara River into Lake Ontario. But a mirage of the town was. From the deck of the steamer he observed — and then described — the mirage of Toronto which hovered oddly over the waters of the Lake.*

JUNE 14, 1842. — From Queenston we embarked in a fine steamer for Toronto, and had scarcely left the mouth of the river, and entered Lake Ontario, when we were surprised at seeing Toronto in the horizon, and the low wooded plain on which the town is built. By the effect of refraction, or "mirage," so common on this lake, the houses and trees were drawn up and lengthened vertically, so that I should have guessed them to be from 200 to 400 feet high, while the gently rising ground behind the town had the appearance of distant mountains. Given the ordinary state of the atmosphere none of this land, much less the city, would be visible at this distance, even in the clearest weather.

The Travelling Rocks

Lord Dunraven

The classic description of the so-called Travelling Rocks of Nova Scotia was composed by the noted Irish politician and sportsman W. T. Wyndham (1841-1926), the Earl of Dunraven. His account of "this extraordinary phenomenon" appears in the section devoted to moose-hunting in Newfoundland and Nova Scotia in 1879 in his book of memoirs, Canadian Nights: Being Sketches and Reminiscences of Life and Sport in the Rockies, the Prairies, and the Canadian Woods *(1914).*

Do rocks travel uphill? What agency sends them from sea to shore? To these questions Lord Dunraven had no ready answers. As well, he failed to specify the sea shore in Nova Scotia where "the unheard-of spectacle" occurred. His account, which first appeared in the journal Nineteenth Century, *was judged of sufficient scientific interest to warrant republication in the* Scientific American, *41:88, 1879. William R. Corliss reprinted it in* Unknown Earth: A Handbook of Geological Enigmas *(Glen Arm, Md.: The Sourcebook Project, 1980).*

Corliss could answer the question that Lord Dunraven believed unanswerable: "Anyone familiar with ice action in our northern lakes and rivers will have no great difficulty in accounting for the rock movement described. It takes place in various ways, depending on the depth of water, the breadth of the pond or river, the force of the wind and waves, variations in water level, and other conditions. Just which of these causes, alone or combined, operated in Lord

Dunraven's Nova Scotia lake it is impossible to say from the description he gives. Probably the last named, and the wedging of the ice-masses against the larger rocks, when rising and falling with the water, had most to do in moving the boulders on shore."

A STRANGE SCENE, which came within my observation last year, says his Lordship, completely puzzled me at the time, and has done so ever since. I was in Nova Scotia in the fall, when one day my Indian told me that in a lake close by all the rocks were moving out of the water — a circumstance which I thought not a little strange. However, I went to look at the unheard-of spectacle, and, sure enough, there were the rocks apparently all moving out of the water on to dry land. The lake is of considerable extent, but shallow and full of great masses of rock. Many of these masses appear to have travelled right out of the lake, and are now high and dry some fifteen yards above the margin of the water. They have plowed deep and regularly defined channels for themselves. You may see them of all sizes, from blocks of, say, roughly speaking, six or eight feet in diameter, down to stones which a man could lift. Moreover, you find them in various stages of progress, some a hundred yards or more from shore and apparently just beginning to move; others, half-way to their destination, and others again, as I have said, high and dry above the water. In all cases there is a distinct groove or furrow, which the rock has clearly plowed for itself. I noticed one particulary good specimen, an enormous block which lay some yards above high-water mark. The earth and stones were heaped up in front of it to a height of three or four feet. There was a deep furrow, the exact breadth of the block, leading down directly from it into the lake, and extending till it was hidden from my sight by the depth of the water. Loose stones and pebbles were piled upon on each side of this groove in a regular, clearly defined line. I thought at first that from some cause or other the smaller stones, pebbles, and sand had been dragged down from above, and consequently had piled themselves up in front of all the large rocks too heavy to be removed, and had left a vacant space or furrow behind the rocks. But if that had been the case the drift of moving material would of course have joined together again in the space of a few yards behind the fixed rocks. On the contrary, these grooves or furrows remained the same width throughout their entire length, and, have, I think undoubtedly been caused by the rock forcing its way up through the loose shingle and stones which compose the bed of the lake. What power has set these rocks in motion it is difficult to decide. The action of ice is the only thing that might explain it; but how ice could exert itself in that special manner, and why, if ice is the cause of it, it does not manifest that tendency in every portion of the world, I do not pretend to comprehend.

My attention having been once directed to this, I noticed it in various other lakes. Unfortunately my Indian only mentioned it to me a day or two before I left the woods. I had not time, therefore, to make any investigation into the subject. Possibly some of my readers may be able to account for this, to me, extraordinary phenomenon.

A Narrow Ray of Light

Alexander Graham Bell

Alexander Graham Bell (1847-1922) was a tireless investigator and inventor. Most widely remembered as the inventor of the telephone, he was also a pioneer in the field of aerial navigation, for he arranged test flights of early airplanes over the Bras d'Or lakes near his summer home, Beinn Breagh, near Baddeck, Cape Breton Island.

Bell was also a keen observer of meteorological phenomena. His attention was attracted by an odd and unusual "narrow ray" of light which illuminated the sky above Baddeck, N.S., the night of 11 September 1891. He pondered the peculiar auroral display for some weeks before deciding to describe it in a letter which he dispatched to Nature, *the British scientific journal. The letter was published in the issue of 26 November 1891 under the heading "A Rare Phenomenon."*

I HAVE READ with much interest the accounts of "the rare phenomenon" observed by several of your correspondents (published in Nature, vol. xliv, pp. 494, 519), as I noticed a similar appearance here in Nova Scotia, at about the same time (September 11).

A narrow ray — apparently of auroral light — spanned the whole heavens from east to west, passing overhead a little to the south of the zenith. There was little or no display of auroral light in the north at the time.

A "harvest-home" was held here on September 11, and I noticed the appearance, I think, the same evening about 11 o'clock.

A number of persons in the town of Baddeck observed the same or a similar phenomenon "very shortly before September 12."

Alexander Graham Bell,

Bein Breagh, near Baddeck, Cape Breton, N.S.,
November 6.

The Fiery Shower
Growing More Dense

Thomas Conant

There is nothing miraculous about a shower of meteors. Or is there? Truly phenomenal is the effect on the trained and untrained observer alike of the sight of the night sky illuminated like a stage or a screen and playing host to a spectacular meteorological display.

One such nocturnal moment was described by Thomas Conant (1842-1905), a writer of reminiscences of rural life based on the experiences of growing up in the Oshawa area of Ontario. The passage below records the family tradition surrounding a shower of meteors. It comes from Upper Canada Sketches *(Toronto, 1898).*

A reference to this passage appears in the article "Stars Fall over Canada" in the Journal of the Royal Astronomical Society of Canada, *Volume 61, Number 5. The authors of the article, two astronomers, Peter M. Millman and D.W.R. McKinley of the National Research Council, explained that this account "well illustrates the lasting impression made by the great Leonid meteor shower of 1833, an impression wide-spread in eastern North America thanks to generally clear weather on that night."*

ONE OF THE MOST important occurrences of the time, and one from which many reckoned their local history, was a remarkable display of falling meteors. The following account is taken from memoranda left by my mother, and as told by my father:

On the night of the 12th November, 1833, my father, then a young man, was salmon-spearing in a boat in the creek, at its outlet into Lake Ontario, now Port Oshawa. One of his hired men sat in the stern and paddled, while he stood close beside the light-jack of blazing pine knots, in order to see the salmon in the water. He, in common with the inhabitants generally, was laying in a stock of salmon to be salted down for the year's use, until the salmon "run" again the following fall.

At or about ten o'clock of this evening, as nearly as he could judge, from out of an intensely dark November night, globes of fire as big as goose eggs began falling all around his boat. These balls continued to fall until my father, becoming frightened, went home, — not forgetting, he quaintly added, to bring with him the salmon already caught. On reaching home, Lot 6, B.F. East Whitby, the whole household was aroused, and frightened too; but the fires ceasing they went to bed, to pass a restless night after the awe-inspiring scene they had witnessed.

Getting up before daybreak next morning, my father raked over the embers of the buried black log of the big fire-place and quickly had a blaze. Happening to glance out of the window, to his intense amazement he saw, as he said, "the whole sky filled with shooting stars." Quickly he called to the men, his hired help in the lumbering business, to come down stairs. They needed not a second invitation, and among them was one Shields, who, on reaching the door, dropped in a twinkling upon his knees and began to pray. The balls of fire continuing, his prayers grew more earnest, if vigour of voice could be any index to his religious fervour. Of the grandeur of the unparalleled scene my father said almost nothing, for I am led to think they were all too thoroughly frightened to think of beauty, that being a side issue entirely. The fiery shower growing more dense, my father went out of doors and found the fire-balls did not burn or hurt. Then he went to a neighbour's — a preacher of renown in the locality — having to pass through the woods, and even in the darkness, he affirms, the fire-balls lighted his way quite distinctly. The preacher, already awake, was seated at the table beside a tallow dip reading his Bible, with two other neighbours listening and too frightened, he said, to even bid him good morning. He sat and listened to verse after verse, and still the star fell.

The preacher gave no explanation or sign, but read on. Looking eastward, at last my father saw a faint glimmer of breaking day. Once more he came out into the field and made his way homeward. Before he reached there daylight broke. Gradually the fire-balls grew less and less, and, with the day, ceased altogether. To find a sign of them he hunted closely upon the ground, but not a trace was left of anything. Nor was any damage done. What became of the stars that fell he could not conjecture.

Fall of Enormous, Unknown Ants

Charles Fort

When it comes to the study of anomalies, it is unnecessary to refer to Charles Fort by his full name. His last name is sufficient. All that one has to do is describe an event or a behaviour as "fortean" and specialists in such matters will understand precisely what is meant.

A "fortean" phenomenon may be described as an event that would have delighted Charles Fort (1874-1932), the American researcher and writer who spent a lifetime collecting and publishing accounts of "damned facts" — that is, reports of odd occurrences that are dismissed by the scientific establishment because they fail to fit the known facts and current theories.

Fort was by inclination and training so deeply anti-theoretical that he could be described as the skeptic's skeptic. He dismissed all the theories evolved by all the world's scientists. He felt and argued that the scientific establishment was so interested in inclusiveness that it excludes whole categories of "damned facts" because they do not sit well. Fort despised the theories but cherished the "damned facts." To cherish them and keep them from being "orphaned," he evolved his own bizarre and sometimes whimsical hypotheses. One such hypothesis was evolved to explain the disappearances of two men, Ambrose Bierce in Mexico and Ambrose Small in Toronto. Fort suggested, no doubt tongue-in-cheek, that "someone is collecting Ambroses."

Fort is at full strength discussing "falls" — not things that bump

183

in the night, but animate and inanimate objects that reportedly drop from the sky onto the ground, often in vast numbers, at regular or irregular intervals. He discussed the nature of "falls" in The Book of the Damned *(1919), the first of his four books in the collection called* The Books of Charles Fort *(New York: Henry Holt and Company, 1941). These four books form the fortean gospel, and the research materials that were left unpublished at the time of Fort's death constitute the lesser books of that Bible. As the patriarch wrote: "As to falls or flutterings of winged insects from the sky, prevailing notions of swarming would seem explanatory enough: nevertheless, in instances of ants, there are some peculiar circumstances." He ended the discussion of insect "falls" with the following surprising suggestion:*

> *That wingless, larval forms of life, in numbers so enormous that migration from some place external to this earth is suggested, have fallen from the sky.*
>
> *That these "migrations" — if such can be our acceptance — have occurred at a time of hibernation and burial far in the ground of larvae in the northern altitudes of this earth; that there is significance in recurrence of these falls in the last of January — or that we have the square of an incredibility in such a notion as that of selection of larvae by whirlwinds, compounded with selection of the last of January.*

Fort drew his readers' attention to a Canadian report: "Fall of enormous, unknown ants — size of wasps — Manitoba, June, 1895 (Sci. Amer., 72-385)."

The report below is the one in question. It is reprinted from Scientific American, *"A Weekly Journal of Practical Information, Art, Science, Mechanics, Chemistry, and Manufactures," Volume LXXII, No. 25, 22 June 1895. The source cited by the editors of* Scientific American *is simply "Winnipeg Free Press." Short of scanning the back issues of that publication, and employing a perpetual calendar, it should be possible to narrow down that day in June when the city was visited by falls of "large black ants." The date is presumably June 5, 12, or 19th.*

A Shower of Black Ants

The warm, thunderous state of the atmosphere, Wednesday evening, presaged a heavy downpour of rain in the city and vicinity, but this expectation was not realized, and the rain passed off with a slight shower. Instead of the rain a shower of another kind resulted, which is one of the most curious visitations in the history of the city. On the sidewalks, in the roads, upon the roofs, and the insides of the houses there was seen, yesterday, numbers of large black ants crawling about. They were found as plentiful in the outskirts of the city as on the main streets, and from the fact that some of these insects have wings while others have dropped or shed them, it is natural to conclude that they have migrated from some district to the south of the province, and have come to say. They are large, black-bodied specimens, about the size of a wasp, and have the strong nippers of their race. They are not native of Manitoba, and are similar to the African ant.

Nature's Illumination

John Flint Roy

*O*ccasionally one experiences a moment in time and place that is so rare, so unusual, and so encompassing that at the time or in retrospect it acquires a numinous patina. There may be nothing mystical about the experience itself; nonetheless, it will be sensed, felt, understood, and intuited to be magical and mysterious all the same. Such moments, being uniquely private, are ineffable in the sense that they defy communication. The natural world, unaided by man, is in possession of the power to bring such moments to fruition in the human species.

One such moment of experience was brought about by the quality and the continuity of light — "Nature's great reservoir of illumination" — in the Qu'Appelle Valley of Southern Saskatchewan. The perfect moment was experienced in 1938 and described in a brief memoir written for the present editor on 21 August 1987 by John Flint Roy.

At the time of the illumination, Roy was a young officer with the RCMP. In later years he was widely respected as an authority on the writings of Edgar Rice Burroughs and a leading collector of pulp literature. He was active as a fan of fantastic literature until his death, from heart failure, at the Chatham General Hospital, Ont., on 8 Dec. 1987.

IT WAS A BEAUTIFUL Summer evening in 1938, and in the Qu'Appelle

Valley, just out from Regina, Saskatchewan, a group of young people were enjoying a weiner and marshmallow roast.

My girl friend and I strolled to the top of a nearby knoll and sat looking down on the campfire below us. This is what we saw, as we sat entranced.

The sun was just dropping below the horizon and to the east a full moon was beginning to rise.

Overhead, stars were appearing, and the odd meteor flashed briefly and disappeared.

Far to the north-east lightning streaked from a small black cloud, while to the north the Aurora Borealis flickered and rippled.

In the nearby grass, as darkness set in, fireflies blinked on and off.

Here was a magnificent display of Nature's great reservoir of illumination. The only thing missing, we agreed, was the glow from a volcano.

It was indeed a spectacular Summer evening.

6. Human Mysteries

Spontaneous Human Combustion

Peter Schofield

"It strikes without warning, reducing its victim to an unrecognizable char," wrote the researcher and writer Dwight Whalen. "It burns with macabre selectivity, often leaving nearby inflammables strangely untouched. It's a rare and grisly phenomenon known as Spontaneous Human Combustion."

This phenomenon — SHC for short — is not new to history or literature. Cases have been reported over the centuries and across many cultures. Charles Dickens made good use of SHC as a literary device to dispose of an unwanted evil-doer in Bleak House. The consumption of alcohol is not directly related to death by SHC. Yet alcohol is known to be a flammable fluid, and alcoholism is associated with the dissolute and the poor, so advocates of the Temperance movement in 19th-century Canada made graphic use of SHC in their cause.

The first Temperance address heard in today's Canada was delivered on 10 June 1828 in Leeds, a small community in southeastern Ontario. The speaker was Peter Schofield. To astonish his audience he described a case of SHC which he had personally attended. Dr. Schofield was maddeningly vague about details. Just who this man was, and where and when he died, he did not state. The fatal fire, Dr. Schofield added, had not "been communicated...from any external source."

The assertion that alcohol was to blame may seem farfetched, but not so the mystery itself. There is no scientific standing for

SHC. Nevertheless, this anecdotal account is probably the earliest case recorded (or at least mentioned) in Canada. "It's just the kind of story one might like to have a drink to forget," added Whalen, an investigator of the odd and the unusual. Some further details appear in William Henry Leavitt's History of Leeds and Grenville *(Belleville, 1972).*

IT WAS THE CASE of a young man about twenty-five years old; he had been a habitual drinker for many years. I saw him about nine o'clock in the evening on which it happened; he was then, as usual, not drunk but full of liquor. About eleven, the same evening, I was called to see him. I found him literally roasted, from the crown of his head to the soles of his feet. He was discovered in a blacksmith's shop, just across the way from where he had been. The owner of the shop, all of a sudden, discovered a bright light in his shop, as though the whole building was in a general flame. He ran with the greatest precipitancy, and, on flinging open the door, discovered the man standing erect in the midst of a widely extended, silver-coloured blaze, bearing, as he described it, exactly the appearance of the wick of a burning candle in the midst of its own flame. The blacksmith seized him by the shoulder, and jerked him to the door, upon which the flame was instantly extinguished. There was no fire in the shop, neither was there any possibility of fire having been communicated to him from any external source. It was purely a case of spontaneous ignition. A general sloughing soon came on, and his flesh was consumed or removed in the dressing, leaving the bones and a few of the larger blood vessels standing. The blood, nevertheless, rallied around the heart, and maintained the vital spark until the thirteenth day, when he died, not only the most noisesome, ill-featured, and dreadful picture that was ever presented to human view, but his shrieks, his cries and lamentations, were enough to rend the heart of adamant. He complained of no pain of body — his flesh was gone; he said he was suffering the torments of hell; that he was just upon its threshold, and should soon enter its dismal caverns; and, in this frame of mind, gave up the ghost.

Religious Revival Meetings

Michael Gonder Sherk

Religious revival meetings were as much a part of the rural scene in late 19th Century Canada as televangelists are part of urban life in late 20th Century Canada. Camp-meetings may have been part and parcel of the social fabric of the day, yet they attracted the sinner and the saved alike, witnesses all to God's transcending "Power" — to employ the telling word employed by the author of the following reminiscence of revival meetings held late last century in Northumberland County in Eastern Ontario.

The author of this account was an Ontario apothecary or druggist named Michael Gonder Sherk. Although the year and place of his birth are unknown, Sherk grew up in Northumberland County and died in Toronto in his mature years in 1928. He adopted a pen-name for his one and only book, a memoir titled Pen Pictures of Early Pioneer Life in Upper Canada *(1905, 1972). The pen-name he used is the following: A "Canuck" (of the Fifth Generation). Sherk was proud to be a British subject, proud to be a Canadian, and proud to be a descendant of United Empire Loyalists.*

THE CAMP-MEETINGS of the present day are to a large extent social gatherings, with religion and fashion mixed up together, but in the olden time they were times of spiritual outpouring. It was only among the Methodists they were held. Their churches being few and scattered, this was one way they had chosen for getting the people together in the summer time for special revival services, and some of the results were truly wonderful. The zeal of the early Methodist was untiring. He was sincere and earnest, and when these two qualities are combined great results are sure to follow. The camp-meetings usually lasted from one to two weeks. Crowds of people came from near and far to attend them. A great many were attracted out of curiosity. Many that went there to "scoff remained to pray." Some remained on the ground living in tents and cabins made of boards. Provisions were sold on the ground.

People were frequently overcome by the "Power," as it was called, and would lie prostrate on the ground for some time. We are inclined to think that this was only the reaction from the nervous frenzy that they had worked themselves into. Meetings were held nearly every hour of the day. There were mass meetings for all, and prayer and praise meetings in the different tents. The voice of prayer could be heard in all parts of the ground.

No doubt great good came of these meetings.

Narayan Stalked Me

Gordon Sinclair

*F*rom the 1930s to the 1960s, Gordon Sinclair *(1900-1984) was the most widely known Canadian newspaperman and broadcaster. He was as an energetic correspondent with the* Toronto Star, *a lively and controversial radio personality for CFRB in Toronto, and an original panelist on CBC-TV's "Front Page Challenge." He was also loved and hated because he expressed his frequently controversial opinions openly.*

To lift the doldrums of depressed spirits during the Depression, the Star *sent Sinclair on special assignments to India, China, Africa, and the South Seas. These stints resulted in colourful feature journalism as well as such books as* Footloose in India, Cannibal Quest, *and* Khyber Caravan. *In later years Sinclair wrote two volumes of memoirs,* Will the Real Gordon Sinclair Please Stand Up *(Toronto: McClelland & Stewart, 1966), from which the excerpts below are taken, and* Will Gordon Sinclair Please Sit Down *(1975).*

Sinclair first visited India in 1934. It was two years later, on his second trip, that he first met Narayan, the resourceful and persistent young Hindu who become his indispensable man-servant on that and future visits. Sinclair was always puzzled by Narayan's ability to know the whereabouts of the sahib, even when the sahib was at the other end of the country. But Sinclair did not spend much time puzzling over the details, for he saw many curious things in India.

India has been called "the cradle of religion." It gave birth to

Hinduism, Buddhism, and Sikhism. The religious practices of the
subcontinent had the effect on Sinclair of dealing the death-blow to
any idea he might have of a personal deity. "Either way, the idea of
a god who intervenes in human affairs — and I say there is no such
god and never was or will be — is a loser," Sinclair wrote. "Either
god is indifferent to the sufferings of his people, or he is incapable of
help. Take it either way you like, or find a middle course of your
own. I see no answer to man's prayer, regardless of whether that
prayer is to Allah, Buddha, Christ, or ABC, or go down to the
bottom of a long list of deities to Zeus. Wherever the plea goes, it
falls on deaf or uninterested ears."

IT WAS ON ONE of these night-time walks, as I picked my way over
and among uneasily sleeping bodies under the arches, that I met
Narayan. He'd been among fourteen courteous men who had tried
to attach themselves to me as my personal man-servant at ship-
side, each man showing an impressive collection of chits to indicate
that he was equal as butler to Jeeves, as economist to John Maynard
Keynes, and as chef to Escoffier. The chits were in the manner of a
flourish of trumpets to herald the arrival of nobility, written with
Victorian solemnity and praising the bearer in terms that might
normally be used for Florence Nightingale or Albert Schewitzer.

My own feelings of "a man's a man for all that" made the idea of
a personal servant alarming, and I thrust aside pressures from
many sides, including at least half the staff of the Taj Mahal Hotel.
Quietly like the voice of conscience, Narayan stalked me. He would
get into my room and shine my shoes. When I was being brought
breakfast in bed — everybody, want it or not, had breakfast in bed
at the Taj — he would bribe the floor waiter to take the tray to the
sahib. He went with me on walks, staying discreetly at a distance,
knowing that sooner or later I'd get into some bind and need him.

This came when a demented woman of no hands, but raw sores
where her hands should have been, cried for alms in the night, and
pointing up her plight, she tried to rub her bleeding wrists in my
face, or to pretend to do it.

Narayan stepped from the shadows in silence, disposing of the
woman, and in low-key warned that the sahib should really not

walk in these regions at night, especially while wearing a white suit. I engaged this tall, barefooted Hindu at twenty-five rupees a month, about six Canadian dollars at that time. Instantly I was told by people who had long been in India that I was *spoiling* the natives.

Narayan immediately took command, calling for expense money to make me comfortable. I gave it to him, and the results were sensational. The first thing I noticed was that the bearers of other people bowed to me. I was pukka. My hotel room was changed for a better room at no extra cost. Narayan looked over the clothing I'd brought from Canada and said this was uncomfortable, of winter quality, and above all it marked me as a man from another place. We — *we* mind you — should throw it away and get a new outfit. We did. Soon we travelled. We had the best rooms on the best trains. Narayan kept accounts. He came to me at least twice a week wanting more money and usually (but not always) I gave it to him. Others kept telling me I was being swindled, so one day in a burst of irritation I asked Narayan if he was cheating me. "Certainly," he answered.

We got along wonderfully, and when I left India, never expecting to return, we were friends. By a strange quirk I was back in India within five months. I didn't tell Narayan I was returning for the simple reason that I didn't know his last name and had no idea where to get in touch with him.

I had sailed away from Bombay, where I had first met Narayan, and on the second journey I landed, at the other side of the country, in Calcutta. In the customs shed there, I heard a familiar voice giving orders as to where the sahib's luggage was to be put. That was Narayan, immaculate in white turban and black pantaloons, barefoot as always, and with his account book handy. To this day I don't know how he knew I was coming. He suggested that his pay be doubled on this tour. It was. So were his expenses.

With Narayan, I criss-crossed India numerous times, sometimes by plane, once by car, but usually by train. These journeys resulted in three books about India, of which two sold well. Some impressions remain as strong as if they had happened yesterday.

✿

Even in the most remote sections of the jungle you'll find a place to sleep in India; generally a mud bungalow inhabited by bats, mosquitoes, and lizards, in that order; but some are clean and neat, with such luxuries as tiled bathrooms and electric stoves....

After the second day you're sure to be visited by fakirs, magicians, mind readers, snake charmers, story-tellers, and all the rest of these quick-witted wise guys who play on the superstitions of the Indians. Generally away off in the jungle you meet far more genuine magicians than in town.

This trip I saw one man apparently cut deep gashes in his arm or leg, call for his wife who bustled up with a needle, thread, and bandage. She sewed the man together again, bandaged the wound, went through a lot of mesmeristic hocus-pocus, then took the bandage off. There was no scar of any kind.

This woman also sewed buttons all over her own face. This is a tough enough job even from the standpoint of the sewing, let alone the physical pain of the thing. After she'd sewn four buttons one on each cheek, I was invited to pull them and see if they were the genuine article fit to hold up a man's pants. They certainly seemed to be real buttons sewed on to real skin with real thread, and I never did find out what the secret was. I didn't, however, pull them off.

✳

...But the most prominent and recurring thought was that the Indian peasant people are the most hospitable in the world. The backwoods Indian who never owns so much as forty cents at one time in all his life is honoured and flattered if you drift in his poor mud shack, and often as not, if you have no other place to sleep, he'll move out, turn his whole place over to you and scorn any payment whatever. All you need in such case is a copper-lined stomach and insecticide for blood.

This was written in either 1934 or 1936. Except for higher prices, there is little I'd change in 1966.

Nothing Ever Happens to Me!

A.R.G. Owen

A.R.G. Owen and Iris M. Owen are the country's leading parapsychologists. (The initials A.R.G. which appear before Owen stand for Alan Robert George; the initial M. which links Iris and Owen stands for May.)

Today they would be another Cambridge don and professional working wife, but for the fact that they were drawn to Canada with the offer of the opportunity to establish their own centre for psychical research and parapsychological investigation. The husband-and-wife team accepted the offer, and in Toronto in 1970 they established the New Horizons Research Foundation and the Toronto Society for Psychical Research. For two decades the groups were active. Their work has been continued since 1989 by the Society for the Study of Anomalies.

George Owen was born in Bristol in 1919. He was awarded a Doctorate from Cambridge University where he taught mathematics and genetics. He is the author of numerous abstruse scientific papers as well as books written in a more popular style, including studies of poltergeistery. One of his major works is Psychic Mysteries of Canada (1975).

The following passage is reprinted from the book Science and the Spook: Eight Strange Cases of Haunting (New York: Garrett Publications, 1977) written with Victor Sims. Some emendations were made to the passage by the author for publication here. In the passage he refers to his wife, Iris M. Owen, the author of Conjuring

Up Philip: An Adventure in Psychokinesis *(1976), a landmark publication in the history of parapsychology.*

It was the British author Colin Wilson who coined the phrase "ESP dense." He used it to refer to his own lack of psychical powers or abilities. Apparently George Owen considers himself to be "ESP dense" — or, in his own words, "a psychic moron." Whether this is true or not, Iris Owen may be the one who is "ESP subtle."

NOTHING EVER HAPPENS TO ME! I have no psychic powers! Only once in my life do I appear to have played any part in a telepathic episode. That involved a dream and is rather amusing. Some years ago we had a cat who was a night rover, and was usually given his supper in the kitchen before being allowed out on his travels. One very chill January night, as I had done on many a previous occasions, I put on an electric fire so that he could get warm while eating his repast. Eventually he had had his fill and went happily out into the dark. I went to bed where my wife was already installed and asleep. About three in the morning she awoke having had a "non-sense" dream. She had found herself back in the East Anglian farmhouse of her youth, and in the kitchen where a fire blazed in the old-fashioned coal range, universal in those days in the country. Everything was quite normal abut for one striking exception. A refrigerator had been fitted into one side of the coal-range. My wife, in her dream, turned to her father who was present and declared, "What a silly place to put a fridge! It's too hot, the fridge is too hot!" Waking with this thought in her mind she went down to the kitchen where she found that the door of the refrigerator was, in verity, too hot. I had forgotten to turn off the electric fire — a portable one — and had left it blazing full blast directly opposite the refrigerator whose door was now noticeably warm to the touch. One may, if one desires, ascribe this to coincidence. However it is odd that in my recollection that was the only night in a long and cold winter that I had left the fire on, and the only night in which my wife developed an anxiety about the matter. I like to think that my wife had a telepathic dream inspired by a guilty conscience I had about it, but active only in subconscious layers of my mind.

Relics of the Buddha

David Ryshpan

David Ryshpan is a business consultant who has travelled widely and worked extensively in the Far East. He was born in Montreal in 1932 and now resides in Thailand.

This interview with David Ryshpan was conducted in August 1989 during his return visit to Montreal. It was conducted by David's older brother Howard, a well-known theatre director and instructor at Dawson College in Montreal. In the interview David repeated for Howard the story of his involvement with some relics of the Gautama Buddha. The experience took place in Colombo, Sri Lanka, in November 1981, at the time that a new Buddhist shrine was being inaugurated.

Howard noted that David was wearing around his neck a small gold case. For the significance of this observation, read on....

DAVID, WHEN YOU WERE in the Orient, you experienced some interesting things. You have told me about stories about your experiences. You were there for sixteen years. When you were first in the Orient, what did you experience? Were you prepared for a different culture, a different sensibility, a different awareness of things?

It gradually came about. I was thrown into an entirely new culture which had a certain air of mysticism. There were animistic religions and there were so-called philosophical religions, like Buddhism. They honestly believe that there are spirits, there are

200

ghosts, there is power in horoscopes and astrology — much more than we do.

When you first went there and you heard some of these stories of the supernatural and of ghosts and of how they bring in fortune tellers to decide how your business is going to be run, were you skeptical at first?

No, because I had previous experiences here, in Canada, and in the States, where I was witness to so-called apparitions or ghosts or poltergeists or what-have-you. So when people started talking about these things, I took an interest — as an observer rather than as someone who participated.

One of the most fascinating stories that you told me was about your first stay in Sri Lanka. Could you give me a little bit of background? Why were you there?

The company I was director of was invited to participate in a venture in the new free-trade zone which was being established across the road from the airport at Colombo, Sri Lanka. Our future partner was one of the largest corporations in the capital, a very diversified trading-manufacturing concern. We were invited to come in as a partner to manufacture garments. When I went there, there was nothing except coconut trees growing on a former coconut plantation. There was no infrastructure — no water, sewers, or electricity. We had to cope with those problems and put up a factory in the quickest possible time because we had made certain commercial commitments for our production.

I remember when we had our ground-breaking ceremony. Something that was something new to me was the religious aspect. There was a so-called auspicious time for the ground-breaking ceremony. Buddhist monks and Catholic priests were invited to participate, and there were certain blessings and so on that were said at the time. Our Sri Lankan chairman was a Roman Catholic.

Was the primary religion Buddhism? Any particular sect?

Yes, Theravada, the same as the Thai and the Burmese. It's different from Tibetan, Japanese, and Chinese Buddhism.

After putting up the factory, I travelled all over Sri Lanka and I had a chance to observe their various religions, beliefs, customs, etc. I felt there was something lacking, there was something that I wanted to do for the workers. So I started asking questions. I found that the workers in our area were predominantly Catholic, but I found that as far as their customs went, they were particularly Buddhist. In fact, very often people were married in a Catholic church with a Buddhist monk present, or even married in the registry by a Buddhist monk, even though both parties were Catholic. So there was an intermingling of religions.

I decided I would like to build a shrine or a place of worship for the workers. At that time I was friendly with the then ruling family — my girlfriend there was the niece of the President of Sri Lanka. Her father had entered a Buddhist monastery after his wife had passed away. He was a lawyer by profession, a superior court circuit judge, and a sports car enthusiast. He had started various other sports enterprises. I found him entirely interesting, and I spent many hours talking with him about many aspects of Buddhism and culture and even the politics of the culture.

I mentioned to him that I was interested in doing something for the workers. The chairman of our Hong Kong company was born in Thailand and was a Buddhist by birth, so I had raised with the directors the possibility of building a small shrine, equivalent to a small temple, on the grounds of the factory in the free-trade zone. They thought it was a good idea out of respect for their father and mother who were Buddhist. In order to pursue this venture, I went to my girlfriend's father for advice. He said, "Well, it is very difficult to import images of the Buddha, because that requires not only religious but also government approval." Anyway, he assisted me in importing two images of the Buddha from Thailand. These were about three feet tall, cast in bronze and then gold-plated. One was for the shrine that was going to be built and one went to the largest temple in Colombo. Both were kept at the temple until the shrine could be built. The Chief Priest of that temple became a personal friend of mine.

Now, I must tell you, I had a lot of opposition when it came to erecting the shrine from the free-trade zone authorities and other members of the government.

Why were they opposing it?

Even though they were Buddhist, they did not think it was wise to introduce religion into the free-trade zone.

But this was going to be something for the workers. How many were going to be employed there?

I eventually had 2,400 workers. The idea of the authorities was that we would then have to build a Muslim shrine, a Hindu shrine, a Catholic shrine, a Protestant shrine, and so on. I felt we were living in a predominantly Buddhist country; the customs and beliefs were Buddhist, even though some of the people may not have been practising Buddhists. I thought this was the least I could do for the workers. Finally, the brother of the President, who was assisting me through all of this, persevered along with me and we prevailed and we got what we wanted.

This allowed you, then, to proceed to built the temple?

That's right. I designed it not in Sri Lankan style but more in Thai style out of respect to the Buddhist image, which was a Thai image, and also out of respect to our chairman who was born in Thailand. You have to remember that Theravada Buddhism in Sri Lanka came from Thailand. At one point in history the Portuguese and the Dutch completely converted all the Singhalese people to Christianity, out of Buddhism, and it wasn't until the late 18th century that Theravada Buddhism was brought back into the country. In Sri Lanka it has become almost a state religion, as it is in Thailand and Burma. There is a long relationship between Thailand and Sri Lanka when it comes to Buddhism.

We proceeded with the building of the shrine, or temple, which took approximately four months. During this period of time the President's brother, the father of my girlfriend, passed away. It was a very sad thing because he wanted to see this particular temple completed. When it came time to inaugurate the temple, the normal procedure calls for sixteen monks, with several senior monks, to chant Buddhist scriptures. This goes on for a twenty-four hour period, day and night, and only after that are the image of the Buddha and the temple consecrated. For the inauguration, the chairman of our company and his wife came from Hong Kong. Various members of the free-trade zone authorities were invited, but they refused to attend. My girlfriend and another brother of the President, a lawyer of international reputation, both came to the inauguration.

Did they do anything outwardly to oppose the opening of the shrine?

No. We were the first company to do anything like that in

the free-trade zone, and they finally said, "Okay, we'll see what happens." What happened was that several other manufacturers put up shrines for their workers, and an annual night of chanting was started.

At the time of the inauguration and consecration of the temple, the Chief Priests from the temple in Colombo officiated. We used to call one of them Podi Hamdru, which means Small Priest, because for many years the Chief Priest of the temple was blind and deaf and the Small Priest acted as his assistant but in fact ran the temple. As we could not call him Chief Priest or High Priest, we called him Small Priest. His full name was The Venerable Gnanissera Thera. He was named after the district he came from. He took me aside and he showed me a small dagoba or pagoda or chedi made of bronze. This is basically a tiny stupa, a structure where sacred relics of the Buddha are kept.

A stupa is a repository for relics —

— and scriptures of the Buddha. This was a miniature one done in bronze or brass. He opened it up and showed me inside that there was a piece of cloth, which was folded in a special way, and inside the piece of cloth there was what looked to me like a grain of rice. He said, "Do you know what this is?" I said no. He said, "This is a relic of the Buddha." This means that when the Buddha was cremated, his bones shattered into numerous slivers or pieces that look like grains of rice but which are actually pieces of bone. The most sacred of all the Buddha's relics are several strands of hair of the Buddha, which are kept in Thailand, and the tooth of the Buddha, which is kept in the Temple of the Tooth in Kandy, Sri Lanka. He said to me, "This is a very sacred relic because it is a bone of the Buddha." He wanted to give it to me. He explained that for safe-keeping it had to be kept under the Buddha's image. To any Buddhist these are very holy objects. To Catholics it be as sacred as a portion of the True Cross.

Why did he give them to you?

He gave them to me because I had spent the time and energy to build the temple. He felt that was something unique and different. I was a foreigner and a non-Buddhist, and yet I would do something for the people of Sri Lanka. This particular High Priest was always doing something for the people, and he found it unusual that a foreigner would come to their land and do something for the people — never mind giving 2,400 people jobs, but also looking after their spiritual needs or customs or beliefs.

He opened up this piece of cloth and showed me this little piece of bone, which looked like a grain of rice, and he said, "Make sure it is kept under the image of the Buddha in a particular way." Then he explained to me that I should find a fairly heavy wooden board and should then find a glass bell —

A glass bell...?

...a bell-jar, the kind you sometimes see in a laboratory where it is used to create a vacuum, and place the relic in the bell-jar to make sure it is kept secure so that no one can steal it. I asked, "Why would anyone steal it?" He answered, "Even if someone offered a million dollars for such a relic, they could not obtain one."

I was flabbergasted. Taken aback. The fact was: Here I was, being given such an honour and being shown so much respect by the Buddhist clergy, that they would entrust me with a sacred relic of the Buddha! It was priceless. These relics were handed down from father to son through many generations. They were kept in temples and were always the property of the temple until a new temple was built. Normally they were only taken from whatever reserve they were in and given by one high priest to another high priest whenever they inaugurated a new temple. Here all they had was a shrine room.

I assured the Chief Priest I would do my utmost to make sure that it would be kept safe. I appointed my chief gardener, who was a Buddhist, to proceed with making this particular wooden coffer with the bell-jar in the prescribed manner. Then it would be placed under the Buddha's image, so that when anyone pays homage to the image they were also worshipping his bones and making various other religious commitments. Two or three times a year the relics have to be paraded before the people — on religious festivals like the birthday of the Buddha and the day he attained Enlightenment, etc.

I promised to do this and I made sure that my chief gardener was made the keeper of the shrine. We tried several times to screw bell-jars onto the wooden board but the bells always broke. It wasn't until three months had passed that we had the right coffer where we could deposit the sacred relic.

All this time where was it held?

For the whole period of three months it was held in the company safe. Only three people had the combination of the safe. I was one of them. My general manager, who was a Hong Kong Chinese and totally irreligious, was the second. And the third was the accountant, who was a Christian by birth and not really interested in anything. Besides the combination there were the keys to the safe. To open it you still had to use the two keys. The general manager held the keys. Any time the accountant wanted to go into the safe, he would ask the general manager, and it was opened only when the general manager or I was present. For the three months nobody went into the safe without a witness. The whole significance of this is, after three months, when we were ready to deposit the relic in the coffer under the image of the Buddha, we took the brass dagoba or chedi out of the safe and, just to make sure the relic inside was safe, in front of my chief gardener, I proceeded to unfold the cloth which held the relic.

Had you, at any time, or had any one of them, ever checked the relic?

No. It was totally my responsibility, and I left instructions that nobody, except myself, could touch the relic. My general manager assured me that nobody except the accountant ever went into the safe during those months. The general manager was the witness whenever the safe was opened. To my amazement, when I opened the cloth, there wasn't relic there. There were two relics there.

Identical ones?

No, one was like the original, although I feel that it had changed. It wasn't the same shape. It wasn't any bigger or smaller. It just didn't look the same. And next to it was another relic, not of the same size, but smaller.

What was your reaction?

My reaction was one of shock and amazement. The first thing I did was to run to the telephone and call the Chief Priest and say, "Hey, remember the relic you gave me? Are you sure you didn't give me two — because now I have got two."

And his reaction was, "Oh, don't worry. This happens all the time."

"What do you mean this happens all the time?"

He said, "The relics have been known to materialize or dematerialize or travel to other temples or other places of safety."

He said these things are not uncommon? I don't imagine that they happen that commonly. Do they happen that commonly?

He mentioned to me one instance in which there were two temples in adjoining parishes, and they were within about two miles of each other, and one temple had two relics and the other temple had only one relic. There was some animosity that developed between the temples, the reason being that the parishioners felt that at the one with the two relics the priests were not being faithful in their work. They were running little businesses on the side and were being a little bit hypocritical. A year went by. When the elders of the temple inspected the relics, which they did on a yearly basis, the one that had one relic was found to have three relics and the one that had the two relics was found to have nothing. No one would explain it. No one would say why. The feeling was the relics had dematerialized in one temple and then rematerialized in the other temple which was more faithful to their beliefs.

What did he explain had happened in your case?

We were surrounded by three or four temples, and one of their relics could have been transported to our temple. His feeling was that it was very possible that for all the work I had done in building this particular shrine room and in taking an interest in the worker's welfare in a spiritual way, as well as in their physical and mental welfare, had earned me merit. Consequently, we felt that those relics, both of them, really belonged to me, and not to the temple or to the company I worked for. He said if ever I should leave the company or leave the country, for whatever reason, I must take those relics with me and carry them with me at all times.

Well, it so happened that three years later I did leave the company and the country. But before going I went to see him and I said, "I would like to return the relics to you. What do you want to do?"

He said, "No, you are to take the relics. Have a small gold case made for them, and carry them around your neck for the rest of your life. You can leave them in your will to your relatives, or you can will them back to the temple."

I promised to do that. And still, to this day, I carry the relics.

Before they came into your personal possession, where were they kept?

They were kept under the Buddha image for three years.

Was there any reaction from the authorities when you removed them?

No. They felt that the power of the relics had transferred partly into the Buddha image itself. To them the Buddha image is not only sacred — it was consecrated — it still retains a certain power from the relics that were kept under it. And they also felt that the relics really belonged to me. The workers themselves never knew about the so-called miracle, as we never told them in order to avoid any hysteria.

The keeper of the temple knew about it and some rather prominent people in government. And every time I went to the Colombo temple, the Chief Priest, now called Loku Hamdru, who had become Chief Priest after the old High Priest had died, used to recount the story of the relics to any visitors who were there at the time, including visiting High Priests of other temples in other countries.

What were their reactions?

Their reaction was one of acceptance that here was a miracle that had happened.

Didn't it bother them that the relic would go to someone who was a non-Buddhist and a foreigner in the country?

It didn't matter. The Chief Priest would tell them about all the work I used to do to the temple, the various donations I made.

A very large rubber plantation of eight hundred acres was willed to the temple. Profits derived from it would be used for Buddhist meditation and spiritual purposes and also to buy books and scriptures. I thought what they were doing was a terrific thing. I went and bought ten thousand clove trees, seedlings, for them. It would take seven or eight years before they would earn any money. Then they would earn about five million dollars a year for them.

So that was a substantial gift.

It was a gift on my part, but I saw it as a continuing type of thing. Every year there would be substantial revenue to continue their work.

Are they deriving that revenue now?

Yes. It is more than seven years since I donated the trees.

The amazing thing now is to see the Buddhist monks working in a rubber plantation and also setting up day-care centres for the workers' children, food kitchens, growing their own fruits and vegetables. I thought, over all, it was a tremendous thing.

This Chief Priest did tremendous work. I could see that he didn't ask for anything. He used to work sometimes twenty-four hours a day, so I supported him any way I could. His appreciation was shown in giving me these particular relics at the time I built the shrine.

How did you feel when he gave you these things, not being raised in that part of the world, so far removed form that form of culture?

Well, initially, when you think of Buddhism, you think of it as a religion, and usually with religions there are all forms of mysticism and so on. But after talking with various Buddhist monks and with the father of my girlfriend, who had become a monk and who was a very learned person, I learned that it was not a religion but a philosophy. I am very much interested in Buddhism as a philosophy and not as a religion because I am not a religious person. And things like miracles and sacred relics did not register on me.

They were far removed from your own sensibilities.

I have been to various shrines, like the shrine to Brother André in Montreal, with their miracles and holy oil and holy water, etc. I am not saying I am an atheist. I believe in some form of divine being. I can't put my finger on it. But being exposed to the mysticism of the East, initially in Hong Kong, Thailand, Japan, Korea, and India before going to Sri Lanka, and being immersed in the Buddhist culture, I just found it interesting. So when this so-called miracle happened to me, my attitude was, "Okay, so you either believe or you don't."

It happened to me. I have vouched for the fact that it happened. I have witnessed who were there when it happened. And, okay, I laugh it off. It was a miracle. It happened. I can't explain it.

What happens when you tell this story to other Buddhists?

When I tell it to other Buddhists, they say, yes, we can understand, we have heard of similar stories. Whether I tell it Thailand or Sri Lanka, it doesn't matter, they all believe me. It doesn't bother them.

Are they interested in seeing the relic or touching it?

Several people, who claim to have various powers of ESP or clairvoyance, etc., put their hands on it and say, "Yes, tremendous power comes out of it." Well, I take that with a grain of salt.

I can't say it has hurt me. I can't say it has given any benefit tome. All I know is something happened, I was witness to it. The relics are very precious to me.

When you tell this story to Westerners or to non-Buddhist people, how do they react?

I find that most don't believe in it. The only ones I found who do believe in it happen to be Roman Catholics. They are also supposedly witnesses to various miracles, not personally, but through their indoctrination or the fact that most things could about because of a miracle. The idea of a miracle is not that foreign to them.

Describe the size of the gold coffer.

It's about three-quarters of an inch long and about a quarter of an inch in diameter.

How large are the relics?

The relics are...one would be about, I'd say, a quarter of an inch long and maybe a millimetre wide...the other one is about half the size in length but the same width.

You still carry the relics with you all the time around your neck?
Yes.

Current Control at Will

George D. Hathaway

George D. Hathaway is an independent researcher with a special interest in non-conventional technologies, especially theories and devices that touch upon his specialty, electrical engineering.

He was born in 1951 in Newmarket, Ont. In 1974, he graduated from the University of Toronto with a degree in Electrical Engineering. He has worked with the Ontario Science Centre but is now a private researcher and consultant. One of his long-range projects is a study of the lore and theories of levitation. One investigation which he would like to undertake is the study of the peculiar talent of Alfred Yeske, a man from Prince George, B.C., who is apparently able to demonstrate the ability to control electrical current at will.

The account which follows was written by Hathaway on 18 Feb. 1982, ten days following his initial meeting with Yeske. He watched with astonishment as Yeske manhandled a dangerous level of Alternating Current with impunity. Hathaway is on the lookout for an individual or an organization willing to undertake a scientific study of "current-handling." If Yeske is able to demonstrate this capability under controlled circumstances, and if he is able to teach this ability to others, the benefit to mankind should be obvious and apparent to all. So far Hathaway has been unable to find a sponsor for this research.

I AM A PROFESSIONAL Electrical Engineer registered in Ontario whose work is the analysis for a wide range of clients of the technical feasibility of novel energy conservation and renewable energy techniques and devices.

On a business trip to Vancouver, I had the privilege of interviewing a singular individual who demonstrated several abilities which, as far as I know, are unique. The name of the individual is Alfred Yeske. An associate of mine had heard of this man and, knowing I would be interested in seeing him and watching him in action, arranged a meeting at my uncle's home in Vancouver, where I was staying. The meeting took place on February 8, 1982.

Alfred Yeske is a simple, gentle man, about forty-five years of age. He seems a sincere and honest person of reasonable intelligence. Apparently, in his late teens, he was struck by lightning. At the time he was standing in a forest ranger's tower near the city of Prince George, B.C. The lightning bolt did not kill him, but it melted the change in his pockets, blew his boots off his feet, and pitched him outside the tower onto the compass — or platform — which surrounds it. He came through the ordeal dazed but otherwise unharmed.

A short time later, while in the employ of B.C. Hydro, he thought for some unknown reason that if lightning had not killed him, perhaps high voltage A.C. — Alternating Current — would not harm him either. Holding two bare wires of 120 volts A.C., one in each hand, he found that he could vary at will the amount of discomfort — hence the current — that passed through his upper body. It is not recorded how well he was insulated from the ground for this experiment.

Over the years he incrementally increased the voltage and current he was handling. One day he stood in a field repairing downed power lines of 20-40 kilovolts A.C. — apparently without any protection whatsoever. A fellow worker approached him from behind to warn him that the lines might be live. The poor fellow tapped Alfred on the shoulder and was instantly killed. Alfred told me that, had he known that this person was going to touch him, he would and could have controlled the current flow so that the person would not have been harmed in the slightest. At the subsequent inquest, the judgement was that the cause of the worker's death was accidental electrocution. The opinion was expressed that it was only a miracle that Alfred himself was not killed.

It was no miracle, said Alfred!

Soon thereafter Alfred was demonstrating to others current control at will. By this time he had left the employ of B.C. Hydro. A few local radio and television shows popularized his various feats, including this eye-catching one. Alfred would stand in a grounded tank of water, light 120 volt A.C. bulbs with his bare hands, and then plunge the bulbs and wires into the water. He performed this feat without even popping the circuit-breakers in the television studio. Several times he actually welded together pieces of iron. In one hand he held a standard electric welding rod. He completed the series circuit by holding in his other hand the hot lead from the welding set. Indeed, several newspaper reports and news photographs attest to his ability to weld like this. In addition, he showed he could control at will conventional ammetres that were in series with himself and high A.C. voltage. Not only was he able to control the flow, he claims he is able to teach others how to do the same. I learned all this from Alfred himself and from his extensive collection of press clippings, etc.

When I met Alfred he was carrying with him an electrical plug — a two-pronged, house-main type with two free leads attached to it in standard fashion bared about one inch from the free ends. Upon plugging this into a standard 120 volt A.C. socket, he proceeded to grab the leads, one in each hand, between thumb and forefinger. I recall at the time that he was wearing black overshoes which could have been made of rubber. This demonstration took place with him standing on a shag carpet in the living-room of the house. He explained that he needed to concentrate or else he would feel the effect of the current. He proceeded to bring the wires into contact with various parts of his hands, apparently with absolutely no effect whatsoever.

In another demonstration Alfred asked me to take a lead, which I did. I was wearing leather-soled shoes at the time, and my hands were somewhat sweaty due to a slight nervousness. I held one lead in my left hand, and with my right hand I took his free hand. His other hand still held the other A.C. lead. Thus we completed a simple series circuit through our four arms and two chests and, perhaps, with a trickle of current through our shoes. I felt nothing at all. Then Alfred told me he would raise the current, bit by bit, until I could feel it. He proceeded to do so, making no movements at all. Slowly I began to feel the familiar tingle of Alternating Current. (I had inadvertently experienced its unpleasantness many times in the past.) I felt the A.C. tingle run through my wrists, my arms, and then my hands, until I asked him to bring down the current. He accomplished this almost instantaneously. During this demonstration, neither of us moved or changed our grips. The whole episode lasted several minutes.

Several people in the room at the time witnessed this demonstration. The observers included my uncle and my father and a young woman who was also investigating Alfred's abilities. At one point she joined Alfred and me to form a human circuit. The same effects were observed. My father also joined us and experienced this feat of "mind over electricity." Needless to say, I could detect no fraud or trickery. I could find no ways in which the current was being bled off. At the same time I am unable to account for Alfred's ability to control current or at least its effects on him and on others.

Alfred also stated that he could exert some control over circuit-breakers and fuses. He could prevent them from blowing if he was holding a dead short with his hands. He took an ordinary 60-watt bulb and held it together with one wire in his hand, being careful not to touch the bulb's screw-base to both of the wires simultaneously. He took the other wire in his other hand and proceeded to sweep it over the bottom terminal of the bulb, being careful not to touch the wire to any other part of the bulb. The lamp flashed on and off as he made these motions. Then he touched the movable wire to the screw-base and held it there for several seconds. A large flash was seen and a pop was heard but no circuit-breaker cut off and no fuse blew. There was some damage, however. The screw-base of the bulb now had a large gash in it, one-eighth of an inch in diameter. We filmed these episodes in Super-8 with sound. I still have the light bulb. Despite its pocked base it still works.

In addition to maintaining that he is able to teach his feat of concentration to others, Alfred states that he is willing and wishes to be examined in a purely scientific manner. His goal is to assist others who work with high-voltage equipment and show them how to minimize the risk of electrocution. This is the reason I was initially contacted. I hope in the near future to perform preliminary experiments on and with Alfred using 110-220 volt, single-phase Alternating Current. Not only is he willing to co-operate with me, he is willing to indemnify any researcher against any harm that might come to him as the result of these experiments. Like Alfred, I want to get to the bottom of this phenomenon to see if it might be beneficial to those handling high-voltage equipment.

Tests of Psychic Abilities

Chris A. Rutkowski

Chris A. Rutkowski *is an astronomer and writer in the employ of the University of Manitoba. He is also a researcher and investigator with a special interest in anomalous phenomena. One project he has underway is a mammoth study of "mysterious Manitoba." He plans to give full coverage of the province's paranormal activity. In fact, the passage below comes from the unpublished manuscript of that study.*

In this passage Rutkowski refers to his friend, the late J. Allen Hynek, the American astronomer who devoted the last half of his professional life to the study of UFOs. Indeed, Dr. Hynek coined the phrase "close encounters" of the first, second, and third kinds to refer to degrees of closeness to unidentified flying objects. He appeared (as himself) in the Hollywood film Close Encounters of the Third Kind. *In that film the character of the ufologist, played by the director François Truffaut, was modelled on the UFO theorist Jacques Vallee.*

Here is an oblique look at Dr. Hynek who was no stranger to the television camera. In this instance the camera comes from the set of Beyond Reason, *a weekly network program that was hosted by the writer and broadcaster Allen Spraggett.*

TESTS OF PSYCHIC ABILITIES have been performed many times. There was at one time a Canadian television show called *Beyond*

Reason, for which a panel of psychic "experts" (including an astrologer, clairvoyant, and two other "sensitives") would try to determine the identity of a hidden "mystery guest." On some episodes, some of the panel members would definitely appear to be able to divine the names of the guests; on other occasions, they were less than adept. One remarkable event was when an astrologer became puzzled after casting the horoscope of a mystery guest; he was baffled as to why a "break" seemed to have occurred in the guest's life. The guest was revealed to be a noted celebrity who had had a sex change.

The natural question arose as to how "secret" the mystery guests really were. After all, a bit of backstage bribery could enable a panel member to have inside information. The strictness of the security was noted when my friend Dr. J. Allen Hynek, the renowned astronomer and UFO investigator, was selected as a guest. Though he normally spoke with me when he visited Winnipeg, I only learned of his visit after the program had been taped. He told me to watch the show, as it was "very revealing." He also explained that the producers of the show had taken great pains to ensure no one knew he was in Winnipeg, and even gave instructions to the hotel operators not to reveal his presence to anyone who might have been inquiring.

The show was broadcast a few months later. On it, the panel members struggled with the mystery guest's identity, until it came to the turn of the clairvoyant. She held the guest's watch in her hand, and after only a few seconds said she felt "vibes" that the guest could only be Dr. J. Allen Hynek! It seemed truly amazing. But the next time Dr. Hynek was in Winnipeg, I asked him about the show. He explained how he had been approached by the producer just minutes before going on the air, and had been asked to give an item of jewelry or clothing for the clairvoyant to hold. Without thinking, he took off his watch, then proceeded to the booth where he was to be secreted. He realized he had made a mistake. He showed me the watch that he had given for use by the clairvoyant. It had been given to him as a gift, and was clearly inscribed: *Allen Hynek*.

"Betty Louty"

Jo Atkins

George Gamester, *a lively columnist with the* Toronto
Star, *has an odd range of enthusiasms. From time to time he invites
his readers to contribute to a series of theme columns.*

*"Tell Us Your Eerie Tales" is the theme of one of his series. Here is
how Gamester began the series on 16 June 1989:*

> *Forget it, Rod Serling. Get lost, Vincent Price. Dry up, Edgar
> Allan Poe. We have all the spooky stories we need right here —
> thanks to* Star *readers' incredible response to our invitation to:*
> *Tell us your eerie tales.*
> So who needs fantasy?
> As we learn from our first $50 winner, Jo Atkins of North
> York, real life is strange enough....

Here is Jo Atkins, a writer in Willowdale, Ont., telling the amazing
story of "Betty Louty."

WHEN ELIZABETH WAS SMALL "Betty Louty" appeared as an imaginary playmate. She came every afternoon for a friendly visit. We
arranged the coffee table for Betty's visit: lace tea cloth, tiny cups
and saucers, cream and sugar, and the inevitable cookies were part
of the ritual. Elizabeth held her one-sided, polite, somewhat-
comforting conversations with her unseen guest and played the

sympathetic friend. Before my older child was due home Betty Louty would depart.

"Where does Betty live?" I asked.

"A long way away," was the only answer I ever got.

No one in our family knew anyone by that name. It was unusual and we often wondered what had prompted Elizabeth to invent it. We put it down to the vivid imagination of a creative high-strung child who had suddenly found herself without her closest friend and ally...her sister.

A few years later we all went to Jamaica for a holiday. In Kingston, a visit to the famous strawmarket was mandatory, as they each wanted a doll dressed colourfully in the traditional costume, balancing a basket of fruit on its head.

Our older girl chose a doll from the first stall in the market. But not Elizabeth. She moved from stall to stall but did not find a doll she wanted. No! No! was all we heard. We became a little fractious: She became more determined.

"I want that one," Elizabeth said finally, pointing most definitely in the direction of the farthest corner of the top row of dolls.

"Take one form the bottom row," I said. "They're all the same." The heat in the market and the intractability of my daughter were getting to me.

"I want that one," she insisted, still pointing.

The old lady moved her pole along the row, first to one doll then the next. She turned to look at me.

"They are not all the same. Each one is signed by the person who made it," she said reproachfully.

"That's her!" said Elizabeth suddenly, eyes alight.

With a great deal of patience the old lady hooked the doll down for her. She patted the child on her head.

"This one is made just for you, darlin'. This lady is not makin' dolls any more. This is the last one she made. She's been waitin' here for you."

"I know she's special. I'll look after her," said Elizabeth as she hugged the doll tightly and covered her with kisses.

Throughout our holiday, that doll never left Elizabeth's side. She slept, ate, walked with her, and would prop her gently on the sand before going into the water.

"She would like to swim too, but she's afraid of the currents in the water," said our young one.

"Currants are in cake," I said jokingly. How could she possibly have known about ocean currents since she was so young and not familiar with the seashore?

"She's tired and needs a nap," Elizabeth announced as soon as we returned home.

"I think you do too," I said. "Why don't you undress her and get her ready for bed?"

It was so quiet in Elizabeth's room, I thought she must have fallen asleep, but when I peeped in I found the doll had been carefully undressed by my little girl. She had taken off all the clothes and had only the bare ragdoll in her hands, cradling it gently as if it were a new-born child.

"Your bath's ready but you can't put your doll in with you. She'll get too wet," I said.

"She's afraid of water. She told me so," said Elizabeth very defensively. This game was getting to be too much for me!

"Well, let's pick up her clothes anyway," I said. "After your bath you can put her clothes back on."

As I picked up the clothes, I remembered the old lady in the Kingston market. I could not see the signature of the maker. Good saleswoman, I thought!

"I wonder who made this doll," I said.

"Betty. It's writing; I can't read it," said Elizabeth as she handed me the doll's apron.

There, on the inside band, was the maker's name..."Betty Louty."

The imaginary playmate never appeared after that holiday in Jamaica. My daughter has her own home now but she still has the doll. For all these years she has treasured her.

It seems that "Betty Louty" finally came home.

7. Ghostly Mysteries

Appearance of the Lake Steamer

Rowley W. Murphy

Rowley W. Murphy, a former seaman and a distinguished marine historian, was vouchsafed the vision of a ghostly lake steamer off Etobicoke at the western end of Toronto.

The event took place on Lake Ontario in Aug. 1910. Murphy was a youth at the time, but he was not alone in experiencing the vision or apparition. It was observed by at least ten other experienced sailors and seamen. Murphy recalled its appearance in considerable detail in his two-part article "Ghosts of the Great Lakes" published in Inland Seas, Summer 1961. *Even a half-century after the experience, he was still of two minds as to the nature of the ghostly lake steamer.*

EXPERIENCED GREAT LAKES SEAMEN have, like the writer, seen curious and extraordinary sights which remain clear in the memory. Could not some of these members record impressions of strange or wonderful occurrences which they have seen afloat, and yet appeared to be outside the boundaries of fact?

*

Another appearance from the past was seen by the crews of three yachts one beautiful night with full moon (like cool daylight) in August, 1910. My father, a cousin, and I were on a holiday cruise around the west end of Lake Ontario, and as we were late getting

222

underway from Toronto Island, and were running before a light easterly, decided to spend the night in the quiet, sheltered and beautiful basin at the mouth of the creek, spelled "Etobicoke" — but always pronounced "Tobyco" by old timers. (This seems hard for present residents of that area to tolerate, as they insist on trying to pronounce each syllable.)

In 1910, the Tobyco Creek was really a small river which made an abrupt turn westward and widened into a small lake, with a good beach held by poplar trees, between this harbour and the Lake. There was perfect shelter in this excellent harbour from wind from any direction, though in a hard easterly, it was not easy to reach Lake Ontario through the narrow harbour entrance.

At the date of this cruise, there was one brick farm house to westward of the harbour entrance and no buildings at all among the walnuts and oaks on the lovely grassy banks of the creek, except one ancient landmark, known as "The Old House," from the veranda of which Lieutenant Governor Simcoe is said to have shot a deer in 1794. This house was in good condition, when a few years ago it was torn down to increase parking space for a supermarket! The whole area is now completely built up, but in 1910 the beautiful grassy plains contained no buildings from Lake Ontario to the Lakeshore Road, except the landmark mentioned.

Our crusing yawl, with a larger sister of the same rig and a still larger Mackinaw (one of several "fish boats" converted to cruising yachts with great success), were the only occupants of the harbour this perfect night. The crews of the three yachts numbered eleven in all, and as is generally the case, after dinner was over and dishes done, gathered on deck in the moonlight to engage in the best conversation known to man.

All hands turned in earlier than usual, there being no distractions ashore, and by midnight were deep in happy dreams, helped by the quiet ripple alongside. At what was about 1:30 a.m., the writer was wakened by four blasts on a steamer's whistle. After waiting for a repetition — to be sure it was not part of a dream — he put his head out of the companionway.

There, flooded by moonlight, was a steamer heading about WSW. — at about half speed, and approximately half a mile off shore. She had a good chime whistle but not much steam — like

Noronic on that awful night of September 17, 1949, who also repeated her four blasts many times.

But who was she? On this amazingly beautiful night, with memory strained to the utmost, it was difficult to do more than think of who she was not! She was considerably smaller than the three famous Upper Lakers, *China*, *India*, and *Japan* (about this date under Canadian registry, known as *City of Montreal*, *City of Ottawa*, and *City of Hamilton*). She was not as small as *Lake Michigan*, but like her, did not appear to be of all wooden construction. However, there were many in the past, of quite related design and size. The vessel seen had white topsides and deck-houses, and appeared to be grey below her main deck, like the Welland Canal-sized freighters (at this date, the big wooden steamers of the Ogdensburg Line of the Rutland Transporation Company). *Persia* and *Ocean* were like her in size and arrangement, but were all white and came to known ends, and of course *Arabiana* was of iron, and was black.

In this appearance off "Toby Coke" (a variant of spelling), the starboard light, deck lights and some seen through cabin windows, had the quality of oil lamps; and her tall mast, with fitted topmast, carried gaff and brailed up main-sail. Her smokestack was all black, and she had no hog beams — but appeared to have four white boats. Her chime whistle was a good one, but was reduced in volume as previously mentioned, and was sounded continuously for perhaps ten minutes. Very soon all hands now watching on the beach decided that something would be done. So a dinghy was quickly hauled over form the basin, and, with a crew of four mad up from some of those aboard the three yachts, started to row out with all speed to the vessel in distress, to give her what assistance might be possible.

As the boys in the dinghy reached the area where something definite should have been seen, there was nothing there beyond clear and powerful moonlight, a few gulls wakened from sleep — but something else, impossible to ignore. This was a succession of long curving ripples in a more or less circular pattern, which just might have been the last appearance of those caused by the foundering of a steamer many years before on a night of similar beauty. In any case, the four in the dinghy returned in about an hour, reporting also small scraps of wreckage which were probably just old driftwood, seldom seen with any fresh breezes blowing.

But something more there was. This was the appearance to the visual and audible memory, which those on the beach and those afloat had seen and heard, of something which had occurred in the more or less distant past, and which had returned to the consciousness of living men after a long absence.

Whatever the cause, the experienced crews of the three yachts mentioned were of one mind as to what had been seen and heard. At least eleven lake sailors would be unlikely to agree on the character of this reappearance without good reason! And the reason was certainly not firewater working on the mass imagination, as no one of the three yachts had any aboard. So, reader, what is the answer?

The Vision of Walt Whitman

Lieut.-Col. L. Moore Cosgrave

Old Walt is the nickname of an immense ridge of precambrian rock in Ontario's Bon Echo Provincial Park. The rock acquired its nickname in 1919 when it was dedicated to the "democratic ideals" of the great American poet Walt Whitman. The dedicatees were a stalwart band of Canadian Whitmanites who were led by Flora Macdonald Denison, pioneer feminist and mother of the writer Merrill Denison.

Horace L. Traubel (1858-1919) was among the guests who were assembled for the dedication ceremony at Bon Echo on 23 Aug. 1919. This was only appropriate; Traubel was the poet's close friend in life and his devoted biographer in death. Traubel kept vigil at Whitman's bedside and was present at the poet's death in 1892 at Camden, N.J. Whitman placed a premium on loyalty and friendship, and Traubel was nothing if not a loyal friend.

Traubel reported experiencing a series of visions of Whitman at Bon Echo before his own death there on 6 Sept. 1919. The third and final vision occurred on his deathbed, two days before he succumbed, and it was witnessed not only by Traubel but also by Lieut.-Col. L. Moore Cosgrave, one of the Canadian Whitmanites. As Cosgrave later explained, he and Traubel saw "the likeness of Walt Whitman, standing upright beside the bed.... "

Cosgrave's statement took the form of a letter written from his residence in Toronto in late May 1920. It was addressed to Walter Franklin Prince, the well-known psychologist and psychical *researcher, and Prince reproduced the statement in his book* Noted Witnesses for Psychic Occurrences *(Boston: Boston Society for Psychic Research, 1928; New York: University Books, 1963). Thus the statement of Whitman's "likeness" rests not only on Cosgrave's statement but also, as Prince shows, on corroborative evidence from Flora Macdonald Denison and others who were present at Bon Echo that fateful summer.*

WITH REFERENCE TO your communication of May 25, in connection with the psychical occurrences connected with the passing of Horace Traubel I hereby state as follows:

During the months of August and September, 1919, I was in close touch with Mr. Horace Traubel, well known for his numerous writings and spiritual plane of thought; previous to that time I had not known him personally, nor had I a deep knowledge of the works and ideals of Whitman, this I state to show that my mind, conscious or subconscious, had not been engrossed in their works or belief, in addition, my long service in France with the Canadian forces, practically continually in the advanced lines from January, 1915, to the Armistice, had, naturally, made me familiar with the presence of death and the atmosphere around the dying, though imbuing me with natural reverence, created no unusual tension or emotional excitement such as is common to those unfamiliar with death, this is also stated to indicate that I was in a normal condition when the occurrence took place to which Mrs. Denison alludes, and I beg to corroborate in toto the statements made by her in reference to myself. Briefly, it was as follows: During the three nights previous to the passing of Horace Traubel, I had remained at his bedside, throughout the latter hours of darkness, momentarily expecting the end, my thoughts at all time were very clear and spiritual, owing to the quietude of the surroundings, the close touch of nature and the peculiar clean magnetism that seemed to surround this remarkable selfless man, who had given his whole life to the service of humanity, I had felt this curious spirituality surrounding but few great people, and never with ordinary beings.

During this long watch, Horace Traubel, who was suffering form paralysis and debility, was without visible pain, and semi-conscious, unable to articulate owing to paralysis of the tongue. His eyes, however, which were remarkably brilliant and expressive, gave us the clue to the majority of his needs. On the last night, about 3 A.M., he grew perceptibly weaker, breathing almost without visible movement, eyes closed and seemingly comatose, he stirred restlessly after a long period, and his eyes opened, staring towards the further side of the bed, his lips moved, endeavoring to speak, I moved his head back, thinking he needed more air, but again it moved away, and his eyes remained rivetted on a point some three feet above the bed, my eyes were at last drawn irresistibly to the same point in the darkness, as there was abut a small shaded night lamp behind a curtain on the further side of the room. Slowly the point at which we were both looking grew gradually brighter, a light haze appeared, spread until it assumed bodily form, and took the likeness of Walt Whitman, standing upright beside the bed, a rough tweed jacket on, an old felt hat upon his head and his right hand in his pocket, similar to a number of his portraits, he was gazing down at Traubel, a kindly, reassuring smile upon his face, he nodded twice as though reassuringly, the features quite distinct for at least a full minute, then gradually faded from sight. My eyes turned back to Traubel, who remained staring for almost another minute, when he also turned away, his features remarkably clear of the strained expression they had worn all evening, and he did not move again until his death, two hours later. I reported the occurrence to Mrs. Denison, who entered the facts in her diary at once, as she had records of several other psychic phenomena to date. I am thoroughly convinced of the exactness of the above statements, and did not regard it as extraordinary, owing to the fact that I had experienced similar phenomena at crucial movements during heavy casualties in France.

The Idol

G.S.F.

*F*rom time to time I am a guest on a radio program or a television show to talk about "the unexplained." I find that each appearance evokes a response of some kind. Sometimes it is immediate: a researcher or a program assistant or a technician buttonholes me in the studio and relates a curious experience. But usually it is a delayed reaction: I receive a phone call later that day or early the next, or a letter arrives in the mail a week later, that sets forth an inexplicable event.

After talking on one Toronto radio program, I received a letter from a gentleman who lives in Sutton West, Ont. It began: "I understand that you are interested in 'anything not believed to be irrational, the unexplained.'" It continued, "I have such a story to tell. It is such a grotesque story I am sure that you will not believe it, but I assure you that it is true. In a way I hope you will just throw this letter in the wastepaper basket.... "

Needless to say, I was delighted to receive this letter, which was written and signed by G.S.F. (The name has been withheld upon request.) I have never met the correspondent, but for some time in late 1988 and early 1989, we conducted a lively correspondence. It is from these letters that his story (set in the India of the early 1930s) emerged. Here is my correspondent's story told in his own words. It is a true story, but a strange one, the stuff of occult fiction.

I have one disagreement with G.S.F. He concluded one of his letters with the following words: "Friends and relations constantly

229

urge me to write a book, but I am so poor at paperwork that I contribute wholeheartedly to the dictum that there is a book in every man — and that is the best bloody place for it to remain." He should write that book.

I AM AMAZED AT some of the references I read to such places as Quetta and Rawalpindi being hot, dusty, god-forsaken places. Quetta is cold and stands at the head of the Bolan Pass as a protection against the Baluch tribes of Persia and raids across the border from Afghanistan. The Staff College is located here and many of Britain's top generals filled positions of one kind or another. Fruit orchards stretch away in all directions. Move eastwards across the North West Frontier to Peshawar at the head of the Khyber Pass and then one hundred miles south to Pawalpindi. Hot and dusty yes, but god-forsaken — you be the judge.

Rawalpindi (or Pindi) is the headquarters of Northern Command and bristles with the military. The northern suburb of Westridgte is home to a large railway colony and where you have a railway colony, you can be sure of something going on all the time. The suburb to the south — across from Tolpi Park — is Chaklala with the troops. Pindi Cantonment is the Administrative Centre with Posts, Telegraphs, and all such ancillary services. More rogering takes placed in Topi Park than in all of Toronto's (better policed) parks, with positions going from the normal through the other sixty-four to the missionary.

Troops and European civilians live in Cantonments established by the British. Perhaps five miles down the road is the Indian City which has been there for centuries. The bungalows in the Cantonments are owned by wealthy Indians from the City. A variation on the South African apartheid existed. The Garrison Engineer rented all the bungalows. Bungalows left over after apportionment were used as offices or for storage. No Indian who applied to live in Cantonments was ever refused *provided* he could find accommodation!

Bungalows were large and built to cope with the heat. They could have as many as twenty rooms with sixteen-foot ceilings and with at least four skylights to each main room. Situated in huge compounds amidst a variety of tropical flowers, they rented for a maximum of seventy rupees per month (about seven dollars at the time), which included stables, garage, and outhouses for a dozen servants. Through the years people lived in them, died in them, and in many instances were murdered in them. This is where my story comes in and is the worst of my many encounters with the unexplainable.

One house in particular stood back, solid and sullen, a hundred feet or so from one of the two roads connecting the Railway station to the centre of the Cantonment. No one knew how old it was or who its original owner had been, but the consensus was that it had played its part in the Mutiny of 1857. The front faced the side and the side faced the road. A deep and gloomy archway provided entrance into this place. It was occupied by the ASP, the Assistant Superintendent of Police, his wife, and their two small children. Well read and widely travelled, he was the antithesis of the popular conception of the policeman. An excellent raconteur, he held one in thrall with his stories of out-of-the-way places. When I told him that I was about to be married and was looking for suitable accommodation, he graciously agreed to rent me a third of the bungalow. This one third was entered through the archway in the side that faced the road.

His sergeant was an ex-BOR (British Other Rank; *i.e.*, a private). Coarse and ignorant, his one redeeming feature was his devotion to his daughter, a lovely little girl three to four years of age. He shared a less-pretentious bungalow closer to the Bazaar. Somewhere, somehow, Mr. BOR stole an object of veneration from a place of worship. It was a thing of sinister beauty. Mr. BOR didn't have it in his home too long when his daughter started to display unusual symptoms. Then she started to convulse. The convulsions grew worse and, despite all medical care, the child died. Distraught, and beginning to connect the death of his child with the idol, he went to his boss and confessed to the theft. Mr. ASP should have fired him on the spot, but he was a gentle man so he reprimanded him and took possession of the idol with a view of returning it. But how does one get an idol back where it came from without causing another mutiny? He was also cognizant of the fact that the Great Indian Mutiny of 1857 started in this Cantonment.

So the idol took up residence in our bungalow and Mr. BOR disappeared without a trace.

All went well for a few days. Then Mr. ASP started to display some queer symptoms. He grew detached and morose and skidded into convulsions. He would froth at the mouth and writhe on the floor and had to be restrained from causing himself bodily damage. The doctor would be sent for, but on his arrival Mr. ASP would sit up, quite normal, wondering what all the fuss was about. When this had happened a few times, the doctor was reluctant to attend. Mr. ASP's condition grew worse. He lost interest in his person and in his surroundings and, as a result of his not going to work, his District fell into chaos. Finally he lost his job. I heard some years later that he had been seen begging in the streets of Delhi, while his poor wife worked at menial jobs to put food on the table.

But to step back. His wife managed to convince him that there was some connection between the idol and his recent illness. In a lucid moment he turned to me and said, "George, you are interested in these things. Would you like to take the idol over?" In a not so lucid moment I said yes. My wife was horrified, but I was able to persuade her that it was illogical to allow our lives to be governed by some vermilion-painted piece of terra cotta. So the idol moved from Mr. ASP's side of the bungalow to ours.

We continued to live like any other young married couple in a Cantonment Station. We enjoyed the odd movie, visits with friends, and long walks with our two bull terriers. But there was a sense of foreboding, and joy had definitely gone out of living. Now I want now to be as clear and accurate as possible. What follows has to be accepted as fact or it has to be rejected as mere fantasy.

It was a hot night bathed in brilliant moonlight. Our beds were outside in the compound, with the feet pointing to the road and our heads to the archway that formed the entrance to our portion of the bungalow. My wife's bed was to the left of mine, and to her left was a tree I didn't remember ever having seen before. It was shedding most exotically perfumed petals in a wide circle. My wife had dozed off but I was wide awake enjoying the beauty of the night. Suddenly I began to realize that we were not alone. I turned over and slowly raised my head and looked into the depths of Hell.

An enormous black figure stood over me with arms outstretched. The monster and I looked at each other. Then it slowly retreated into the archway and disappeared into a Dante's Inferno of its own making. The otherworldliness of the scene preempted fear.

It was pointless waking my wife, but when I mentioned the affair to her at breakfast, I didn't have to elaborate. She too had experienced some kind of vision of an alien world.

Later that day the Manager walked into my office, pointed to the blueprints and estimates on my desk, and said, "Put them all away for now. An emergency has arisen in Pindi, and you are to report there immediately." A similar thing had happened a few days before the date set for our wedding. An emergency had taken me to Simla, and I had got back just a few hours before the marriage ceremony. Now it was happening again. My wife had so looked forward with anticipation to spending our first Christmas together, but it wasn't to be. I was being dispatched to the deserts of Rajputana from the end of November to the middle of January, and she would be all alone hundreds of miles away.

After all that had happened, how could I possibly leave my wife in that cursed bungalow and go off at a moment's notice to Pindi five hundred miles to the north? I protested that Rawalpindi was outside our territory, etc., which surprised the Boss. "Good heavens, man, why all the fuss? You will only be gone for a few days." It was not that I was indispensable but I had been attached to the Pindi Office in my bachelor days and probably knew the territory better than the men in Delhi or Karachi. I contemplated resignation but my wife pointed to the fact that I had a good job, the Depression was lingering, and I would be home again before we knew it. She assured me that she would take all precautions and contact me immediately if necessary.

Here I must describe my wife, for without her there would be no story. She is a small woman. She doesn't smoke, doesn't drink, is a vegetarian who, literally, eats less than a sparrow. People describe her as frail. Actually, she is made from hob-nails and is as stubborn as a mule, an original assessment that I have had no reason to modify over the ensuing fifty-five years! The three children tower above her and, as can be readily guessed at, I left their upbringing to her.

The Manager of the Pindi sub-divisional office was a wimp, the nephew of a gloomy prelate, and wealthy enough to buy, bring out, and drive a straight twelve (or was it sixteen?) cylinder Standard Swallow. He removed his monocle, expressed the thought that some construction as going on somewhere between Srinagar and Gilghit and that this was the reason why I was here and I had better get to Kashmir as soon as possible. All went well, and in a few days I was ready to commence the return journey.

Roads in Kashmir and in the Hill stations of India are just wide enough to take tow cars abreast, but traffic is not heavy. You could leave Srinagar after breakfast and make Pindi before dinner. Driving through gardens and orchards between avenues of popular trees, I made it in good time to Baramullah. From here the road gets tortuous and treacherous and speed is reduced till you bypass and get to the other side of Murree. I got to Domel where I was dismayed to learn there had been heavy rains in the mountains causing landslides and that it was impossible to proceed farther. I got a small room in the Dak Bungalow which was in a state of bedlam.

There was a very reserved British Colonel and his lady friend and a group of American tourists who would have been quite at home in Topi Park. They jabbered all through dinner and later made sleep impossible with their caterwauling. Despite my urgency to get moving, I delayed having breakfast till after everyone had left. The khansamah informed me the road had been repaired and reopened and the other residents had made an early start. It was in a very buoyant mood that I resumed my journey.

Alas, a few miles out of Domel the same crowd was lined up at the side of the road. Another landslide had closed the road. I took my place at the end of the line. One of the American women came up, jumped up on the tailgate of my station wagon and spread her legs wide apart, quite oblivious of the peeping and giggling of the coolies squatting on the ground close by. Since I was in no need for frivolity, she departed and presently the Colonel walked over. He was unhappy. He would be late reporting back to his Regiment and what explanation would his companion give for her absence? He felt the delay in clearing the road was quite unnecessary and suggested we walk over and examine the site. Everything was quiet so we set off and almost immediately discovered why it was taking so long. From where our cars were parked, the stones looked like pebbles. Among them we realized there were jagged boulders, some large enough to tear chunks of road out as they went hurtling into the gorge of the Jhelum River hundreds of feet below.

Sidestepping boulders, scrambling over debris, we were about half way into the slide when the mountain started to shake, releasing an avalanche of mud and stones. I am quite unable to give a coherent account of what happened next. All I can say is that I found myself free, and on the far side of the slide. But where was the Colonel and what was all this sticky matter on my face? It was his brains, and he was lying crumpled up behind a boulder with a jagged hole in his skull through which the rest of his brains were oozing out. He was a big man. I couldn't lift him. I don't know whether he felt anything, but he kept repeating "Oh God!" as he spent the rest of that night on a narrow shelf with the wind howling like a banshee around us.

When I eventually reported into the Office in Pindi, Mr. Prissy calmly announced, "You have been transferred to this Office." I contacted my wife, rented a very nice bungalow, settled the usual preliminaries while I waited for her to join me. By the time she arrived, I had visited the most southern of the stations in my territory, a place called Jhelum on the river of the same name. It was here that Alexander the Great was supposed to have fought and won the battle of the Hydaspus and where his troops mutinied and forced him to return home.

I helped my wife to settle in with the dogs and the idol and I went off to the Khyber for a few days. On my return, Mr. Prissy produced another downer. I was wanted back in Kashmir. I had been in Kashmir more than a dozen times, and I had had my fill of orchards, Moghul gardens, snow-capped peaks by moonlight, clear blue lakes, and living in houseboats of five rooms, two servants, and three meals a day for fifty cents a day.

Anyway, I drove back over the spot where the accident had occurred without giving it a second thought. On the return journey I couldn't resist getting out of the car and walking over the ground in question. And now strange feelings started to assail me. I was rooted to the spot and had to be helped back into the car. Somehow

I got home and went to bed. It would be along time before I would be out of bed again, my senses dulled by laudanum.

Had my "friend" of the archway killed the Colonel by mistake? Was it now going to rectify the error, not by a quick, merciful death, but by degrees? If so I could not stand the ticking of a clock, and any light set off a wild tantrum. We lived in a soundless, sightless world, and only my wife's strength kept me from destroying myself. She just carried on as though all this horror was the most natural thing in the world.

There had been an occasion when she and I had been tossed around in a violent earthquake and then, in trying to escape, been kidnapped. As far as she was concerned, there was nothing to it. Mr. Prissy came to see me, took one look, and said, "My God, he's gone crackers!" and fled. At this stage my wife's nerve seemed to give. She insisted that we get rid of the idol. At first I resisted, then compromised by suggesting that we ask her father to keep it for us. He was a very religious man to whom all this superstitious pagan nonsense was anathema. He agreed. So the idol was transferred to him. Two weeks had barely gone by when he was yelling to be relieved of its presence. He could stand it no more. My wife was now adamant. The idol had to go. I agreed. To this day it lies buried in a little Christian cemetery somewhere in Pakistan.

Did the malign influence stop there? No. There were a few more incidents, one of which resulted in injury to me, but the influence diminished. The company (a multinational oil company) had put me on six months' leave of absence without pay, and we went to live with my wife's father. It didn't seem as though I would be able to get back to work, but with the rise of Mr. Hitler the company as prepared to retrain me in another job. I completed my retraining in record time, went from strength to strength, and before the War ended was appointed Labour Officer of a thousand-man Terminal and, damn me, if in this capacity I didn't run into my first poltergeist. But that is another story.

An Experience in India

Marina Loan

David Schatzky, the lively and likeable host of CBC Radio in Toronto, has a special feeling for the supernatural. He hosted an early afternoon talk and phone-in show which was popular with listeners throughout Ontario, and he took special pleasure in scheduling a guest suitable for the occasion. The present editor has served as his guest on a number of Halloween programs, chatting with David, his listeners, and his callers about their experiences with ghosts and spirits.

One of the callers on the Halloween show of 1988 was Marina Loan. She is an Anglo-Indian who has lived in Canada since 1964. She dramatically told us of an incident from her past...a "ghostly experience" that occurred to her in India near the village of Radsol in 1962...an incident she has been unable to forget or to explain.

She enthralled the listeners to the program with her straightforward account, so I asked her on the air if she would be kind enough to write up the experience. She did so and sent it to me a letter from her home in Scarborough, Ont. The account is dated 7 Nov. 1988.

AS YOU REQUESTED, I am relating the ghostly experience I had some years ago. This happened in India in the Province of Orissa.

My husband worked in the bamboo jungle for a paper company. Our bungalow was situated at the edge of the jungle. It was built on the slope of a hill and at the foot we had a mango grove. Amongst the trees there was growing one of the tallest mango trees that I had ever seen. It bore no fruit.

On questioning the servants, I was informed that it had borne fruit but it stopped doing so when an unfortunate accident occurred. I assumed that the accident had occurred to the tree, but was told, "Oh no, lady, not the tree. A young man climbed the tree to pick mangoes, and the branch he was standing on broke, and he fell to his death. This man was unmarried, and since then there has never been any fruit."

I didn't think any more of this story till one evening, at dusk, on Diwali, the Hindu festival held in October-November, when small oil lights are put in doorways and windows to keep out the evil spirits. I was walking with my terrier, Rex, when he stopped and growled. His fur stood up on his neck, and he turned and bolted back to the bungalow. Brave dog! I was curious to see what had scared him. I continued to walk a little farther to the barren mango tree. I looked up, and on a branch that had not been there before there stood a youth, about seventeen years of age. We looked at each other. I was quite unafraid. I turned and slowly walked back home with a feeling of sadness.

I heard, later, the apparition had been seen before, and the mango grove was given wide berth on Diwali night.

The Above Is Strange Enough in Itself

Thos. J. Muckle

*D*uring *the course of a radio interview, which was conducted by Jeff Howatt of CHUM-FM in Toronto, I discussed a handful of the unusual events and experiences that are dealt with at greater length in my book* Mysterious Canada. *I extended an invitation to listeners — and readers — who had unusual experiences of their own to communicate with me.*

One listener who took up the invitation was T.J. Muckle, M.D., F.R.C.P.(C.), Director of Laboratories, Chedoke Division, Chedoke-McMaster Hospitals, Hamilton, Ont. Dr. Muckle phoned me and identified himself. He politely inquired if I really wanted more accounts of strange experiences. He had in mind the fact that as I had already published a book about the paranormal I might no longer be interested in collecting such accounts. I assured him that I was busy amassing material for future books in the field, and that I would love to hear his story, especially as his medical training required that he be precise and objective, indeed clinical, in recording events.

Dr. Muckle related the events described below. I asked him if he would be willing to prepare a detailed account for publication. He agreed to do so, and indeed did so in his letter dated 20 Dec. 1988. Here is his account of the apparition — or "apparition" — of a family pet.

IN THE SUMMER OF 1976, I took my wife and three girl children to Camp Oconto on Eagle Lake, northwest of Kingston, for a vacation (for them) and a working holiday (for me). I was the "camp doctor."

In the middle of the afternoon, several days later, I was sitting in an easy chair, reading a book on the verandah of our small bungalow. The chair was sideways-on, so that in the corner of my eye I could see the living-room through the open door. Quite suddenly, but at the same time with no sense of dramatic suddenness, I could see our pet cat walking slowly across the room, apparently quite unconcerned, calmly looking straight ahead. It took me a couple of seconds to realize that she was walking along a foot and half or so above the floor level. She ambled across to the other side of the room and, just short of the far wall, disappeared — not quite instantly, but within a fraction of a second.

This "apparition" had been present, I suppose, for about fifteen seconds. I would like to emphasize, however, that there was nothing about what I saw to suggest any form of apparition. The cat was normal in every detail, completely opaque and moving in her accustomed fashion. She was not surrounded by any dark aura, or glow, and I have to say that in every way, apart from being a foot and a half off the floor, appeared absolutely normal. At the time of the "apparition" I had no sense of dread, or fear, no sensation of cold or heat, or any other unusual sensation whatsoever.

My first thought, within a second or so of her appearing, was the following: How did she manage to travel all the way from Hamilton? Then I realized that she was, in fact, a foot and a half off the floor, and it couldn't be her. By this time she was about one-third of the way across the room, and for the remainder of her walk I just watched her with my mind blank. My sense of blankness persisted for maybe a minute or so after she had disappeared. Then I began to "re-run the tapes," and take a closer look at the living-room to see if, by any faint chance, it could have been some sort of optical illusion and that a cat very like ours had in fact been walking on something which I hadn't perceived. However, I couldn't find anything to substantiate this.

I called two of my children from nearby to tell them what I had seen and to give me a hand to see if we could find any cat anywhere in or near the bungalow, just in case I was losing my mind. We couldn't. During this exercise I began to wonder not whether or how I had seen this, but why. Immediately, of course, I was reminded of having read of similar sightings and that the associations were usually bad. Half an hour later, telling my wife and my other children of the occurrence, the only strong impression I had of the whole event was a feeling of the absolute reality of this "apparition."

The above is strange enough in itself, but the real impact came about two and a half hours later, when we went into supper and I was told that there had been a telephone message for me at the Camp Telephone Office from our neighbours in Hamilton. I went across and, on the way, the uneasy suspicion that something bad had indeed happened recurred. I telephoned our neighbour, and she told me that our cat had been run over by a car about three hours before, which was pretty near the time I saw the "apparition." She also added that the cat had not been killed instantly but had lived for a few minutes after being hit. I immediately wondered whether I would have seen the apparition had the cat died instantly — the implication I trust is obvious.

This is the only experience that I have had that I would really call paranormal, although I have had other experiences such as "some places give me the creeps," and on two occasions I have been overwhelmed by a fainting sensation when somebody nearby was, unbeknown to me, in the process of fainting. Please feel free to use this experience as you wish.

The Shuter Street Apartment

Isabel Germiquet

Isabel Germiquet prepared this detailed report of the poltergeist-like disturbances that she has experienced over the five or so years while living in her own apartment. For the record, the apartment is located in the building at 295 Shuter Street in downtown Toronto. She prepared this report at my request on 19 Dec. 1988. She had contacted me after learning that I was on the look-out for accounts of hauntings, strange sightings, etc. The report was keyboarded and printed by Mrs. Germiquet's son on an Apple computer. I have minimally edited it for publication here. It takes a hardy soul to endure such disturbances!

I MOVED INTO THE ONE-BEDROOM apartment in which I am now living on August 13th, 1983. As I was moving from a large, two-bedroom apartment, I had too much furniture. So I hung my clothes in the closet in the bedroom, and I put away my things in dresser drawers there, but at first I didn't actually sleep in the bedroom. I could hardly reach the bed for all the furniture and things. Whenever I worked my way through the bedroom to get a change of clothing, I could hear a male voice groaning form within the closet.

During the weeks that I couldn't use the bed, the door was kept closed because the bedroom was such a mess of furniture. In spite of this, I found that the door was frequently open. This happened many times a day, and I knew that I had not left it open. One particular day, when the door was shut, I tried to push it open, but it felt like someone was holding the door tightly shut. Suddenly it gave way, and I stumbled into the room. This was just the beginning. The following is a list of the phenomena that occurred in my apartment over the last five years, and continue to occur to this day.

Aug.-Oct. 1983. The day after I moved in, I began to hear tapping noises in the bedroom whenever I entered it. These noises spread over the entire apartment. Then snorting sounds came from the oven and spread all over the apartment. The first night that I slept in the bedroom, all the coat-hangers in the closet started to rattle for no apparent reason. Snorting came from inside the closet. These sounds continued on a nightly basis. Occasionally growling noises came from behind the television set.

Dec. 1983 - Jan. 1984. My granddaughter and grandson moved from Vancouver to Toronto. They spent a considerable amount of time in my apartment and experienced some of the following phenomena. We were touched on the arms and had our hair tweaked. We heard snoring sounds from the oven and the rattling of the oven-racks. My daughter suggested taking pictures of the open oven. The film showed faces and figures. About this time I was hugged by an invisible presence. On Christmas Day, rapping was heard on the headboard of my bed, and my daughter, sleeping over that night, was struck in the back. Banging was also heard on the inside of the closet door.

My daughter and I saw a male shadow moving out of the dining-room. There were no males present in the apartment at the time. The next night, on the advice of the Psychic Centre, we decided it was wise to sleep at my daughter's apartment on Wellesley Street. When leaving my place, we heard footsteps behind us, as we walked down the corridor to the elevator. We turned and looked, but no one was there. While we were at my daughter's, some plastic bags began to rustle, as if someone was moving them.

During this month I read the book *Supernature* by Lyall Watson. It said a man in Sweden was getting spirit-voices on his tape recorder. I decided to borrow a tape recorder form my son. We turned it on and recorded a voice saying, "Strange one, Jimmy. Find me, Jimmy. Jimmy, find me if you can."

April 1984. My daughter moved from Wellesley Street to an apartment in a building next to mine. One night, she left my place at 7:30 p.m. Just after she left, my apartment door opened and closed by itself. At 9:00 p.m., my daughter telephoned to tell me she could hear a man humming in her apartment. At midnight I could hear him humming in my apartment. On one occasion, I heard the sound of someone flicking the light-shade. When I looked up, the light-shade was vibrating.

May 1984. I found an enormous hand-print on the kitchen cupboard. A mysterious formation of moisture appeared on the wall without explanation. I called 100 Huntley Street, and a Minister came to my apartment. After the Minister left, the bottom of the drapes over the sliding balcony door were flung about one or two feet above the level of the floor, and I heard growling and scratching, as if an animal was trying to escape.

July 1984. My eight-year-old daughter and I saw many quarter-moon shapes of light moving about the living-room. Later that month I saw two flashes, orange-like flames shooting across the walls. The flames were about 16" by 4" in size. At the time all the doors, windows, and drapes were closed. Also during this month, I sat on the sofa reading and heard a male voice whistling a tune a few feet away.

Aug. 1985. My granddaughter, aged nine, was alone with me one day when I put on the tape recorder. I recorded a male voice that said, "Go out on the 29th. Look up, Trudy. Don't worry, everyone is coming back — your Dad, Ethel, friends." My nickname is Trudy, and my Dad and Ethel have been dead for thirty-five to forty years. Another time, when I was alone, I heard a noise. I turned on the tape recorder and a different male voice said, "Come, child...find thy rest...ending from thee."

Sept. 1985. While taping, I recorded a woman speaking Italian. I asked three different people to translate the words for me. They all said the woman was telling me to read the books in my library. Later that month, my granddaughter was sitting on the floor watching TV. We heard the noises that generally accompany the phenomenon. Then we both heard a child-like voice saying aloud what sounded like "boak...boak." We decided that the male voice was saying, "Book...book."

As I was wrapping gifts, I heard the rustle of a Simpsons bag on my sewing machine. I turned and saw a large handprint form on the surface of the bag. As I watched, the handprint on the bag relaxed. On closer examination, I could see the sharp indentations left by the finger-nails. A variety of unexplained smells occasionally occurred in the apartment — everything from perfume to rotten meat. On investigation, they did not appear to be coming from air ducts or from other apartments.

Feb. 1986. One day I saw three golden balls of light in the living-room. They were moving around about a foot from the floor.

Aug. 1986. My youngest son was staying over for a few days. One night, while he was listening to music on the tape recorder in the bedroom, I heard the buttons on the machine being pushed, one after the other. I was about to ask him what he was doing, when he shouted for me to hurry into the room. He was very upset and he told me that something he couldn't see was pushing the buttons on his tape recorder. It was now turned off. I turned on the tape recorder and watched as something turned it off again. I could feel a presence in the room, and I shouted at it in anger to go away. There was a swooshing sound and a sharp banging on the inside of the closet door. Thereafter the tape recorder operated normally.

Oct. 1986. One day my son was visiting me and we had a quarrel and I called him a stinker. He left, and a few minutes later I heard a lot of tapping sounds, so I turned on the tape recorder. I recorded a woman's voice saying, "Let stink out the door... walk in the bare." I wondered if the voice was telling me not to let my son come back.

Jan. 1987. One night my granddaughter was visiting. She wasn't feeling well and went to bed about 9:00 p.m. About five minutes later she started screaming, "Nanny, Nanny, help me! Get me out of here!" When I got to her, she was hysterical. But she told me what had happened. She had turned out the light and pulled up the covers, with the top part folded to about the middle of her chest. Suddenly the covers were yanked down to the bottom of the bed. I looked and I could see the spot where they had been grabbed.

Feb. 1988. I was sitting in the living-room and I saw a bright flash of light in the kitchen area. As I watched, it flashed repeatedly in the direction of the apartment door. The flashes looked like balls of light. They made whoomp sounds, as if they were hitting something. Suddenly the balls of light started to make a sudden, ninety-degree turn and rush straight toward me. They seemed to flatten out a few feet from me, and make the whoomp sound as if they were hitting something there. This continued until seven o'clock the next morning.

One kind or another of the above phenomena has occurred continually in this apartment over the past five years. There has never been a break of more than three weeks between occurrences. Usually there is an occurrence very night.

Our House on Pape Avenue

Gertie Sequillion

"*Enclosed please find the story of Pape House,*" *wrote Gertie Sequillion in her letter to me dated 23 Dec. 1988. "I hope that this story is all right, as I have not attempted to write for publication before."*

The story is indeed all right. It is being published here in Mrs. Sequillion's own words. The account arrived in a carefully prepared, six-page typescript which I have minimally copy edited. Mrs. Sequillion originally phoned me in response to an invitation that I issued on an open-line radio program. I had asked listeners and others to share with me any paranormal experience that they may have had.

Mrs. Sequillion contacted me by phone the following day. She had not heard the program, but a friend of hers had, and the friend then encouraged her to relate to me this account of living in a haunted house at 557 Pape Avenue in Toronto's East End. The events occurred in 1969. I encouraged Mrs. Sequillion to write out an account of the episode and mail it to me. A week or so later, the six pages of typescript arrived. The reader is invited to make of it what he or she will!

IT ALL STARTED INNOCENTLY ENOUGH. I was doing the dishes at the sink, like most new mothers-to-be, while waiting for my husband to come home for dinner, when there came a knock on the door and there descended on me my whole family from Newfoundland.

Well, you can imagine my surprise, and all the noise and inconvenience in a one-bedroom flat, with five more people in it! That, however, was not all, as they had news to relate. My Mother had sold our family home, which my Father had built. My Father had had a heart attack over the idea of the move to Toronto. He was still in the hospital in St. John's. Annie, the youngest, was with Mom, waiting for news of his release. Then they too would descend on us, with Dad to follow thereafter.

To save time and confusion later, I will here introduce my family: Dad (Chesley), Mom (Annie Clara), Jessie, who was married and away with the Armed Forces (thank God!), Rod, Chesley Jr., also married and thus saved the ordeal, Ed, who could tell his own story of the place, and Rich who decided to leave rather suddenly, myself (Gert), Marina, John, who was slightly retarded, Lily, Bernice, and Annie, named after my Mother and the youngest since our baby sister Celeste had died at the age of two and a quarter years.

Thus we are a big family like steps and stairs. If it had not been so, my experience would have been of more fright, but as the human mind tends to rationalize things supernatural, so did I at the time.

However, I had no idea of this when Rod first said, "Gert, your flat just won't do. Mom wants us to find a place for all of us. That includes you and Fred." I thought, "My husband, poor man, this is something you aren't going to like!"

Most people would say "no" right then and there, but I must confess I was not the "no" kind. I had never said "no" to my Mother about anything in my life, so true to form I said "no" in my heart but not in the open. So I found myself with the problem, which to everyone else was so simple. I just had to tell Fred, when he came home, that we were moving. But, oh, how unsimple it was to me!

You see, my husband was not a patient man by any means of the word. He was good-looking, and thus his appeal to me, but patient or understanding of anything but his own comforts he was not. Rather verbal he could be, but not, thank God, to a person's face. Thus I knew the brunt of it would be felt by me alone. Still, he wasn't home yet, so I had time to think just what I'd say. I decided food was my best bet, so dinner turned into something special and lots of it!

To say he was surprised to find a whole houseful of family, all of them mine, is to lighten an otherwise ghastly ordeal. I introduced them much the same as I have to you, with the exception of Dad, Mom, Jessie, Marina, Chesley Jr., and Annie.

"Gert, we don't have room for all these people," he said, and he was amazingly calm. But you just knew he was trying to figure a way of getting rid of them as quickly as possible.

"Honey," I said, as a way of softening the blow, "you can get a newspaper after dinner." Whereupon I was interrupted by Rod who said, "You mean supper, don't you, or have you turned into a bunch of Torontonians?"

This interjection lightened everyone's mood, and soon we were all laughing about the differences between being a Newfie and a Mainlander. This merriment was short-lived, however, when our landlord got wind of the matter and notice to leave was given. Fred, being a man to take care of his money, saw that it would be a profitable venture to move in with my family. Thus the difficult problem for me was solved without me having to tell him anything. And to this day he doesn't know that moving in with my family was already a foregone conclusion.

To us, then, the ad in the paper for the Pape Avenue house seemed a godsend at the time. It read something like this: "Three storey house for rent in the East End of the city. Kitchen, bath, living-room, and possible five bedrooms. Immediate occupancy. Phone -------."

We called and made arrangements to see the place. It had really large rooms. Everything had been newly painted, and to us the price per month seemed like a steal. Once the first and last months' rents were paid, we still had a little left for more furniture, as ours alone wasn't enough. The packing and moving were done very swiftly. Still, we were not yet all moved in when Mother and Annie arrived.

"Happy birthday!" she shouted from behind us, as I was carrying a box out the door. It wasn't my birthday, of course, but she had bought me a gift and couldn't wait any longer to give it to me. It was only the first of May and my birthday was not till the eighth.

When it did come, only my brother Rich and I remembered, as his birthday is the same as mine. By then I was in the new house already a week, and what a sleepless one it was!

The house was clean and nice, large enough for all. I don't think we've ever had so much room in our lives. But the noise was driving me crazy.

Let's see. The kids were in the middle bedroom, the one with that awful stain on the floor. Yes, that's right, and Dad and Mom had the larger bedroom across the hall. I just couldn't stand the noise from the kids' room any more, and neither could Fred. I was going to kill the kids if they didn't go to sleep. We had tried to keep quiet about the racket they made, but Fred did have to work in the morning, and as pregnant Mother I needed my rest, didn't I? Mom and Dad would just have to be mad at me. Fred was very close to leaving me altogether. Living with relatives is bad enough, but the man couldn't get any sleep at all.

It was the same thing every night, always noises like people fighting, and then running up and down the stairs after one another like a herd of elephants, and then in their bedroom it was like they'd fight and even knock one another down. Sometimes it was as if one of them was seriously hurt. But as the noise kept up all night, I guess they weren't.

Well, tonight it was going to stop or else! That's just what I was thinking that night, but I was not prepared for what I found out. I went into their bedroom, prepared to kill, but like little angels they were sound asleep. In fact, I went all over the house, even up to the third floor, where my older brothers were sleeping. My, it was an eerie place! I felt like someone was watching me, but though I turned around two or three times, the only thing I saw was sleeping men. Still, I got out of there fast. I felt weird up there.

Upon returning to our bedroom, Fred was mad at me. "I thought you were going to quiet them down. Well?"

"Honey," I said, "you and I are the only people awake in this whole house."

"Gert, that's garbage. You can hear that racket," he said, waving towards the stairs.

"Fred, everyone is asleep," I nearly screamed at him. "I'm cold," I added, tucking myself back in bed. "If you don't believe me, you can check for yourself."

Fred grumbled under his breath, but he didn't do anything about getting up. I didn't know what time it was, but I do know I must have fallen asleep from exhaustion, for in the morning, when I awoke, it was nearly ten.

This was the routine, for routine it became, until Fred could take it no longer. He himself decided to go check on the kids. He was cold when he returned and quite determined to leave this house. He said it was the strangest place in the world, where people make a noise and no one is supposed to be doing it.

Telling my Mother wasn't going to be an easy chore. But Fred was my husband, and a wife had to go along with her husband, didn't she? So the news was given and accepted with bad feelings all around.

It was about our last night. We all sat at the TV after supper. For that matter, the TV in our place never seemed to be off. Ed mentioned quite jokingly that he would return to the third floor to sleep up there with the other boys. Apparently for the last week he'd been sleeping on the sofa downstairs, because he didn't feel comfortable up there. Rod and Johnny were joking with him about it, and at first he didn't want to tell why, but afterward he did.

"I don't want you guys to think I'm afraid to be on my own or anything, but last night something woke me suddenly, and so I was getting up to see what it was, when my face turned to the window and I saw a hideous-looking face staring at me. Well, you know I'm not one to go crying about ghosts or anything, but I don't want some guy looking in at me sleeping either."

Well, what a shock it must have been for him. So it was decided, with a lot of good ribbing, that he'd return upstairs. Funny, no one had mentioned it to us.

Well, the noises never stopped. In fact, they just seemed to us more sinister than ever. So two days later, my husband and I moved out, amid Mother's groaning and reproaches.

My time came and I was finally delivered of a son, healthy, happy, and bawling. After leaving the hospital, my Mom was the first to call with the news that they had moved into a new house and I was to come over and show her the baby. So to Mother's house went, baby and all, that very night, and everyone loved Fred Jr.

It was while we were checking on the baby that Mom and I had a good chance to talk. She wasn't mad at us anymore, and she said so. She then showed us around her new house. "Isn't it marvelous, Gert, and there's no ghosts in it, either."

"What, Mom?" I asked.

"Oh, dear, your Father told me not to tell you. But I suppose it is all right to tell you now that the baby's come an' all."

"Tell me what, Mom? What about the ghosts?" I was all questions, and my ears were ready to hear anything, but not what she said.

"Well," she began, "when you left, we took over yours and Fred's bedroom. Honey, we started hearing what you and Fred heard. We were not aware that you were going through so much and hearing so many noises. Your Dad recognized it right off, as spirits living in the house. You see, our bedroom wasn't so noisy, but the third floor was terrible, and the boys couldn't stand it up there. Ed and Johnny saw all sorts of things, men mostly, and we tried to keep the knowledge from you, by making you think it was one of us who caused those noises. We were afraid you would be frightened and something would happen to the baby. We didn't want you to move out, though, as we were intending to get another place anyway, when the money situation was a little better for your Father.

"Anyway, we didn't know all about the ghosts. Then we had our doubts, at least until we took over your bedroom. But then we were sure. Your Father says there's no such thing as ghosts anyway. They had to be demons, because the living don't come back. Sometimes demons, however, try to make it appear as if they did. Realizing it was demons, your Father opened our big Bible, but at night the demons seemed to be rustling the pages of it. You could hear them turning in the night.

"So we told one of the Brothers of the Church about it. You remember Mr. — — . He lives down the street. Well, he told us about the house. He said that two brothers had lived there. They had had an argument on the third floor, and a fight broke out, one apparently knocking the other down the stairs, and then ran downstairs to his bedroom, that being the middle one where the children sleep. Well, the other got up and ran after him and found him at the sink, trying to wash or something, and struck him over the head from behind and killed him. There, that is why there's that big stain on the floor there in that room."

"Mom, that sounds just like what we heard," I said. "Are you sure."

"Yes, dear, I am sure that there was something in that house. I was sure the second I came into this one and that eerie feeling was gone. I knew."

"Well, your Father said it's so in the Bible, my dear."

"Yes, honey, we all know that."

Truth, they say, is stranger than fiction, and I know that my mind doesn't want to believe it, but that's just how it happened, and I know. That house is still there today, for anyone to visit and see. I'll show you where it is, and even if necessary take you to the spot, but there ain't no way I'm going back in there.

It Remains a Family
Mystery to This Day

David Peacock

David Peacock, *the author of this letter, is a creative marketing consultant with a background in advertising. He and his wife Suzanne are collectors of old furniture and old houses, as the letter shows. He collaborated with his wife on a book called* Old Oakville: A Character Study of the Town's Early Buildings and the Men Who Built Them *(1979) which features photographs by Patrick Knox.*

The Peacocks still live in the old Ontario community of Oakville where David has his office. But their first house, their dream home, was not as homey as it should have been. It seems they shared it with a spirit, perhaps a poltergeist....

28 March, 1989

Dear John:

Attached is the story of our encounter. It is surely not as dramatic or as frightening as many of the stories you must have come upon, but it was and is very real to us.

We bought the house in question in Oakville, Ont., in 1969. It is a three-storey, frame farmhouse, located on a wooded acre, surrounded by more recently built homes. We purchased the property from an elderly spinster who was the daughter of the original owner. Both of her parents had passed away in the house. Her father had grown quite senile, and her mother had been restricted to the first floor, as she was confined to a wheelchair for much of her later life.

My wife Suzanne and I thought the house would be perfect for us. It was far away from the city and it would be the ideal place in which to bring up our two young children. Fresh air. Tree houses. A creek. An attic. And a rambling old house. All the things that make for a storybook childhood. However, we had not counted on the presence that occupied the house.

We never actually saw a ghost, but we were all very much aware of there being someone else in the house. The children called the presence Grandpa — — — , after the original owner. Hundreds of times we would close a door, only to come back to find it open. Or we would open the curtains, only to return to find them drawn. Once we woke up to find a light fixture missing from the hall ceiling. Later we found it safely tucked into the corner of the cellar behind the furnace. I suppose this was just some sort of a prank.

One evening, after the children had been put to bed, Suzanne and I were sitting in the living room, reading the paper, when suddenly a cold chill ran over me, and the hair rose on the back of my neck. I looked up at my wife, who was sitting across the room, and I could see that she was experiencing a similar sensation. We felt as if the temperature of the room had plummeted thirty degrees. Nothing appeared. But someone was there.

Perhaps the most startling and the most difficult event to explain away occurred during our last winter in the house. The previous owner had left a large pine cupboard in the cellar. It was so large, in fact, that it had been lowered into the cellar as the house was being built. It was a very early piece and it was in excellent condition. It had its original buttermilk stain, inside and out, but unfortunately its exterior had been splashed with whitewash every time the cellar had been repainted.

In my spare time I began to sand the exterior of the cabinet to reveal its natural red pine finish. Over the course of the many weeks that it took to do the sanding, sanding dust accumulated and covered the floor around it. Then, in the midst of refinishing the cabinet, the entire family came down with the flu. At the same time, one of the old lead pipes in the cellar chose to spring a leak. The plumber said that he could not get around to fix it until the next day, so I had no alternative but to shut off the water overnight. Too sick to care, I left the cellar littered with sandpaper scraps which were floating in pools of water. The pools were red in colour from the sawdust that was coating the basement floor.

Feeling better the next morning, I went down to the cellar to turn on the water briefly. I was amazed to find the floor spotless. It had been wiped clean and dry. The pools or puddles were too large to evaporate by themselves. If they had evaporated, they would have left a residue of sawdust. In the middle of the room, next to the cupboard, sat a yellow plastic pail. It was full of water, reddish in colour. On the surface was the scum of red sawdust and a bright yellow sponge.

No one had been feeling well enough to rise from his or her bed to effect the clean-up. So it remains a family mystery to this day how the water got into the pail.

Not long after, we sold the house, and shortly thereafter moved elsewhere in Oakville. Although the presence in the house was not a malevolent one, the house itself never really felt as if it belonged to us.

Good luck,
David

8. Visionary Mysteries

The Beauties of Heaven

Saltatha

Saltatha was a brave of the Yellowknife tribe and the guide and companion of the explorer Warburton Pike (1861-1915), the adventurer and author of an account of their travels across the Northwest Territories. The account is called The Barren Ground of Northern Canada (London, 1892).

Saltatha was appreciative of the land of the North and wise in the traditions of his Dogrib people. Today the Dogribs and other Athapascan groups in the southwestern Arctic are known collectively as the Dene People. Try as he might Saltatha could not imagine how the Heaven promised to the Christians could be more beautiful than the Barren Ground inhabited by his people.

TO THE MAN who is not a lover of Nature in all her moods the Barren Ground must always be a howling, desolate wilderness; but for my part, I can understand the feeling that prompted Saltatha's answer to the worthy priest, who was explaining to him the beauties of Heaven:

"My father, you have spoken well; you have told me that Heaven is very beautiful; tell me now one thing more. Is it more beautiful than the country of the musk-ox in summer, when sometimes the mist blows over the lakes, and sometimes the water is blue, and the loons cry very often? That is beautiful; and if Heaven is still more beautiful, my heart will be glad, and I shall be content to rest there till I am very old."

258

White Man's Heaven

Paul Kane

*P*aul Kane (1810-1871), the explorer and artist, travel-ling between Fort Edmonton and Fort Pitt, in present-day Alberta, spent the night of 13 Jan. 1848 at a Cree encampment of forty lodges. He described the settlement and the experience in Wander-ings of an Artist among the Indians of North America (1859). *Kane recalled that he devoted much of the evening conversing with the local chief, Broken Arm, who was amused that the Christian missionaries among the Cree failed to agree among themselves about "the only true road to heaven."*

HE THEN TOLD US that there was a tradition in his tribe of one of them having become a Christian, and was very good, and did all that he ought; and that when he died he was taken up to the white man's heaven, where everything was very good and very beautiful, and all were happy amongst their friends and relatives who had gone before them, and where they had everything that the white man loves and longs for; but the Indian could not share their joy and pleasure, for all was strange to him, and he met none of the spirits of his ancestors, and there was none to welcome him, no hunting nor fishing, nor any of those joys in which he used to delight, and his spirit grew sad. Then the Great Manitou called him, and asked him, "Why art thou sad in this beautiful heaven which I have made for your house and happiness?" and the Indian told him that he sighed for the company of the spirits of his relations, and that he felt lone and sorrowful. So the Great Manitou told him that he could not send him to the Indian heaven, as he had, whilst on earth, chosen this one, but that as he had been a very good man, he would send him back to earth again, and give him another chance.

A Christmas Vision

Catharine Parr Traill

What could be more Canadian than the Aurora
Borealis at Christmas?

*The pioneer writer Catharine Parr Traill (1802-1899) was ecstatic
when she beheld the Aurora Borealis. She first set eyes on the
Northern Lights — the spectacular display of dancing lights which
illuminate like fairies' lamps the dark norther skies — during in the
winter of 1833. The sight so awed and humbled her that she was
moved to compose what she called "a Christmas vision."*

*Mrs. Traill and her husband Lieutenant Thomas Traill were at
the time a backwoods farming couple working land along the
Otonabee River near Lakefield, Upper Canada, present-day
Ontario. It was here that she wrote her most famous book* The
Backwoods of Canada *(1836) which includes here brief but cele-
brated "vision."*

COMING HOME ONE NIGHT last Christmas from the house of a
friend, I was struck by a splendid pillar of pale greenish light in the
west: it rose to some height above the dark line of pines that
crowned the opposite shores of the Otanabee, and illumined the
heavens on either side with a chaste pure light, such as the moon
gives in her rise and setting; it was not quite pyramidical, though
much broader at the base than at its highest point; it gradually
faded, till a faint white glimmering light alone marked where its

place had been, and even that disappeared after some half hour's time. It was so fair and lovely a vision I was grieved when it vanished into thin air, and could have cheated fancy into the belief that it was the robe of some bright visitor from another and a better world; — imagination apart, could it be a phosphoric exhalation from some of our many swamps or inland lakes, or was it at all connected with the aurora that is so frequently seen in our skies?

The Vision of the Hill of Bears

Anna Brownell Jameson

Anna Brownell Jameson was an inveterate traveller
and an incisive commentator on life in Upper Canada. The quick-
witted, Irish-born lady had no time for the round of duties that so
engrossed her husband, a judge in the colonial administration at
York, as Toronto was called in the early 19th century. So she lived
with him in York for only eight months before leaving to return to
high society elsewhere. Rather than idle away the days and nights in
domestic duties or the social whirl, she engrossed herself in studies
throughout the winter, and during the summer she rode across the
southern part of the future Province of Ontario. Her sole companion was an edition of the works of Goethe in the original German.

Mrs. Jameson's account of her studies and travels is called Winter
Studies and Summer Rambles in Canada (1838). It is a masterwork
of extraordinary detail and outrageous opinion. While it is true
that she spent the winter "in studies," she did not really spend the
summer in "rambles," for she travelled with a purpose, as befitting a
serious student of human affairs and the world of ideas. These two
interests may be seen to coalesce in one passage in her book. It is a
visionary passage, and it was inspired by Mrs. Jameson's surprising
insight into time and humanity's eternal progress. The visionary
experience, the inspiration, or the enlightenment occurred in July
1837 on the Hill of Bears, a natural elevation of land a few miles
outside the town of London. The passage appears below.

"One hundred and forty-six years later, in the comfort of my car,

*I drove to see 'Bear Hill' to see for myself." So wrote the pho-
tographic historical Virgil Martin in his illustrated study* Changing
Landscapes of Southern Ontario *(1988). "Initially, I felt a sense of
disappointment — the hill and road crossing it were still there, but
the view did not meet my expectations. Communications towers
dominate the top of the hill. Its sides have been deeply gouged by
gravel pits. Around its base, farming is giving way to urban sprawl
as the city expands southwards. Gradually, it occurred to me that I
was too late — perhaps 50 or 100 years too late. The future that
Mrs. Jameson had seen so vividly was now mostly history. As I
continued south toward St. Thomas, however, I had to stop as a
mile-long freight train roared past, and then her vision did not seem
quite so dated."*

ON REACHING THE SUMMIT of this hill, I found myself on the
highest land I had yet stood upon in Canada, with the exception of
Queenston heights. I stopped the horses and looked around, and
on every side, far and near — east, west, north, and south, it was all
forest — a boundless sea of forest, within whose leafy recesses lay
hidden as infinite a variety of life and movement as within the
depths of the ocean; and it reposed in the noontide so still and so
vast! *Here* the bright sunshine rested on it in floods of golden light;
there cloud-shadows sped over its bosom, just like the effects I
remember to have seen on the Atlantic; and here and there rose
wreaths of white smoke from the new clearings, which collected
into little silver clouds, and hung suspended in the quiet air.

I gazed and meditated till, by a process like that of the Arabian
sorcerer of old, the present fell like a film from my eyes: the future
was before me, with its towns and cities, fields of waving grain,
green lawns and villas, and churches and temples turret-crowned;
and meadows tracked by the frequent footpath; and railroads,
with trains of rich merchandise streaming along: — for all this *will
be! Will be? It is* already in the sign of Him who hath ordained it,
and for whom there is no past nor future: though I cannot behold it
with my bodily vision, even *now* it is.

But is *that* NOW better than *this* present NOW? When these
forests, with all their solemn depth of shade and multitudinous life

have fallen beneath the axe — when the wolf and bear, and deer are driven from their native converts, and all this infinitude of animal and vegetable being has made way for restless, erring, suffering humanity — will it then be better? *Better* — I know not; but surely it will be *well* and right in His eyes who has ordained that thus the course of things shall run. Those who see nothing in civilised life but its complicated cares, mistakes, vanities, and miseries, may doubt this — or despair. For myself and you too, my friend; we are of those who believe and hope; who behold in progressive civilization progressive happiness, progressive approximation to nature and to nature's God: for are we not in his hands? — and all that He does is good.

Contemplations such as these were in my mind as we descended the Hill of Bears, and proceeded through a beautiful plain....

A Singular and Beautiful Dream

Benjamin Fish Austin

"Dreams may be classed among the most curious and interesting phenomena of our mental life," declared Benjamin Fish Austin in his tome Glimpses of the Unseen (Toronto and Brantford: Bradley-Garretson Company, 1898). Devoting a chapter to the discussion of dream life, Austin suggested that dreams are akin to visions, to revelations, to telepathic impressions, and to instances of clairvoyance. They are a form of new knowledge about ourselves and nature and eternal values.

"A Singular and Beautiful Dream" is the title that austin gave to the description of one of his own dreams or visions. His description is exceedingly lyrical — even literary — a poem in prose. Austin placed the imagery of the dream in a personal context when he wrote about the death of their young child in these words:

"Some months after the 'Reaper' had gathered the fairest flower in our home garden, who seemed to us the brightest, most beautiful, and most loving child God ever gave to an earthly home, our Kathleen of two and one-half years, it was a frequent subject of conversation between my wife and myself why we never dreamed of her, and the desire was frequently expressed by my wife, and as often felt by myself that we might once again behold her, if only in a dream."

ONE EVENING I HAD the following singular and, to me, most beautiful and enjoyable dream. I was riding in a long, narrow boat, which glided noiselessly along a glassy, winding river, stretched like a silk ribbon between green and flowery banks, in a land of groves and forests. In the boat behind me sat a friend, whose name and face I do not recall, who was noiselessly propelling with a paddle our little craft. No word was spoken, the hour being given by mutual consent to feasting our eyes upon the beauty of the ever-changing scene around us and enjoying the music of the beautiful birds, which seemed the only inhabitants of this paradise. The scenery grew more and more beautiful, the music of the birds sweeter, as our little craft swept on along the serpentine river, in and out of the shadows. Beautiful ferns lined the river bank and dipped their tips occasionally into the smooth river at the passing zephyr, and from them fell with musical cadence drops of water transformed by the moving sunlight into liquid gold. Soon our little craft ran noiselessly upon a shelving beach and we leaped to earth to view the scene before us. No sooner had I touched the bank than my eye caught upon a tree before me, and about fifteen or twenty feet from the ground, a small, bright object, glowing with innumerable colours, resting on an upper branch of the tree and swinging with it in the gentle breeze. From the flutter of tiny wings I could see it was a living creature. From the instant I saw it I could see nothing else. It filled my thought, drew me as a magnet, and instantly I started for the tree, seized with a strong desire to possess this creature or view it at nearer vision. Each step its fascinating power increased as it appeared to take on new beauty and power of enchantment, so that by the time I reached the tree I was impelled with a reckless daring to brave any necessary danger to get near the glorious creature that I persuaded myself was awaiting my approach. Drawing near the tree I realized there was no limb of the tree low enough for me to grasp, and so circling around to another tree that stood close by, and without losing sight for an instant of the object of my quest, I grasped a lower limb, then another and another, and swung myself to the tree, and up, up, up, with increasing speed and agility I climbed, hand over hand, until in far less time than I can tell it I was beside it in the tree top. As I drew near in my climbing I remembered I could see it more and more distinctly lying placidly upon a limb, its bright little eyes watching me and its gauze-like wings extended over its body and vibrating gently. I remembered also that it did not strike me as at all strange that it should thus lie perfectly quiet and await my approach. The thought grew upon me from the instant I beheld it that for this purpose I had journeyed to this beautiful land, and that this creature awaited me as truly as I sought it. I was now beside it — hands seizing the two limbs on either side, my face within a few inches of the creature and gazing with such mingled delight and admiration upon it as no words can express. I began at once a most passionate questioning as to its name and nature, and poured forth in language that seemed, till then, beyond me, my love and devotion. Then occurred a strange transformation. For while swaying in the tree top and uttering the most impassioned language to this bright and beautiful creature of my dream, suddenly the gauze-like wings extended, lengthening and widening before my vision until they seemed large enough to cover an adult human body; and, with a tremulous, curling motion the wings lifted themselves up into vapour and disappeared, and beneath them was a face and form of a maiden that appeared half child and half woman, so perfectly were the child-like features blended with the womanly face, and over that face and form there was a radiant beauty such as only the imagination can paint, and that once in a life time. Face to face were we, her long locks of golden hair glittering in the sunshine and streaming in the breeze, her figure one over which the artist, the sculptor and poet might dream a lifetime away; and her voice — I heard it at last — and the music of it will follow me to the last hour of life.... I should fail utterly to give the reader the faintest description of the bliss of that moment by any attempted description. And it was but a moment — for instantly the tree broke and I found myself on the ground again, and the vision had departed.

Three Experiences of the Strangely Familiar

John Buchan

Memory Hold-the-Door *is the title that John Buchan, Lord Tweedsmuir, Governor General of Canada, chose for his volume of memoirs. Buchan wrote the volume in its entirety at Rideau Hall in Ottawa, and it was published by Hodder and Stoughton in London in June 1940. The author did not live to see it in print, however, for he succumbed to a cerebral thrombosis at Rideau Hall and died at the Royal Victoria Hospital in Montreal on 11 Feb. 1940.*

Memory Hold-the-Door *was the favourite book of John F. Kennedy. The American President knew the book under the American title* Pilgrim's Way. *It is one of more than fifty books written by Buchan; a number of his novels and collections of stories are concerned with international conspiracies or supernatural mysteries.*

It does not come as a surprise to learn that Buchan was quite "canny" when it came to unusual experiences. In his memoirs he recorded three "strangely familiar" experiences that had occurred to him over the course of sixty-four years. The first instance of déjà-vu happened in the early 1900s in the African bush; the second, in the Highlands before the Great War; the third, some years later in the office of the Lord High Commissioner in Edinburgh.

On all three occasions Buchan was given "transport" to another age. Was his great gift for imaginative story-telling given full play and working unbidden? Had he once lived at these times and in these places? We may never know the answers to these questions....

THERE ARE NO MORE comfortable words in the language than Peace
and Joy, which Richard Hooker has conjoined in a famous sen-
tence. Peace is that state in which fear of any kind is unknown.
But Joy is a positive thing; in Joy one does not only feel secure, but
something goes out from oneself to the universe, a warm possessive
effluence of love. There may be Peace with Joy, and Joy without
Peace, but the two combined make Happiness. It was Happiness
that I knew in those rare moments. The world was a place of
inexhaustible beauty, but still more it was the husk of something
infinite, ineffable and immortal, in very truth the garment of God.

I had one experience in South Africa which has since been twice
repeated. We all know the sensation of doing something or seeing
something which is strangely familiar as if we had done
or seen it before. The usual explanation is that we have had the
experience in our dreams. My version is slightly different. I find
myself in some scene which I cannot have visited before, and which
yet is perfectly familiar; I know that it was the stage of an action in
which I once took part, and am about to take part again; I await
developments with an almost unbearable sense of anticipation.
And then nothing happens; something appears which breaks the
spell....

I was in the bushveld going from one native village to another
by a road which was just passable, and which followed a sedgy
stream. I was walking ahead, and my mules and boys were about
two hundred yards behind. Suddenly I found myself in a glade
where the brook opened into a wide clear pool. The place was like
a little amphitheatre; on my left was a thicket of wild bananas, with
beyond them a big baobab, and on my right a clump of tall
stinkwood trees laced together with creepers. The floor was red
earth with tufts of coarse grass, and on the edge of the pool was a
mat of ferns.... I stopped in my tracks, for I had been here before.
Something had happened to me here, and was about to happen
again; something had come out of the banana thicket. I knew the
place as well as I knew my own doorstep. I was not exactly
frightened, only curious and excited, and I stood waiting with my
heart in my mouth. And then the spell broke, for my mules
clattered up behind me.

Twice since I have had the same feeling. Just before the War I was staying at a house on a sea-loch in the West Highlands. I was about to stalk a distant beat of the forest which could only be reached by sea, so it was arranged that after dinner I should go down to the yacht and sleep there so as to be ready to start very early next morning. A boatman ferried me out to the yacht. I had dressed for dinner in a kilt, and suddenly in the midst of the shadowy loch I got a glimpse of my shoe-buckles protruding from beneath my ulster.... I was switched back two centuries. I had been here before on these moonlit waters in this circle of dark mountains. I had been rowed out to a ship by a boatman who muffled his strokes, for danger was everywhere. Something fateful awaited me when I got aboard that hull which loomed above the heathery islet.... I sat with my hands clenched in suspense. I leaped at the ship's ladder as if I had been a castaway.... But nothing happened; only the skipper was waiting to offer me a whisky-and-soda!

The third occasion was during my first year of office as Lord High Commissioner in Edinburgh. I had gone out to read in the garden of Holyroodhouse and had chosen a spot close to a shrubbery, where one looked over a piece of unshorn lawn to the old pile. It was a balmy May morning, with the air blowing free from the Firth and great cloud galleons cruising in the sky. The grass in front of me was starred with daisies, and a little further on were blossoming fruit trees, and then the *tourelles* of the most ancient part of the Palace. There seemed to be a flight of white doves somewhere near, but they may have been seagulls from Musselburgh.... I lifted my eyes from my book and was suddenly transported to another age. I was in France at some château of Touraine. I was looking at the marguerites and apple blossom of which Ronsard sang. Once this stage had been set for high drama in which I had had a share, and now it was set again. In a moment I should be summond.... But alas! it was only an aide-de-camp come to remind me that seventy provosts and bailies were invited to luncheon!

Experiences Recalled in Brazil

P.K. Page

The poet and diarist P.K. Page recalled two unusual experiences that occurred to her in South America in her Brazilian Journal *(Toronto: Lester & Orpen Dennys, 1987). Both are described in the entry for 24 May 1958. The first experience derives from the misperception of some metal contraption; the second experience derives from the perception of something less physical.*

Brazilian Journal *is remarkable literary work in that it records in impressionistic detail the colours and configurations of the landscape and the people of Brazil, the country in which Page lived for two years. She was the wife of the Canadian Ambassador.*

AND THAT REMINDS ME of an experience I had at Volta Redonda. We were standing outside the mill, the men talking and I not listening, when I saw, moving on its course through the grass, a metal — what shall I call it? Animal? It was not, of course, like an animal, having neither head nor legs nor feet nor the usual animal characteristics. It was about a foot long and moving as metal moves, with that kind of atomic weight. It was some little time before my mind rejected the concept. And I felt a certain *saudade* for the metal animal when I realized it was merely some man-made mechanical object, moving on a track. Strangely, during the period of thinking of it as a metal animal, there was nothing foreign in the idea. I accepted it as naturally as I would have accepted a rabbit or a bird.

The experience was akin to the time when, in a room with one other person, I gradually became aware of a third being with us. Nothing changed with the awareness of that third person, who sat in a chair on the other side of the room and was as closely with us as I was, myself. It was only when the third person left that the full realization of its having been there broke upon me. Although in no sense unnatural or unknown, it had no sex and no form. It was an entity as natural to me and as much a part of me as was the man who was with me at the time. And with its going there was a kind of absence, an emptiness in a trinity that had had a totality. A sense of loss. I felt a similar loss when the metal animal became a metal object.

Visit to the "Twilight Zone" Truck Stop

Phyllis Griffiths

"Visit to the 'Twilight Zone' Truck Stop" is my title for this account of an eerie experience. The experience itself recalls the decade of the Sixties in such detail that the experience might well have been an episode on Rod Serling's long-running "Twilight Zone" television series.

Yet the event that sparked the shared experience occurred not in the 1960s but in the year 1978. It happened to Phyllis and Don Griffiths. Mrs. Griffiths sent me this account after she heard me talk about "extraordinary experiences" on CFAX Radio in Victoria, B.C.

"I have a story that you may wish to add to your files of strange experiences," she explained in her letter of 27 March 1989. "My husband and I refer to this as our 'twilight zone' visit. If it was a hallucination, then it is one that we both shared. The story is enclosed with this letter."

Here it is. Sky Chief indeed!

IN MARCH OF 1978, we were returning to our home in Lethbridge, Alberta, after spending Easter Week visiting relatives on Vancouver Island. This was a trip that the family had taken many times before, and the route we usually followed was first along Highway 1, the northern route, and then south from Calgary. This time, we decided, just for a change of pace, that we would take Highway 3. We had not taken this southern highway before when returning from Vancouver Island.

As usual with return trips, this one was to be driven straight through. But the route was unfamiliar to us, and the southern route was taking much longer than the familiar northern route. Our two young sons slept cuddled up to their dog in the back seat of the family station wagon. My husband and I drove through the night and into the early hours of the next day without a rest.

At two-thirty in the morning we drove into the town of Creston, B.C. The only place open at that early hour was a tiny service station, where we stopped to refuel the car. Tired as we were, we had no choice but to drive on. There was no money for a motel room, nor were there camp-grounds in the area.

Relief was found about half way between Creston and Cranbrook. It took the form of an old Texaco Truck Stop which we were approaching. It was on the north side of the highway, Highway 3, but it was located in the middle of nowhere. It was a totally unexpected sight, but a very welcome one.

The Texaco Truck Stop had an unusual location, but it also had an unusual appearance. The large old Texaco sign was a solid sign lit by spotlights mounted on top and focused on the painted surface. The gas pumps were also old-fashioned looking, and they dispensed good old Fire Chief and Sky Chief gasoline. There was a diesel pump at the side, but no pumps for unleaded gas were in sight.

The station itself looked as if it had not changed one bit since the year 1960. Even the semi-trailer unit, idling in the truck lot to one side, was of an early Sixties vintage. Everything looked strange indeed. Was this a scene from Rod Serling's "Twilight Zone"?

Nevertheless, my husband and I, tired and thirsty as we were, drove in, pulled up under the pump lights, got out of the car, and locked it. We left our two children asleep in the back seat of the car.

The inside of the restaurant matched the outside to such a degree that everything felt spooky. The interior was frozen in time in the year 1960, yet the decor showed none of the wear and tear that would be found after nearly twenty years of use. We could see nothing that was out of place. There was nothing new or modern about the appointments or the personnel. The waitress was dressed in period clothes, as was the driver of the semi parked in the yard.

The price of the coffee was all of a dime a cup, and a placard advertised the price of a piece of pie as a quarter. The music blaring from the radio dated from the late Fifties, and the d.j. introduced the songs without once referring to the period or to any item of news. No calendar was in sight. But the coffee was good and was appreciated. We felt uneasy in the place, so we were not unhappy to be out and on the road for home once more.

We had driven this stretch of Highway 3 on previous occasions, but it had always been in daylight and heading in the other direction. We had never taken it at night or while returning from Vancouver Island. We had memorized the location of every truck stop on Highway 3, and we thought we knew the location of all the truck stops that were open twenty-four hours a day on this highway as well. But never before had we seen this one. Nor did we ever see it again.

The visit left us with an eerie feeling. Try as we might, we could not shake it off. We asked those of our friends and relatives who occasionally travelled that stretch of Highway 3 if they were familiar with the old Texaco Truck Stop. No one knew anything about it. Everyone was of the opinion that there was no such establishment between Lethbridge, Alta., and Hope, B.C.

The only thing that we could do was re-drive that stretch of highway in broad daylight and watch out for it to see for ourselves whether or not the place really existed. Some months later we did just that. We retravelled Highway 3. Mid-way between Cranbrook and Creston, on the north side of the road, we found the place where we had stopped that eerie night.

The building had long been boarded over. The presence of the pumps was marked only by their cement bases. The same was true of the Texaco signpost. The yard where the semi had sat was overgrown with bush and with aspen poplars which were twenty or more feet in height. It had been many years since that particular service station had pumped gas or served coffee at a dime a cup. But my husband and I know that the old Truck Stop had been open for business that lonely March night in 1978, when a weary family had stopped — in need of a cup of coffee and a bit of rest.

9. Alien Mysteries

The Whole Subject of Saucers Is Classified

Wilbert B. Smith

There are great numbers of people around the world who hold the following views:

Flying saucers (as UFOs were called in the late 1940s and early 1950s) are advanced spacecraft of extraterrestrial origin; in the distant past, and during the last four decades, some of these craft landed or crashlanded on Earth; the U.S. Government has recovered sections of some of these craft as well as the bodies of some of their occupants but has sequestered all the evidence, routinely denying all knowledge of the existence of UFOs and their alien occupants.

One prominent exponent of "the UFO recovery conspiracy theory" is Stanton T. Friedman. The American-born nuclear scientist has for some years been a resident of Fredericton, N.B. His specialty is writing and speaking on the subject of the massive cover-up of evidence of the extraterrestrial origin of UFOs, and his pet phrase to refer to the conspiracy theory is "Cosmic Watergate."

The country's leading UFO enthusiast throughout the 1950s was Wilbert B. Smith (1910-1962). Smith was not a proponent of the UFO recovery theory per se, *but in his later years he believed that he was in communication through a medium with alien intelligences from Venus which operated UFOs. Smith was an electrical engineer who was employed by the Department of Transport in Ottawa. At the time of his death he was Superintendent of Radio Regulations Engineering.*

DOT officials had granted Smith permission to conduct private research into the flight patterns of flying saucers as an adjunct to his official duties. To this end, in 1953, Smith established a "sighting station" at Shirleys Bay, west of Ottawa.

Smith came to the conclusion that the peculiar flight patterns reported for flying saucers could be explained by reference to some form of magnetic and gravitational force or action. He was interviewed at some length about his views and findings by Frank Edwards, the American broadcaster and journalist. In his lively book Flying Saucers: Serious Business (1966), Edwards devoted two chapters to Smith and his work.

One of Smith's revelations is a matter of interest in the late 1980s. This is the record he kept of a "hush-hush" conversation he had with a "top" U.S. Government adviser. This occurred in 1950, during one of Smith's official visits to Washington. The interview was arranged through the good offices of a Lieut.-Col. Bremner of the Canadian Embassy in Washington. Smith returned to Ottawa with anecdotal evidence that flying saucers were real and that portions of them had been recovered.

The handwritten notes Smith kept of this conversation appear below and are reproduced in their entirety. Smith summarized their contents some months later in a memorandum, directed to the Controller of Telecommunications, dated 21 Nov. 1950. Here is what he wrote in that document:

a. Matter is the most highly classified subject in the United States Government, rating higher even than the H-bomb.

b. Flying saucers exist.

c. Their modus operandi is unknown but concentrated effort is being made by a small group headed by Doctor Vannevar Bush.

d. The entire matter is considered by the United States authorities to be of tremendous significance.

Robert I. Sarbacher was the scientist who supplied Smith with this information in Washington. Dr. Sarbacher was then a consultant to the U.S. Government's Research and Development Board and later President and Chairman of the Board of the Washington

Institute of Technology. Sarbacher was still alive in 1983. Replying to a letter from a UFO researcher, he stated that although he had no personal association with any of the people concerned with "recovered flying saucers," he believed that John von Neumann, Vannevar Bush, and Robert Oppenheimer were among the scientists directly involved.

In 1987, some documents came to light which, according to Stanton T. Friedman and other UFO researchers, prove that a "top secret" committee of scientists met regularly from 1947 to 1950 to advise U.S. President Harry Truman on the implications of the recovered materials. This group was called Operation Majestic-12. It was so secret it was classified as "above top secret."

Could the Majestic group be the one of which Sarbacher had heard? The whole business is rather murky. Philip J. Klass and other skeptics regard the Majestic documents — a series of official-looking letters in photocopy form (the originals cannot be located) — as crude forgeries, the whole affair being nothing more than an elaborate hoax.

It is possible that Smith's handwritten notes shed some light on both flying saucers and Operation Majestic-12. It is equally possible that these notes supplied the forgers and hoaxers, if such they be, with additional "background cover." Whichever is the case, the notes were obtained from Smith's widow by the Ottawa-based author and researcher Arthur Bray, and were reproduced in facsimile form in the appendix to Above Top Secret: The Worldwide U.F.O. Cover-up *(Toronto: Macmillan of Canada, 1988). This is a highly readable but also highly partisan tome written by Timothy Good, a British broadcaster, lecturer, and professional musician. Good has travelled widely, amassing a great deal of evidence — all of it circumstantial — to show "that a wide-scale cover-up is in operation." Good dedicated his book to Donald Keyhoe, retired U.S. Army major, one-time Director of the National Investigations Committee on Aerial Phenomena (NICAP).*

"Scully's book," mentioned below, is a reference to a bestseller called Behind the Flying Saucers *(1950). In this breathlessly written study of the phenomenon, which then had the virtue of being novel, the columnist Frank Scully argued that the U.S. Government was withholding evidence of four "recoveries" of flying saucers.*

Sept. 15 - 1950
Notes on interview through Lieut.-Col. Bremner with Dr. Robert I.
Sarbacher.

WBS: I am doing some work on the collapse of the earth's magnetic
field as a source of energy, and I think our work may have a bearing
on the flying saucers.
RIS: What do you want to know.
WBS: I have read Scully's book on the saucers and would like to
know how much of it is true.
RIS: The facts reported in the book are substantially correct.
WBS: Then the saucers do exist?
RIS: Yes: they exist.
WBS: Do they operate as Scully suggests on magnetic principles?
RIS: We have not been able to duplicate their performance.
WBS: Do they come from some other planet?
RIS: All we know is, we didn't make them, and it's pretty certain
they didn't originate on the earth.
WBS: I understand the whole subject of saucers is classified.
RIS: Yes, it is classified two points higher even than the H-bomb. In
fact it is the most highly classified subject in the U.S. Government at
the present time.
WBS: May I ask the reason for the classification?
RIS: You may ask, but I can't tell you.
WBS: Is there any way in which I can get more information,
particularly as it might fit in with our own work?
RIS: I suppose you could be cleared through your own Defense
Department and I am pretty sure arrangements could be made to
exchange information. If you have anything to contribute, we
would be glad to talk it over, but I can't give you any more at the
present time.

Note: The above is written out from memory following the interview. I have tried to keep it as nearly verbatim as possible.

An Object Resembling a Star

P.L. Lewis

Star-like objects, described as "flying saucers," were observed flying over the town of Port Hope, east of Oshawa, Ont. Observed along with them were filaments of a gossamer-like substance which was likened to "spiders' threads." In UFO literature this material is known as "angel hair."

The description here of "an object resembling a star" and "spiders' threads" comes from a statement made by P.L. Lewis of Port Hope. Lewis was a personal friend of P.R. Bishop who included it in his own report called "Cobwebs or Flying Saucers" in the journal Weather, *4:121-122, 1949.*

Bishop was concerned with the "cobwebs," not the flying saucers. In reference to the latter, he added: "No one else seems to have seen them on this occasion, but perhaps Mr. Lewis was the only one to be taking horizontal, post-prandial repose at that time."

The statement is reproduced from Handbook of Unusual Natural Phenomena *(Glen Arm, Md.: The Sourcebook Project, 1978) compiled by William R. Corliss.*

SUNDAY, SEPTEMBER 26, 1948. *Port Hope, Ontario.* This day was warm and the sky cloudless. We had had dinner in the garden and I was lying on my back on the lawn, my head just in the shade of the house, when I was startled to see an object resembling a star moving rapidly across the sky. The time was 2 o'clock Eastern Standard Time.

At first it was easy to imagine that recent reports of "Flying Saucers" had not been exaggerated.

More of these objects came sailing into view over the ridge of the house, only to disappear when nearly overhead. With field glasses I was able to see that each was approximately spherical, the centre being rather brighter than the edges. The glasses also showed quite a number at such heights that they were invisible to the naked eye.

With only a gull flying in the sky for comparison, I should estimate the elevation of the lower objects to be about 300 ft. and the higher ones 2,000 ft.; the size was about one foot in diameter and the speed about 50 m.p.h., in a direction SW to NE.

Also visible every now and then were long threads, apparently from spiders. Some of these were seen to reflect the light over a length of three or four yards, but any one piece may of course have been longer. Each was more or less horizontal, moving at right angles to its length. In one case an elongated tangled mass of these gave the appearance of a frayed silken cord.

These threads appeared only in the lower levels.

It is reasonably certain that these objects were balls of spiders' threads, possibly with thistledown entangled in them, but the way in which they caught the rays of the sun and shone so brightly was very striking.

P.L. Lewis

They Belong to a Different Life Wave

Howard Brenton MacDonald

Not very long ago Dwight Whalen, a friend and fellow researcher who lives in the interesting community of Niagara Falls, Ont., presented me with a booklet he knew I would enjoy reading and owning. The booklet is only thirty-two pages in length but it is attractively printed and smoothly written, and he knew the subject would excite me as much as it delighted him. Dwight haunts used bookstores, and in one such establishment in the Niagara Pensinula, he happened upon this booklet. It was attractively priced at one dollar. Needless to say he bought it with my needs and interests in mind. I must remember to reimburse him the sum of one dollar. It is money well invested, as they say.

I know nothing about the booklet and its author except for the information that appears on the title page:

**FLYING SAUCERS
AND
SPACE SHIPS**

AND THE UNKNOWN PLANETS
FROM WHENCE THEY COME

By Dr. Howard Brenton MacDonald, F.R.G.S.

The initials F.R.G.S. stand for Fellow, Royal Geographical Society. The copyright page supplies a few more facts. It says that the book-

let was printed by Provoker Press, St. Catharines, Ont., and was copyright in 1970.

It seems that Dr. MacDonald's text is the product of sessions with the pendulum. Neither Dwight nor I has set eyes on the booklet "The Pendulum Speaks," which is mentioned below, so we remain in the dark concerning its operation. Yet it is possible that the pendulum in question swings over an alphabet, spelling out words in the same fashion that the planchette seeks out and spells out words printed on the Ouija board. It is an exasperating and time-consuming way to "take dictation," but the results are invariably revelatory.

Revelation is perhaps the right word to use for Dr. MacDonald's account of the two types of space vehicles from the two planets, Jokly and Millokkom. Sections of revelation are interspersed with sections of commentary. I have reproduced the revelatory passages. Perhaps one-quarter of the contents of the booklet appear below. In a section not reproduced here, Dr. MacDonald notes that the standard interpetation of sightings of UFOs is that they signify the End of the World, they mark the start of a New Age, they post a warning "to us humans not to use the Atomic Bomb any more," or they monitor our progress in "the field of atomic fission" so that humans will not go "too far." He goes on to suggest there is a far-simpler explanation — a non-catastrophic one. "Instead," he writes, "my spirit collaborators offered a more simple explanation, which is that the great Space Ships from Millokkom are merely coming here on sightseeing cruises!"

Exclusive Spirit Revelations

AS YET, I have not actually seen a Flying Saucer or a Space Ship; but I have received some exclusive information concerning them.

On the night of May 3, 1952, I discovered, quite by accident, that I possessed the gift of radi-esthesia, or the sensitivity to radiations, and could operate a pendulum. (The complete story of this discovery and my subsequent research in many unknown fields of radi-esthesia is told in my booklet, "The Pendulum Speaks.") And during the course of my early communications with the Spirit

World I learned some interesting and exclusive facts about both Flying Saucers and Space Ships and the heretofore unknown planets from whence they come. It took me about five months to receive the entire story, word for word, thru the pendulum; but the results were worth every effort. The spirit people who supplied me with this information were Penjy, my pendulum guide; William Brenton, my late cousin, who was an amateur pilot during his Earth Life; and my Mother. Frankly, I do not know whether these revelations are 100% true or not. They seem logical to me. Judge for Yourself. I do believe they are genuine spirit messages from the Higher Planes of Life.

What Are Flying Saucers?

The first questions I asked my spirit loved-ones were: What are the Flying Saucers? How do they operate? Where do they come from?
    In answer to the first two, I was told the following:
    The Flying Saucers are genuine flying machines of a revolutionary type not known on Earth. They range in size from little one approximately 25 feet in diameter, to the larger ones of 200 and 300 feet across. They are made of a metal unknown to us. Definitely, they are physical objects and not "ectoplasmic ghost animals" or etheric materializations, as, perhaps, some other types of aerial phenomena may be. They are wonderful pieces of mechanism and incorporate in their design principles of aerodynamic engineering beyond our ken as yet. And they are run by a kind of "condensed energy" which not only can propel them forwards at unlimited velocity, but which can also "reverse gravity" and allow them to rise straight up from the Earth's gravitational zone into interstellar space, where they can, if they desire, join one of the cosmic currents which flow between the various heavenly bodies, and ride on this "magnetic river" to their home star or anywhere they desire.

The Planet from Whence They Came

The answer to my third question came as a distinct surprise to me. I had assumed my spirit collaborators would mention Mars or Venus; but instead the pendulum spelled out:

J-O-K-L-Y

I had never heard of such a planet before, but my guides assured me that this was its correct name. It is a most unusual place, they say. It is a globe, slightly smaller than our Earth, located in the heavens about as far away from us as the Moon. Curiously enough, it is constantly surrounded by a blanket of heavy clouds which make it invisible form the Earth. Thus our astronomers cannot see Jokly, or any evidence of it; nor can the inhabitants of Jokly see us.

Another strange thing is that because of this layer of clouds the rays of the sun cannot reach it. Therefore Jokly has no sunlight; but certain of the rocks scattered along its surface are radioactive and give out an effulgence of their own which serves to illuminate the planet itself. Physically speaking there are no great mountain ranges or continents or oceans of Jokly; merely one large land-mass dotted with rivers and lakes. But it is a fertile place, with abundant crops; which get their nutriment from the radiations of the rocks; and this energy is stored in the plants and furnishes vitality for the people in the food they eat. The Jokly-ites subsist entirely on this vitalized plant food, and always enjoy radiant health.

The inhabitants of Jokly are little people, only about 4 feet tall on the average. They are of dark reddish-brown skin, male and female, very similar to ourselves. They are a highly advanced race, possessing a technical knowledge far outdistancing our own, and having a social organization that is interesting. The populace is divided into a number of small nations, all at peace with each other. The governments of these different nations are essentially the same, consisting of an Aristocracy of the individuals best fitted to rule. There are no wars, no crime, and no poverty on Jokly. They have a language of their own, of course, but in addition a few of the Jokly-ites, the ones who ride the Flying Saucers, can speak a few words of our Earth tongues which, apparently, they have learned clairaudiently. There are modern cities and towns on this little planet, but no wheeled vehicles. For local transportation they use small flying saucers as we do auto-mobiles. Education is universal and comprehensive, and there is one religion for all the people, based on a belief in One God.

Giant Space Ships

So much for the Flying Saucers. Now for my revelations concerning the giant cigar-shaped Space Ships. These, my guides told me, do not come from Jokly, but from another unknown planet named: MILLOKKOM

According to my revelations, these Space Ships are wonderful machines. They run in size anywhere from a few hundred feet, up to 1,000 feet in length, and look very much like huge flying submarines. The big ones resemble ocean liners inside, being luxuriously furnished with staterooms, salons, dining halls, observation galleries, recreation rooms, propulsion chambers, fuel tanks, engine rooms, navigation stations, a master control cabin up front, and many other features designed for the comfort and happiness of the passengers. The ships are operated by a form of energy unknown on Earth. It is "something like" atomic power, only "more so" my guides declared. Perhaps it is the Vril known to the Atlanteans. But whatever it is, it can run these huge, wingless monsters in an incredible manner.

Marvelous Millokkom

In regard to Millokkom itself, my spirit friends assure me that it is one of the most marvelous planets in the cosmos. In size it is a little larger than the Earth, and is located a little further away than the Moon. It is plainly visible from here; but because of peculiar atmospheric conditions and cosmic rays we do not realize it is a planet at all. Astronomers may smile at this statement, but they are the first to admit that they don't know **ALL** the facts about the Heavens; so, perhaps, there is such a planet, after all, unrecognized.

Very similar to our Earth, only infinitely more beautiful, Millokkom has oceans, rivers, lakes, snow capped mountains, giant forests, rolling landscapes, and areas of indescribable scenic charm. Its cities are like ours only more beautiful, cleaner, less congested, and less noisy. They have stunning residential districts, handsome private houses, imposing public buildings, ultramodern factories, excellent schools and colleges, attractive theaters and concert halls, parks, hospitals, churches, and palaces of public assembly. There are railroad trains which seem to run in grooves, as I understand it, motor cars operating by "condensed energy," luxurious vessels on the high seas, and smaller ships for local travel.

Politically, the government of Millokkom is about perfect. There is only one nation of people — literally One World — and it is governed by a Supreme Council of Wise Men. There is only one religion — a form of monotheism — based on profound teachings similar to the Secret Doctrine that is found in our great faiths. The people are happy and intelligent, and have learned how to live philosophically, without fear or hate or worry. There is no crime or poverty on Millokkom, and no war. The people enjoy fine health and only have to go to the hospital in the event of some physical accident. There are animals and birds, some like our own, some exotic; but, oddly enough, there are no fishes or reptiles on the entire planet.

As I have previously mentioned, the citizens of Millokkom resemble us human beings to a marked degree, but with this basic occult difference: they belong to a different Life Wave. Also, their souls do not incarnate on any other planet; nor can these fine people mate with us sexually. Intellectually, they are far ahead of us and possess a degree of spiritual development found in few people on earth. How I wish that I could meet some person from Millokkom! And, as a world traveler who has visited 94 countries on this planet, how I wish I could step into a Space Ship and visit Millokkom! That, for me, would be the Supreme Adventure....

Citizen of the Galaxy

Kenneth C. McCulloch

*K*enneth C. McCulloch *is a resident of The Pas, Man., and is the author of* Mankind: Citizen of the Galaxy. *This is a handsome volume — large in format, with 287 double-columned pages, with numerous illustrations and a fine index. It was privately published in 1985 by Rings of Saturn Publishing, P.O. Box 3440, The Pas, Manitoba R9A 1S2, Canada.*

The theme of the book is lucidly presented and best expressed in the author's own words:

> *The main thesis of the book is that Mankind is descended from a colony planted on Earth at some time in the past, and that we are descended, either partially or entirely, from extraterrestrials.*
>
> *At present we cannot tell exactly when the colony was established. It appears, however, that at some time in the past, there was some kind of natural disaster, which nearly destroyed the civilization then existing on Earth. The survivors were reduced to spending all their time and energy in mere existence; all that remained of their previous high civilization were legends and memories of a Golden Age in the distant past, and a few unidentifiable artifacts. The rebuilding process is still going on.*
>
> *Once the present time of troubles is past, there will be unified world community established on this planet. Only when this is accomplished will we be ready to meet our extraterrestrial neighbours (or relatives). Probably only at that time will they*

*finally want to meet us. At that time we will see that Mankind
has finally taken another step towards becoming a Citizen of the
Galaxy.*

*Kenneth C. McCulloch holds a degree in Astronomy from the
University of Toronto and is an upper-air meteorological observer
whose principal posting has been at Baker Lake, N.W. T. He has
worked there for more than twenty-two years, and it was there that
he began to research and to write* Mankind: Citizen of the Galaxy.
*His interests are wide and range from astronomy to prehistory,
from the ancient-astronaut theory to theories about sunken
Atlantis and the Hollow Earth. The points he makes about these
interests are well researched and well argued, and they are mar-
shalled to support the general thesis that humanity has an alien
origin.*

*McCulloch experienced a UFO sighting in 1976 at the Upper Air
Station at Baker Lake. His description of it appears in an Appendix
to his book, footnoted with the dates of his letters to and from the
noted astronomer, Dr. Brian Marsden: 9 and 25 July 1977.*

THE FOLLOWING IS THE REPORT of a UFO observation made by the
undersigned on 1976 June 26. The object was a bright white light
visible near the northern horizon. There appeared to be no fluctua-
tions in color, except for the effects of heat haze. Initially it was
estimated to be about magnitude -2 to -3, but it faded by about 2 or
3 magnitudes during the hour it was visible. It was difficult to
estimate the magnitude, due to the bright sky and the lack of
comparison objects. It was a point source, even as seen in an 8
power elbow telescope and in 10 x 50 binoculars. It did not appear
to move. The time of observation was from 0545Z to 06455Z. The
sky was quite bright at the time, as the sun was not far below the
horizon. The sky was clear.

I checked the locations of the brighter planets. Venus is too close
to the Sun all month for observation. Mars and Jupiter are about
equidistant from the Sun, and both were too far south to be seen at
the time. It was not possible to use the theodolite to observe the
object, as it was just out of sight behind the Rawinsonde building.

However, by sighting on the power lines just east of where the object was located, it is estimated that the elevation was from 4 to 5 degrees, and the azimuth was about 350 degrees. It is estimated that the Right ascension of the point in the sky behind the object was about 5h 00m, and the Declination was estimated at $+30°$. This is near a point halfway between Capella and Aldebaran. There is nothing bright in that area. In any case, the object was not seen the next night at the same time, with again a clear sky.

There was no skyhook balloon in the area at the time. Cambridge Bay advised that their evening flight terminated in a balloon burst, so it was not a floating balloon. Actually it did not look like a balloon, but it had to be checked. The sky was bright enough that if the light had been held up by a helicopter, the helicopter would have been seen.

I do not know what the cause or source of this light was. It is rather difficult to visualize an astronomical source for it. I don't think that there would be much use in trying to find an observatory reporting something there, as that part of the sky is almost impossible to observe from a southern location at this time of year. It is too close to the Sun. Only in this latitude does the Sun set, but the sky is still very bright.

The sighting was made in Baker Lake, N.W. T.

The following year, I discussed this report with some astronomers, following which I sent a copy of it to Dr. Brian Marsden of the Smithsonian Astrophysical Observatory. Here are excepts from my letter and his reply:

At the time I wrote the report I couldn't think of any astronomical explanation. On thinking it over later, I was wondering if a nova explosion could produce the observed effect. At the recent General Assembly of the Royal Astronomical Society of Canada in Toronto, I discussed this observation with a number of astronomers. Several of them suggested the possibility of it being a sun-grazing comet, and suggested that I send the report to you.

In his reply, Dr. Marsden agreed that it could not have been any of the planets, as they were too far away. Also, he felt that it was not likely to have been a sun-grazing comet, as it was too far form the Sun, and would be unlikely to fade so quickly. He also thought that the fading was too rapid for a nova and probably even for a supernova. As many astronomical explanations were found to be unfeasible, he was unable to explain what I had seen, especially when it was found not to have been a balloon.

More than nine years have gone by since I made the observation, and I am no closer to explaining it now than I was then. I am putting the report in here with the hope that someone can shed light on it.

Odyssey from the Womb

John Charles David

Odyssey from the Womb: A Scientific Appeal from Extraterrestrials *is the full title of an unusual, 116-page booklet. The booklet was written, typed, and prepared for instant printing and limited distribution in Winnipeg in 1979 by Jerry Charles David.*

The booklet is unusual in that its author has combined his own prose and poetry and illustration to express his conviction that between 1947 and 1983 an extraterrestrial civilization established overt contact with humanity for the purposes of "an interbreeding program... to father a number of star children from Earth women so that these children being half from the stars would help bring the Earth to a new order of mind."

The author explained how the program was put into effect in these words:

Scout Craft with special birth producing machines come to Earth and search out females who are in body and mind equal to give birth. When a female is found a fertile ray of light about the size of a small sewing needle is fired into the womb at a fast speed so that no Earth woman could know that she had been made pregnant by The Civilization....

The Star Children are born in groups of 3001. There are 3000 females born for every one male. 2999 of the females are to mate with Earth males and produce offspring. One female is to mate with the male born the same way. By chance this book was finished in 1979, proclaimed as the year of the child.

Jerry Charles David may be knowledgeable about the Star Children, but he himself is not one of them. According to his own account, he was born in Ottawa on 19 May 1954 to parents who gave him up for adoption. He was raised by foster parents in Quebec. After dropping out of high school, he held a series of jobs in Ontario, Quebec, and Northern Manitoba. In the summer of 1974 he met "the most beautiful dream girl." Her pregnancy ended in an abortion.

The following year, after visiting a UFO site in Quebec, he began to take an interest in the notion of extraterrestrial contact. Then he noticed something strange — the beeps. He has described these in the passage below.

David foresees an epic battle between the earthly forces of Lucifer, whose galactic fall happened to occur on the planet Earth, and the newly formed Star Children. The battle will commence some time after 1983.

When the battle is over the Star Ship will come to Earth to refuel. It will land in Northern Canada and a power station on the ship will mine certain minerals which are used to boost the ship into light speed. If the Earth is a united planet living in peace, The Civilization will stay for about three years. In that time they will communicate with our world government and their scientist will teach our scientist new technology never before dreamed about. The Earth will be accepted as part of The Civilization.

The author added the following note: "Thousands are born here by extraterrestrial interbreeding and if you were born in 1947 or any year after, then you could be one of them!"

The booklet is dedicated in part "to the Star Children and world peace, love and unity."

THEN IN MAY 76 my life took on a certain change of events. I saw the light, no just kidding, but what did happen is the evidence of contact, and it is very difficult to explain.

I started hearing beep noises in my right ear. I feel funny trying to explain this because to my knowledge hearing beeps in the head is just not the going thing. I'll try to explain what they sound like as best as possible but it is not easy for I've never heard anything like it. I can say that they do compare slightly to Morse Code beeps that I've heard on some movies. For the last three and a half years I've been hearing them on in my right ear and at any time during the day or night when there is silence around. I can hear them better when I block my ear from outside noise with my hand or pillow. They're coming in at a fantastic rate of speed, about three times as fast as a fast typist. I can hear them better before, during and shortly after a full moon, whatever that could mean? It is at this time of the month that I feel like writing. I know for sure that the beeps are in different tones like the tones in a hearing test machine. They go from low to high pitch levels like this, ..:::""…':::':…and so on. When I first started hearing them my first impression was that I was going in the head. I was afraid to seek medical advice thinking I might end up in the funny house. There was no stress or emotional problem at that time so I decided to wait. Shortly after the beeps started I took a sudden interest in many new subjects and many I had never even dreamed about before. One subject was writing and the only writing I had done before was to scratch down a few poems in school. I'm not claiming now to be the writer of the century, for my only idea of writing is to write down whatever my brain tells me to.

I've told very few people about hearing the beeps and very quietly over the last three and a half years wrote and rewrote this book. I believe, because of the rewriting, that there is a point A start and a point Z stop to the beeps. It may be one month cycle with the full moon. Some part of my brain must have the ability to decode and translate a certain percentage of the beeps every month. This report is possibly about three percent of the beeps. I believe that since I can hear the beeps clearly, then so could a sensitive listening device. Up until now I wasn't going to walk into some place and ask if they wanted to record the beeps in my head. This report may give me a little backing and I feel that the beeps can and should be recorded and decoded. If our technology can get an old rocket up into orbit, then someone should be able to rig up a device that can be placed over or put into my ear. This device should naturally have a feeding line to a recorder or be fed directly into a decoding computer. If this failed, I do not think that I could tap the beeps out under hypnosis for my fingers could not keep pace with the speed of the beeps.

There may be other problems as well. A few months ago during a full moon I was resting in bed one night and listening to the beeps as they were exceptionally loud and clear that night. For a few seconds I thought I could hear something else so I put my hand over my ear, closing the earlobe.

What happened was that I blocked off the loud beeps and was listening to a much sharper set of beeps. When I took my hand away the loud set of beeps returned. Whoever takes on the task of recording and decoding may be faced with the problem of separating the two sets of beeps as they are coming in together. In the latter part of November 79 another unusual event happened. I was in a shopping mall close to where I live and noticed that a Winnipeg radio station had a temporary broadcasting booth set up for store promotions. There was this super beautiful announcer named Lorraine working the booth so I decided to waddle on over to say hello. By coincidence I approached her just a few seconds before she was about to make a broadcast and as I came to within a few feet, her equipment suddenly went wild with interference. She had to ask me to step back about ten feet and then proceeded with her broadcast. Later she said that I must have had something on me which caused the interference, but I didn't. By this experience I now believe that my body might be a storage battery for a good amount of electromagnetism.

Ever since I had started hearing them the beeps I've been hearing the last three and a half years, my attention toward many things has improved and my ability to learn went into overdrive. I hope that the beeps can be recorded and decoded for they are a wealth of information. They should not be recorded under top secret conditions for if they are extraterrestrial, the people on this planet have too many problems to panic. The information they hold could only be welcomed.

Encounter with a Tulpa

W. Ritchie Benedict

W. *Ritchie Benedict is a researcher and writer with a special interest in the paranormal. (One might say that he has "a taste" for the subject.) is articles appear in the pages of* Fate *and other magazines and journals devoted to the unexplained and the inexplicable. He frequently gives talks and lectures on supernatural subjects. He lives in Calgary (as did the late T. Lobsang Rampa of "third eye" fame).*

Like most researchers and investigators of psychical matters, Benedict has been asked innumerable times whether or not he has ever had an experience that he could not explain. To answer that question he wrote an article called "Encounter with a Tulpa." It was published in the Sept. 1987 issue of the now-defunct British publication The Unknown. *The article is reprinted here.*

The word tulpa *is one that is familiar to readers of the exciting books written by the French traveller and mystic, the late Alexandra David Neel, whose specialty was volumes about the mysteries of Tibet. In that country on "the root of the world," she encountered* tulpas, *employing that ancient Tibetan word for materializations or "thought-forms." On one occasion, she wrote, she was able to materialize a* tulpa *of her own. It took the form of a monk, but the imagined monk took on a life of its own, and for six months it refused to dematerialize. Benedict makes an interesting connection between his own subconscious thoughts and actuated Tibetan "thought-forms." In the process he sheds some light on seemingly unrelated UFO sightings.*

I AM A FREELANCE WRITER and I suppose I am as imaginative as anyone else, but what I saw in the sky in 1974 was not the result of any flight of fancy.

To go back a bit and set the stage for what I witnessed, I should explain that I have always been interested in UFOs and psychic phenomena. A *Life* magazine article on the UFO "flap" of 1952 got me started on that topic, and today I lecture on the subject of UFOs and the unknown for the Calgary Public School Board in Alberta, Canada. There is a tradition in my family that my grandfather sighted something highly unusual when he was a mail coach driver in Scotland about 1907-08.

He said that one morning he was passing one of the old cemeteries that dot the south of Scotland, when he saw something white and roughly human-shaped sitting on a wall looking down at him. He picked up a rock or lump of coal, threw it at the figure, whereupon it disappeared. In addition to this, there were the sounds of phantom horses at the old No. 6 Fire Station in Calgary which were heard by him and his fellow firemen at various times, long after horse-drawn engines had gone out of service. Interestingly, in the 1970s, there was a haunted house reported by the media only a block away from the Fire Station, so it appears the area may have been a psychic "hot spot."

My mother once claimed to have observed a figure watching us from the kitchen of our home one evening when we were showing home movies to a group of friends. No one else observed anything unusual, but she said that after a few moments the figure vanished. Another grandson, my cousin, who is today a court reporter in Calgary, once had a bizarre experience in July 1967, while he was walking his collie dog early one morning in the hills north of Calgary. This featured thudding footsteps where nothing was visible. It alarmed both him and the dog and they both hid behind some bushes until whatever-it-was passed by.

I mention this as a prelude to what I experienced, as some experts believe that psychic abilities run in families.

It was Monday, October 21st, 1974, about 4:30 p.m. in the afternoon, when I was walking home from downtown to our house which at that time was located in SW Calgary. It was a relatively short walk — about two miles or so — through busy city streets and I did not expect to see anything out of the ordinary. The newspapers were reporting that some UFOs had been sighted in Priddis, Alta., as well as Turner Valley, and the local television station was going to feature a program on the UFO phenomenon. UFOs were not on my mind at the time as I had been down placing employment applications.

When I neared the school grounds of the old Central High School, something happened to catch my attention and I looked up. I saw what appeared to be a large white hot air balloon about 100 feet above me. It was at least 50-70 feet in diameter. Hot air balloons are common in the skies above Calgary today, and we see them all the time, as there is a local ballooning club that flies them over during the Calgary Stampede. In 1974, though, they were comparatively rare. I looked for a gondola beneath the balloon, but was surprised when I could not see any. Curiously, none of the passers-by on the other side of the street seemed to notice the object, which I kept in sight as I continued walking.

Suddenly, after several blocks, the bottom of the object began to turn black. It was as though a black hole was slowly gobbling up the white balloon. Synchronistically, several days previously, I had bought a science-fiction novel by Larry Niven entitled *A Hole in Space*. That is exactly what this looked like. Curiously, I had the odd feeling that, in some unexplained way, the appearance was connected with me. I remember thinking, *"I see it, but I don't believe it,"* just about the time the blackness appeared.

By this time, I was nearing home and broke into a run. I hoped that whatever it was would stay in sight long enough for me to get a photograph of it. It seemed just my luck that when I did see something unusual that I did not have a camera with me. I burst into the back door and ran for my bedroom, where I picked up my 8 m.m. movie camera. By this time the object had diminished to a small black sphere. I headed for the hillside at the back of our house, and managed to get several feet of movie film with nearby trees for size comparison, before it disappeared completely. The movies did turn out, and while unspectacular (the sphere by this time had become a large black dot), they were enough to prove to myself and everyone else there *was* something there.

When I compared notes with my parents afterwards, I learned that my father, who had just arrived home from work, had not seen anything, but then, he was not looking out of the window. However, my mother had been looking out of the window and saw the object north of our home. This was at approximately *the same time* I first observed the object nearly a mile away and considerably to the east.

This left me with a definite puzzle. Either there were *two* objects, which didn't seem very likely, or else the original object suddenly jumped about a mile nearly instantaneously. Or, there was a third possibility — the object may have been some sort of psychic creation, triggered by either of our subconscious minds, and the other mind picked up on it telepathically.

One thing I was certain of was that the object was no standard nuts-and-bolts UFO. Later, I read upon *tulpas*, or thought-forms, and became convinced that it must have been something of this nature. Perhaps the same conditions that were then producing UFO sightings over southern Alberta were also conducive to a psychic materialization.

I tried to explain the phenomenon away every way I could, but I could not explain away the evidence of the movie film. The only other explanation I could think of was as equally fantastic as all the others — perhaps I witnessed the infusion of energy from another parallel universe. It was not the appearance of plasma, or ball lightning, on a perfectly clear sunny day. It started me thinking about the element of time.

In the thirteen years since this happened, I have wondered whether, in some manner, every time I think (visually) about what I witnessed, I am actually lending a hand in the *creation* of the object back in October 1974. It is rather mind-boggling to think, as I am typing this and remembering, I may be adding energy to that surprising appearance.

Actually, I am rather grateful that the appearance of the object was of something rather harmless in nature. It has occurred to me more than once that such thought-forms may take *any* shape and perhaps be quite terrifying to the witnesses. No doubt this could be the explanation of some (but not all)supernatural events. Whether this would be the case of what my grandfather and mother witnessed, as I mentioned at the start of this account, I have no idea. I have read that some psychics like Ted Serios are able to produce images on photographic film by concentration. It is true I was deep in thought at the time the object appeared, but I was thinking about job prospects, not producing *tulpas*.

It is interesting that I did have a similar experience nearly two years earlier, but wrote it off as possibly being a misinterpreted natural occurrence. Saturday evening, 6 May 1972, I went out to the Westbrook Shopping Mall to buy a record. The mall is about two miles west of our former home. It is bounded to the south by Ernest Manning Senior High School, a parking lot, and a short plaza containing a liquor store and a discount store. It was some- where between 8:00 and 9:00 p.m. and the light was starting to fade. I had not succeeded in finding the record I was after and was heading for the bus stop and home. Several hundred feet high over the garage attached to the Woolco department store, I observed a wing-shaped object. The central part was white in colour with rust- coloured "wings." It moved north over the department store, then back south over the school, finally disappearing over 17th Avenue, the direction from which I had originally come.

As with the first incident I related, I was puzzled that not one of the people walking by to go into the mall bothered to look up. Finally, as I recalled, one man finally did spot the thing, and he seemed quite astonished. I was inclined to think it was a kite, but I could see no strings or children nearby. It would have had to be a very long kite string, in any case, as it was at least 3,000 feet up when it vanished. It appeared to hover most of the time, and was shaped like a bat. At this point, it was the size of the half-moon of the thumb-nail of my right hand when held at arm's length. I took the time to make the comparison.

The question I still have today is was it another earlier *tulpa* or was it a genuine UFO? Both of them were unknown objects in the sky, but neither behaved the way a UFO is supposed to behave. The thing that struck me with the 1972 object is that it appeared to move *against* the wind, which a kite would not do.

Whatever they were, they did a lot to strengthen my conviction that there are a great many things in our world that conventional science has yet to resolve. If such a production can be created by the human subconscious, how great are the untapped resources of our minds? And if they were not *tulpas*, then what were they?

Bernice Niblett's Diary

John Magor

I have yet to meet John Magor, the contributor of this autobiographical memoir, but I have had the pleasure of corresponding with him at some length about UFOs and allied matters. If John is not the most courteous man in the country, it is only because he is the most sensitive and helpful and modest!

He worked as a newspaperman and also as the publisher of Canadian UFO Report, a journal notable for the seriousness with which it treated its subject. He is now living in retirement with his wife Lillian in Duncan, B.C. The project that has occupied him for the last few years is researching and writing his memoirs. These are taking the form of what might be called "a spiritual Roots."

When he learned that I was looking for first-person accounts of the odd and the unusual, he turned from his memoirs to "Pandora's Box." That is the title he gave to the following essay. It tells of his friendship with an usual woman, Bernice Niblett, and it arrived with a covering letter. Since that letter states everything that needs to be added by way of commentary, I am taking the liberty of reproducing it here.

May 5, 1989

Dear John:

Excerpts from Bernice Niblett's diary made a distinct impression when I ran them in CUFOR in 1972, and those carried here *are the bulk of what she wrote. Unfortunately, after living for a while at Gibson's Landing to which she moved from Keats Island, she seemed to have left the area entirely and I never did regain contact.*

However, I am sure these excerpts represent the very heart of the mystery. Sightings were at a peak just then and Bernice was ideally suited to be a medium for them. She was a true UFO mystic and became totally absorbed in what was happening even though it frightened her.

I am confident everything she told me was true as seen through her eyes and do hope this is in time to let you find a place for it. I consider her story a treasure.

With best wishes,

John

Pandora's Box

LIKE PANDORA'S BOX there is, I believe, a capacious chest containing extraordinary instruments and creatures which the gods of supernatural events occasionally open for reasons as mysterious as the chest itself. When the contents spill out there is a surge of strange incidents. There are sightings of unexplained vehicles in the sky and, as it seems in this case, humanoids on the ground, and sometimes a rare animal of the wilds, as we also learn here.

For me and, to a lesser extent my wife Lillian, there was just such a period in 1967 when we had a phase of strangeness we will never forget, though for me the exposure was more memorable because as a writer I wished to learn more about it. I was to discover it seemed to be like a contagion, spreading as it went, and apparently stemming from someone particularly sensitive to the Pandora effects.

In our case the effects became noticeable some time after we moved into our present place on Vancouver Island. We do not live in a haunted house, I am sure, but for a while at least the mystery almost certainly had something to do with a small wooded island a few miles away in the Gulf of Georgia. More specifically it had something to do with a person who had lived there until strange events apparently forced even her to leave the confined area in which she found herself.

For Bernice Niblett obviously was someone whom psychics would call a "sensitive spirit." She attracted unusual incidents in the same way certain children are said to attract poltergeist activity. She was aware of singular happenings that might go completely unobserved by others.

Yet Bernice was not a child. Far from it, as I discovered on a visit to meet her. She was a slender, fair-haired woman of about thirty who, having learned that I published *Canadian UFO Report*, had the initiative to write to me saying that from a cabin she was renting she had been observing and sometimes hearing unusual illuminated flying objects. Since her place on Keats Island was difficult to reach by a rough path through woods and bush, would I be interested if she mailed me accounts of what she saw? All she asked in return was a subscription to my magazine.

So it was that I not only began to receive the most mystifying letters of my life but, for the first time ever, had UFO sightings of my own, as if Bernice had indeed opened a magic box.

Luckily CUFOR, to give the magazine its identifying initials, was by then operating well enough to provide an assured means of recording her reports. Working in her cramped one-room cabin, she laboriously transposed them from a diary she had started in 1967.

"On Jan. 27," the first entry said, "the cold woke me at 6:00 a.m. It was still dark and the stars were glittering. As I looked out a very white star moved into view from over the roof. It made two spirals down, zigzagged parallel to Earth a couple of times, then stopped for about ten minutes. It then took off at great speed, turning yellow, then pink. It did not seem to be following Earth's curvature but to be flying off into space.

"I decided to keep a lookout from then on…

"The very next evening I saw another flying object from the front window. It travelled very slowly over the water, only a few hundred feet up. This one seemed to be a long dark body with dim red and yellow lights at both ends. It weaved from side to side, stopping two or three times with its lights dimming almost out.

"Next afternoon two men in neat dark coveralls came down the path to the cabin, saying they were Hydro men and how surprised they were to find someone living here.

"They asked if I needed help, which I did, as I had some new stove-pipes which I hadn't been able to put up myself. While I held the pipes steady inside, one of the men got on the roof and added the new pipes. I heard the man on the ground directing him and the one on the roof would answer, 'Yes, Master.'

"They then came in for tea. They asked if I liked living here, did I go hunting, and didn't I get frightened at times? Asked what there was to be afraid of, the men looked at each other and the 'boss' finally answered, 'Oh, things.'

"Although the men were friendly enough, they were a little 'stiff' and just not the kind to discuss UFOs with, so I didn't mention them.

"Feb. 17. Woke up about 6:00 a.m. again (still dark) and saw one travelling inland over Keats. It was below tree tops most of the time as it went up the hill behind the cabin where it was lost to view. This was definitely a long, dark body with two or three yellow lights at each end.

"I was feeling uneasy and less enthusiastic about seeing these things now. They were definitely interested in the ground and must be picking up things...? I just might end up as a 'sample'!

"Feb. 21. Had just walked to the front window. Something about sixty feet about the water, with 'frosted' yellow lights at the sides and a bright red in the middle, slid over from the left to my rocks, then back again. It slid up and back as if on a rail.

"My knees turned watery and my stomach filled with butterflies! I realized I'd seen several of those same things many times, but through the trees as I sleepily observed them from my bunk window. Because they were over water I'd presumed they were boats but I had never seen the bodies of these machines, just the arrangement of lights. Now what I saw from the bunk window had no discernible body either...

"After seeing the thing slide up and away again, it took me some time to get over my fright. Curiosity finally made me brave enough to venture out to the edge of the rocks where I could get a wider unobstructed view.

"On the other side of Ragged Island and more than half hidden by it appeared to be a big boat well lit up with neon lights. As I wondered 'Why there?' threee balls of scintillating light flew up from it. Eventually there were five or six of them, and I kept glancing back for fear one of the lights would get between me and the cabin, cutting off retreat! Then the balls travelled slowly over tree tops, dropping down amongst them.

"Running back to the cabin, I locked the door. This was all too much! This was a nest of UFOs! How could I have been so unobservant to miss all this before? In moving to Keats I had probably moved right into their midst from the beginning!"

Later, using the island's public phone, Bernie called the local police department.

"Knowing it would be easy for them to give me a brush-off if I told them about UFOs, I told them instead that there were prowlers about and would they please come over?

"On board their boat and under the cool gaze of two young policemen I felt rather foolish. To them I'd be just a nutty woman seeing things. I heard much later that the RCMP had received several UFO reports but these men didn't tell me about it to make me feel less foolish about mine."

When a spell of windy wet weather hit the West Coast, Bernice thought she might have some relief from UFOs, but it was not to be. She wrote:

"On one of those blustery nights I heard a sound like an enraged hornet approaching. It seemed to hover close over the cabin, move away, then back again. The sound of a large hornet flying around is enough to give anyone goose pimples. Combined with a stormy night it was almost too much! When it seemed overhead my eyes were riveted to the ceiling, expecting something to come boring through the roof. I was too frightened even to take a peek out the window at it.

"For at least two weeks that 'hornet' was around. It was a bright white ball, as far as I could make out, and it went back and forth in a small rocky area across from Ragged Island. Next day I went to look at the rocks where I presumed it had been. They were covered with a thick mat of moss, and two chunks of about a foot each had been knocked off. The drill holes I thoroughly expected to find were not visible to me."

Later Bernice had a chance meeting with one of the "Hydro"

men she had met before, and still later she encountered four company men who had a much more casual and authentic appearance than the others. When she told this group about her earlier meeting with the "Hydro" men, they said, "Somebody has been pulling your leg."

That was the last I ever heard from this bravely independent and very reclusive young woman. My last note to here was returned with a post office note that she had moved and there was no forwarding address. I felt then that somehow I had failed her.

But had she gone as completely as it seemed? About a month after receiving the postal note I had two singular UFO sightings of my own in one week. They were all the more surprising as I had never seen a UFO in my life before. Nor had Lillian who was with me during the first incident.

On that occasion we watched with neighbours as a brilliant orange light appeared low overhead and moved erratically about before vanishing beyond a group of trees. It looked so strange a small girl with us burst into tears.

The second object seemed more purposeful. Arriving about two hundred feet above our house when I was outside alone, it flew straight ahead with a spectacular trail of sparks until it was lost to view against a star-filled sky. It seemed to have no body and moved much lower and slower than a shooting star.

At first I thought of those two remarkable incidents as separate from anything related to Bernice. But then I began to think she had been the central figure of a larger episode even more mystifying than I had realized. In particular I thought again about the last lines of her diary in which she wrote:

"Every human is different. We expect it, so when we exchange a word or two with someone whose phraseology is different, we only wonder what country he's from, not what planet. Maybe that's a mistake."

When I first read that, I supposed Bernice was referring to the so-called Hydro men. But the total strangeness of her presence seemed to extend far beyond them and linger when she had gone. Now the picture that comes to mind of someone who might have need from another world is that of Bernice herself… and there is another more mundane reason why that picture comes to mind.

A few years ago Keats Island became part of the scenic background for a TV series called *The Beachcombers*, which centres on the fictional adventures of life around Gibson's Landing across a narrow strait. That is where I arranged to meet Bernice and where she lived briefly when the cabin became "too much." So almost every week now there is something on the screen to remind me, however slightly, of that life close to Pandora's Box.

Also from time to time I am reminded of "Pandora effects" in other ways, and here I think particularly of a truly extraordinary incident in the same general time-frame of my correspondence with Bernice. More accurately, it happened before I knew her and had nothing to do with Keats Island. Instead, it was like an eerie pre-staging of events. It was as if, a year ahead of time, the gods of supernatural affairs were arranging the scenes.

The first and only act of their drama happened while Lillian and I were commuting between Prince Rupert, where we lived at the time, and Vancouver Island, in search of a home where I could continue my newspaper work. We had stopped in a lovely wooded area outside the town of Terrace, and there was nothing to concern us except the serene beauty of the place. Then, as if at the stroke of a witch's wand, all had changed. From the trees across the dirt road, a sinuous black shape appeared. It was like a mould made from the blackest of tar. It began with huge green eyes at the head and tapered back to a graceful tail that somehow escaped the dust of the road.

We whispered to each other that it looked like a panther. More transfixed than frightened, we watched every movement and noted every detail, as the magnificent animal moved slightly down the road and back into the woods. In its majesty it never deigned once to glance at us.

As we learned, our guess that it was a panther was a good one. But I don't think we fully grasped what a rare experience we had had until the recent visit from Doris and Bud Simpson, parents of Lillian's daughter-in-law, who were en route to their summer home in the Yukon.

Doris and Bud had spent most of their lives on the Pacific Northwest, where wild game bounds. So I saw a chance to raise the topic of our black panther. To our surprise, they had only one incident of such an animal to report and that was a sighting by Doris.

"They are very rare," she explained, "and the one I saw was small. His stomach almost touched the ground."

I thought again of the marvelous, full-bodied specimen we had seen, and it seemed more unreal than ever. Was it, after all, the product of some pre-arranged magic to introduce the eerie show which for Bernice became "too much"?

Not So Close Encounter

Pierre Pascau

J. Allen Hynek referred to encounters with UFOs as "close encounters" of the first kind, the second kind, and the third kind. (Someone suggested that alien sex was the fourth kind!) Then again there are encounters of the "zero kind"...the kind that are hopelessly unrevealing.

Pierre Pascau, acting host of "Canada A.M.," CTV's national morning show, learned about close encounters of the "zero kind" when he interviewed — or attempted to interview — a guest on the show about an alleged UFO sighting. The guest was a not terribly eloquent farmer, to express it diplomatically. Pascau never forgot the close non-encounter on camera.

He recalled the incident when he was interviewed by Paul McLaughlin, author of Asking Questions: The Art of the Media Interview *(Vancouver: Self-Counsel Press, 1986).*

I WAS INTERVIEWING a farmer from Regina who had seen a flying saucer land on his field. It was a remote interview — I was in Toronto and he was in Regina.

He appeared on the screen and he looked like a farmer hillbilly. He was called Thud, so I said, "Farmer Thud, how are you?"

Grunts.

"What did you see?"

Nothing.

I said, "Didn't you see a flying saucer?"

"Oh, that."

I said, "What was it like?"

"Well, like any flying saucer."

It became comedy. It was hilarious, because it was like a game we were playing, me trying to make him speak and him refusing to speak.

And the audience loved it.

Postface

The most beautiful experience we can have is the mysterious. It is the fundamental emotion which stands at the cradle of true art and true science. Whoever does not know it can no longer wonder, no longer marvel, is as good as dead, and his eyes are dimmed.

Albert Einstein, "The World As I See It" (1931), Ideas and Opinions *(New York: Crown Publishers, Inc., 1954, 1982), translated by Sonja Bargmann.*

313

Sources

Every reasonable attempt has been made to contact the individual copyright owners of the selections included in this anthology. In not every instance has this proved to be possible. The editor and publisher hereby acknowledge their use of previously copyright passages written by the following authors.

Mark Abley: *Beyond Forget* (Vancouver: Douglas & McIntyre, 1986). Reprinted by permission of the publisher. / Henry H. Bauer: *The Enigma of Loch Ness: Making Sense of a Mystery* (Urbana-Champaign & Chicago: University of Illinois Press, 1986). Pp. 1-8 copyright (c) 1986 by the Board of Trustees of the University of Illinois. Reprinted by permission of the author and the University of Illinois Press. / Jerry Charles David: *Odyssey from the Womb* (Winnipeg, 1979). Permission requested. / Howard Brenton MacDonald: *Flying Saucers and Space Ships and the Unknown Planets from Whence They Come* (St. Catharines, Ont.: Provoker Press, 1970). Permission requested. / Najla Mady: *Simply Psychic* (St. Catharines, Ont., 1983). Permission requested. / L.M. Montgomery: *The Selected Journals of L.M. Montgomery: Volume II: 1910-1921* (Toronto: Oxford University Press, 1987), edited by Mary Rubio and Elizabeth Waterston. Entries: July 19, 1918; April 13, 1919. Reprinted by permission of the University of Guelph. / P.K. Page: *Brazilian Journal* (Toronto: Lester & Orpen Dennys, 1987). Reprinted by permission of the publisher. / Pierre Pascau: *Asking Questions* (Vancouver: Self-Counsel Press, 1986) by Paul

McLaughlin. Reproduced courtesy of the publisher. / James Randi: "Cold Readings Revisited," *Paranormal Borderlands of Science* (Buffalo: Prometheus Books, 1981), edited by Kendrick Frazier. Originally published in *The Skeptical Inquirer*, Vol. III, No. 4, Summer 1979, pp. 37-41. Reprinted by permission of *The Skeptical Inquirer*. / Gordon Sinclair: *Will the Real Gordon Sinclair Please Stand Up* (Toronto: McClelland & Stewart, 1966). Used by permission of The Canadian Publishers, McClelland and Stewart, Toronto.